Agents of Change: Professionals in Developing Countries

PRAEGER SPECIAL STUDIES IN
INTERNATIONAL ECONOMICS AND DEVELOPMENT

Agents of Change: Professionals in Developing Countries

Edited by

Guy Benveniste
Warren F. Ilchman

Published in cooperation with the
Professional Schools' Program of the
University of California, Berkeley

PRAEGER PUBLISHERS
New York • Washington • London

The purpose of the Praeger Special Studies is to make specialized research monographs in U.S. and international economics and politics available to the academic, business, and government communities. For further information, write to the Special Projects Division, Praeger Publishers, Inc., 111 Fourth Avenue, New York, N.Y. 10003.

PRAEGER PUBLISHERS
111 Fourth Avenue, New York, N.Y. 10003, U.S.A.
5, Cromwell Place, London S.W.7, England

Published in the United States of America in 1969
by Praeger Publishers, Inc.

Library of Congress Catalog Card Number: 73-95698

Printed in the United States of America

ACKNOWLEDGMENTS

This book is based on the papers presented at an international conference held at the University of California, Berkeley, in May, 1968, under the auspices of the university's Professional Schools' Program. This program is supported by a grant from the Ford Foundation, and its main purpose is to provide new opportunities for the professional schools at the university, to internationalize their outlook and to expand their research and training activities in other societies and cultures. The editors wish to acknowledge the generous support of the Ford Foundation, which made this conference a possibility. They thank the Fellows of the Professional Schools' Program, who have consistently served as a keen intellectual sounding board; they thank their colleagues William Alonso, Donald Hansen, Peter Marris, and Harold Wilensky, who in different ways have helped with editing this book; and they also thank Miss Helen Rudy, who carried much of the administrative burden of the conference and who has typed several versions of the manuscript of this book.

CONTENTS

Page

ACKNOWLEDGMENTS   v

Chapter

1   INTRODUCTION   3

    Guy Benveniste and Warren F. Ilchman

Aims   4
Cross-Professional Communication   7
Part I: Experts Abroad   9
Part II: Thinking Anew   11
Part III: Education and Training   13
  Four Major Needs   15
Part IV: Collaboration   21
Summary   23
Notes   25

PART I: EXPERTS ABROAD

2   DILEMMAS OF PROFESSIONALS ABROAD   29

    Warren F. Ilchman and Guy Benveniste

The Professional's Resources   31
The Roles He Plays   33
  Agent of Professional Knowledge   33
  Agent of a National Culture   36
  Agent of an Organization or Regime   36
  Agent of a Superior Power   37
Notes   40

3   RELATIVITY IN DEVELOPMENT: AN EXAMPLE
    FROM CRIMINOLOGY   41

     Nils Christie

Which Crimes? Treated How?   41
Punishments and Social Institutions   42
The Natural Level of Crime   46
Alternatives for Social Stability   47
Ethical Dilemmas   47
Notes   49

Chapter		Page
4	THE DEVIL'S ADVOCATE VIEW	50
	Adam Curle	
	Advisors As Imperialists	50
	Advisors As Educators	51
	Advisors As "Educatees"	54
	Changing Attitudes and Behavior	54
	Changes in the Third World	55
	Worldwide Change	56
5	EXPERTS ABROAD: PROBLEMS OF THE APPLI-CATION OF SOCIAL SCIENCE TO FOREIGN AID	59
	Harold L. Wilensky	
	Parochialism of Professional Culture	61
	The Technical Nature of Professional Tasks	62
	The Service Ideal	65
	Implications for Agents of Change	67
	Broadening the Knowledge Base: Social Science?	68
	Technical Knowledge and Skills	68
	Social-Political-Ideological Knowledge	77
	Three Success Stories	78
	Four Sources of Success	83
	Refashioning the Model	93
	Notes	95

PART II: THINKING ANEW ABOUT
PROFESSIONS AND CHANGE

6	THEORETICAL MODEL OF THE ROLE OF PROFESSIONALS IN COMPLEX DEVELOP-MENT SITUATIONS	103
	Eugen Pusić	
	Techniques and Interests	103
	Three Stages of Social Development	105
	Stage 1: Group Society	105
	Stage 2: Power Society	106
	Stage 3: Functional Society	106
	Professionals As Related to the Stage	108

Chapter	Page

The Professional: Transitional 110
Professionals as Propulsion for Change 112
Prospects 114
Notes 119

7 PUBLIC ADMINISTRATION AND CHANGE:
TERRA PAENA INCOGNITA 122

C. Dwight Waldo

Implications of Instrumentalism 123
Origins as Context 123
Ambivalence toward Change 126
Universality and Efficiency: Conundrums 127
Administration in an Age of Revolutions 129
Steps Toward Theory 131
Notes 135

8 THE CONCEPT OF INNOVATIVE PLANNING 137

John Friedmann

Goals and Methods: The Tao 137
The Sense of Time 138
Limits of Knowledge and Effort 139
The City As Agent of Change 140
Notes 145

PART III: PROFESSIONAL EDUCATION FOR
WORLD RESPONSIBILITY

9 THE EXPERIENCE TO DATE 153

Irwin T. Sanders

New Goals, New Roles 154
The Professional School in the University Complex 155
Rethinking Technical Assistance Programs 157
Learning about the Infrastructure 157
Transferring Technology 158
Success 158

Chapter   Page

    The Professional School in the World   159
      Business Administration   159
      Engineering   160
      Law   161
      Medicine   164
      Education   164
      Agriculture   165
      Public Health   166
      Public Administration   167
    The Professional As World Citizen   168
      Increasing Administrative Commitment   169
      Liberalizing the Students' Environment   170
      Influencing the Professional System   171
      Developing Faculty Competence   171
    Notes   172
10 TRAINING ECONOMISTS FOR SERVICE
    IN DEVELOPING COUNTRIES   173

      Gustav F. Papanek

    Seminars in Problem-Solving   173
    Supervised Experience   174
    Some Examples   175
    Experience in Policy Advising   176
    Maintaining Professionalism   177
    Specialization and Teamwork   179
      Pakistan: An Example   180
    The Technocratic International   182
    The Clinical Year   183

11 GUIDELINES FOR PROFESSIONAL SCHOOLS   186

      Kenneth R. Hansen

    The Transfer of Technology   187
    Some Unlearned Lessons   190
    Some Suggestions and Some New Approaches   192
    The Professional School As Critic   195

Chapter   Page

12 THE INTEGRATED EDUCATIONAL INSTITUTION:
    TEACHING, SERVICE, AND RESEARCH   197

        Antonio Medina

    Clinician or Public Health Doctor?   199
    From Line to Staff   200
    Service-Oriented Teaching   201
    Curriculum Guidelines   202
    Teaching-Service-Research   203

13 A LOOK TO THE FUTURE AND A BRIEF
    PLEA FOR THE COMPARATIVE APPROACH   205

        Brian Holmes

    Two Major Problems   205
    Two Issues   207
    The Problem Approach   208
    Notes   209

            PART IV: INTERNATIONAL PRO-
                FESSIONAL COOPERATION

14 INSTITUTION BUILDING IN DEVELOPING
    COUNTRIES   213

        Raúl Devés Jullian

    Building A University   213

15 THE INTERNATIONAL INSTITUTE APPROACH   220

        Vernon W. Ruttan

    The Institute Model   221
    Mexico: Agricultural Sciences   221
      Multidisciplinary Teams   222
      Internship   223
      Disengagement   223
    The Philippines: IRRI   224
    The Organization of Resources   225
    Notes   227

Chapter   Page

16   THE INTERNATIONAL CONSORTIUM   229

        P. K. Kelkar

     Reciprocal Visits   231
     Separate Administrative Office   232
     Recruitment   233
     Importance of Personal Qualities   234

17   EPILOGUE: PROFESSIONALS AND
        DEVELOPMENT   238

        Jack C. Westoby

     Scope of Tasks   238
     Avoiding Illusions   241
        Institutional vs. Technical Problems   241
     Notes   245

ABOUT THE CONTRIBUTORS   246

Agents of Change: Professionals in Developing Countries

CHAPTER **1** INTRODUCTION

Guy Benveniste
Warren F. Ilchman

The old maxim that travel is broadening has particular
relevance for persons in professions in the United States.
Like most maxims, however, it is only half true. The encounter with the world through technical assistance or other
service abroad which many American professionals have
experienced has required considerable soul-searching into
the adequacy of theory and education as applicable to these
unfamiliar settings. Such encounters have occasioned this
book, whose central question is: What do we know about professionals and professional education that will help us to
meet the world-wide involvement that seems to be ours?
In this sense, travel has been broadening. On the other hand,
the same encounters have produced a contrary result, a
retreat back to fortress America and a determination to roam
no more--a decided narrowing of view. Why, it might be
asked, does work abroad inspire in professionals such extreme responses: an enthusiasm for greater involvement or
the desire for virtually unqualified withdrawal?

An equally interesting question, however, arises from
the marked similarity of certain responses of many American
professionals to this world encounter. Some aspects of their
behavior abroad are in direct contrast to what is expected of
them domestically. It has become customary for sociologists
to rank professional persons in America politically as con-
servatives or as neutrals. [1] By income, education, and social
status, most professionals can be numbered among those in
our society who have a stake in the established order and are
resistant to changes that do not arise through legitimate
channels and by accepted means. With the possible exception,

3

perhaps, of social workers, this generalization seems to hold across all professional fields.

Practicing their professions abroad, especially in low-income countries, American professionals from all fields seem to become far more concerned with political issues. Quite often they espouse a radical stance. They usually advocate substantial public programs and the use of government coercion in ways and to degrees they would find unthinkable in the United States. Amusingly, even those who swear never again to travel east of Suez or south of San Diego do not depart their host countries without uttering prescriptions for "thorough-going social revolution" or "a coup by a strong progressive military leader"; if their language is not that strong, they will at least call for land reform, more effective tax collection, and a thorough bureaucratic renovation.

What accounts for these extreme responses to the world encounter generally, and, what accounts for the extraordinary contrast between the American and foreign behavior of our professionals? A simple answer to the first question might be that it is a case of personality differences-some like to live aborad and some do not; to the second, that the absence of certain prerequisites for professional effectiveness necessitates a different political stance in different countries.

These answers are as common as they are unsatisfactory. They are unsatisfactory because they represent a lost opportunity to examine the nature of professional life to see the extent to which much of the difficulty is inherent in professionalism itself, and because they fail to point out the limits of professional knowledge, particularly the often repeated misunderstanding of what is flexible in the political and social life of the host nation.

AIMS

This book is addressed to several ends:

First, to the growth of the professional's self-knowledge, so that he may see more clearly and choose more optimally,

at least in terms of the objectives he may be pursuing in cultures and social systems that are not identical to the ones in
which he was trained.

Second, to providing a better awareness of the limits of
professional knowledge in a world where science and technology cannot hope to resolve all political issues.

Third, to examining the implications of the viewpoint
expressed here for professional education and training.

Fourth, to discussing the institutional implications of
undertaking action-oriented research in developing countries.

When we first began to think about an international conference on the professional serving abroad, we made a number
of assumptions. First of all, we recognized that all professions are becoming more and more international. Professional careers are increasingly pursued in a world market;
the probability is high that today's student engineer, lawyer,
doctor, or economist will spend some months or some years
or it may be his entire professional life in a culture or a
society different from his native culture.

We were also aware that American professional schools
are not only training Americans for service in their country
and abroad, but are serving a large demand from students
coming from other countries; and we assumed this demand
would continue as long as American professional schools had
something to offer which might not be available in the countries
from which foreign students originate.

We recognized that professions are social activities; We
assumed, therefore, that one could expect some differences
in the way each profession is practiced in different societies,
and we were not convinced that some professions, for instance
engineering, are immune. We wanted to explore the nature
of these differences. We also wanted to stress the implications such differences might have on the training provided in
American professional schools, on the ideologies infused in
students, and on the expectations bred in the minds of young
professionals on their way to their first overseas assignment.

As we started to think about these themes in the somewhat
vibrant atmosphere of Berkeley, where, at our own doorstep,

we could see the beginnings of a quest for a new moral order and an anti-bureaucratic revolution, we were reminded of a fact so self-evident that it is easily forgotten: Professional roles are social activities that take place in social systems, and social systems change over time. The question therefore arises, To what extent are professions agents of social change? Or, contrarily, to what extent do they tend to reinforce the status quo?

As we thought about the roles which American-trained professionals play in other cultures, we began to suspect that it is not always clear to them that because they come from a different culture they practice some kind of manipulation, work some kind of external change on the other culture; that wittingly or unwittingly, professionals serving abroad are agents of social change even if they are unaware of this dimension of their activities. This lack of awareness, we suspected, would be far truer of professionals whose body of expertise depends on the physical sciences; engineers or industrial experts, for example, would probably assume that the technical aspects of their role are the only significant ones to consider, the universal aspects of building bridges or manufacturing steel making any cross-cultural analysis a waste of time and energy. But we were concerned to see to what extent other professions, for example social welfare, criminology, economics, were aware of the social relativity in which they work and to what extent they would be willing to think along these lines.

Thus, we decided to organize an international conference on the subject of the professional as an agent of economic, social, and political change in low-income countries. A useful and generous grant from the Ford Foundation allowed us to invite a number of experts from the United States and from other countries to prepare summaries of their views and come to Berkeley to share their experience with their colleagues in Berkeley's professional schools. We asked each professional school* to select these experts and for three days we discussed preliminary drafts of the papers.

---

*The professional schools and departments at Berkeley represented at this conference were those of Agricultural Economics, Architecture, Business Administration, City and Regional Planning, Criminology, Education, Engineering, Forestry, Public Administration, Public Health, and Social Welfare.

CROSS-PROFESSIONAL COMMUNICATION

The group that came to Berkeley bridged many barriers.
They came from different disciplines and professions. One
man came from a socialist country, Yugoslavia; three were
professionals from developing countries; three were Europeans; one served with an international development agency
of the United Nations family; the others were Americans.
Of the seventeen persons assembled, thirteen, including ourselves, were affiliated with institutions of higher learning;
the others were working with development institutions or as
consultants in their area of expertise. But even among the
group of thirteen one could distinguish those more oriented to
theory and those who, in one way or another, had spent many
years in the field working in developing countries.

Since the participants had been selected by the professional
schools at Berkeley, some were unknown to us, others were
old friends with whom we had studied or worked. To be sure,
the wide range of professional backgrounds of the members
of the group helps to explain why some had never met or even
heard of each other. It is customary to assume that the professions do not talk to each other; that this is true becomes
quite evident when a group of varied experts working on like
concerns are brought together. The conferees at Berkeley
were often surprised during discussions to find their own concerns expressed by other professions: "You mean engineers
are also concerned with this problem?" became a routine
statement.

A number of faculty members and students from the
various professional schools at Berkeley participated in the
discussions. Here again it was somewhat amusing to observe
the lack of communication that exists on a large university
campus between the various professions. Yet, as someone
remarked, problems are not tailored to the narrow confines
of the expertise of each profession. If the professions were
truly oriented to problem solving, would it not be more logical to expect various professions to work together on a single
problem? But lines of communication between professions
are not reinforced by the cloisonement fostered by separate
professional schools. This is in itself a problem, one to which
the conference addressed itself during discussions.

The reader should therefore keep in mind that the views
presented in this book are those of individuals from different
professions who are attempting to bridge gaps between professions and disciplines to talk about common concerns. The
reader should also keep in mind that certain professions,
such as those based on the social sciences, find it quite
natural to discuss the role of the professional as an agent of
change and discuss it from a theoretical point of view simply
because the subject matter falls within the domain of their
professional concerns. Other professionals have to perform
greater mental gymnastics to expand their concerns simply
because their conventional domain of expertise may be limited
to, say, road building or the expansion of agriculture. The
large-scale social consequences of road building or the expansion of agriculture are, of necessity, beyond the usual day-
to-day concerns of these experts. Not that the expert is
privately unconcerned with such consequences; but he necessarily recognizes the need for specialization and assumes
that other experts are concerning themselves with problems
he may know exist but does not feel he can master within the
time constraints of a single life span.

Thus, the reader should regard the views collected in this
volume, not as the product of social scientists concerned with
the issue of professionals as agents of change, but as documents written by members of different professions. The
question really is; What do various professions, some based
on the social sciences, some based on the "hard" sciences,
think about when asked about the role of professionals as
agents of change? Evidently the way the problem is handled
will differ. For some professionals, the discussion takes
place at the empirical level of experience; they are actors
in the situation and their reflections are based on action.
For others, the problem is removed to another conceptual
level. They are examining the professions as part and parcel
of their subject of study. Of the professionals herein presented as authors, some base their works on direct personal
experience, and some on theories and empirical facts--the
result of research. All write out of a concern with action and
an awareness of the magnitude of the unsolved problems faced
by the developing countries. In editing we have attempted to
reduce repetition and overlap between the various contributions
to this book, and some chapters are, therefore, shortened
versions of the originals read at the conference.

The book is divided into four parts.

Part I deals with two questions: Is the professional, or should he be, an agent of change in developing countries? How can he be more effective?

Part II seeks to provide new conceptualizations of the relationships between professions and change.

Part III is concerned with the education and training of professionals for service in developing countries.

Part IV examines the need for international collaboration for institution building in developing countries.

PART I: EXPERTS ABROAD

In Chapter 2, Warren F. Ilchman and Guy Benveniste set the discussion by pointing out that, wittingly or unwittingly, foreign professionals are agents of change in low-income societies, if only because they acquire, with their role, assets that have different values in other societies. The American or European professional in a developing country is not only a technician known to have access to a codified body of knowledge; he is also an actor with access to sources of power he may not have at home. In fact, in low-income countries the American or European professional may play several roles: First, that of agent of professional knowledge having the legitimacy and authority of international scientific or professional status; second, that of agent of a national culture judged desirable; third, that of agent of particular organizations with access to economic, financial, or other material resources; fourth, that of agent of a superior power in the world's political stratification.

Therefore, these authors argue, the problem is not whether American or European professionals in low-income countries should or should not be agents of economic, social, or political change; The problem is one of recognizing that professional actions abroad can have great unforeseen social or political consequences simply because of the great assets

available to the expert; professional choices, or the technical
ability to optimize, may be hindered if foreign professionals
take certain social or political factors for granted on the
basis of irrelevant experience at home.

Both Nils Christie, a Norwegian criminologist who writes
with fresh candor, and Adam Curle, a British educator (also
a Renaissance man), are concerned with the potential exces-
sive influence of foreign experts in developing countries.
In Chapter 3, Christie argues succinctly that it is difficult to
evaluate the consequences of altering some aspect of an on-
going social fabric and that the expert should move with great
caution--always doubting the sources of his own wisdom,
always attempting to foresee the implications of his recommendations. In Chapter 4, Curle stresses the collegial role
of the expert. Given the uncertainties alluded to by Christie,
which Curle recognizes in his own experiences abroad, Curle
points out that the responsibility for development and change
lies in the hands of the people of a developing country. The
role of the expert is that of an understanding friend, a colleague
who can sit back and assist here and there when his assistance
is felt to be needed. At the Berkeley conference, Adam
Curle was truly concerned that the conferring group would be
insensitive to the growth of expert talent in developing countries and to the need for collaboration. He was genuinely
concerned with the title of the conference, since he did not
think it appropriate to conceive of American professionals as
proseletizers for the new religion of development. He was as
concerned with arrogance as with power and suggested that
"success" in development calls for humility, patience, and
detachment.

In Chapter 5, Harold L. Wilensky, a distinguished sociologist and student of the role of men of knowledge in society,
takes a fresh look at the issue of "success" in development
work. Wilensky is quick to point to a paradox of development
theory, that "at more sophisticated levels, development theory
based on social science inspires pessimism." The argument
he makes is important: the more we professionals understand
about society, the more we can perceive the many by-products
of any recommendation or policy decision; and the more we
can perceive the many effects of recommendations or policy
decisions, the more difficult it becomes to evaluate what
decisions are desirable for building a nation. Having said that

much, Wilensky is nevertheless willing to examine three
"success stories": the Cornell University project in Vicos in
Peru, the technical aid program of Israel, and the U. S.
Peace Corps. He generalizes from some of the lessons of
their experience. To be sure, Wilensky assumes these three
cases to be "successes," and this assumption was disputed
during our discussions. But his paper is hard-hitting when
he points to the flexibility and imagination demonstrated by
these three programs. Wilensky reminds us that commitment
is one of the significant assets of the professional. He points
out that the problem of training developers for this country
or for service abroad consists in socializing individuals into
the professions who know something, but who are also tolerant
of the approaches of other specialists and are always willing
to learn again, to refresh their knowledge, to invent new
approaches.

PART II: THINKING ANEW

        The three chapters in Part II are written by three men
with a wide reputation in the fields of public administration
and development. All three are concerned with theory.
Eugen Pusić, a well-known Yugoslav social scientist, presents a theory of the role of professionals in complex development situations. C. Dwight Waldo re-examines the
theory or lack of theory of public administration and change.
John Friedmann presents his concept of innovative planning.

        Pusić is concerned with the centralization of power in
societies as they become increasingly technological. He is
justifiably concerned with the possible rise to power of a
minority when technology provides increasing means of coercion. But he is not pessimistic. He sees also, counter-
balancing this process, the rising influence of a movement
toward rationalization based on the articulation of interde-
pendent professions which generate the knowledge from which
development derives. For Pusić the professions have a
special role to play in the process of development, that of restraining man's control over man. But this role will not be
played unless the professions become conscious of the situation
in which they find themselves. Then, and only then, will the

professions development movements for social action which
are based on participation instead of domination. Pusić's
vision provides a larger framework in which to consider the
role of the professional as agent of change. For Pusić the
issue is what type of change one is talking about. If it is
change imposed by a minority on a majority, if one attaches
a negative value to this type of change, then of course one
may begin to perceive a new dimension for the role of professionals.

Waldo picks up the thread of Pusić's argument by examining the evolution of the ideology of one profession, public
administration. Waldo traces the development of this ideology
in the United States where, in the context of a rapidly changing
society, the profession has maintained not only a non-partisan
stance, but also a neutral technical stance oriented to the
values of a middle class, that is, to the ideals of efficiency,
which are perceived as a means toward the unquestioned goal
of "progress." In that perspective Waldo questions the
universality of the profession. Are the norms of the profession
applicable everywhere or are they the product of a particular,
historical, limited period in the life of Western Europe and
North America? If it is not universal, then of course the
profession cannot remain intellectually unconcerned with the
revolutions taking place throughout the world--whether these
are taking place in developing countries or even right here at
home. There follows a need for a theory of change and a
technology of change. Waldo returns to Pusić's call for a
new consciousness of the profession which stresses an awareness of change at two levels: First, at the level of theory and
practice, so that the profession can help reduce some of the
unfortunate consequences of unplanned change; second, and
significantly, at the level of commitment and belief, a level
which has more to do with setting goals than with optimizing
means toward these goals.

The concern with theory is taken up by Friedmann, who
writes about planning from his wide experience in city and
regional planning both in the United States and abroad.
Friedmann takes the argument one step beyond Waldo's and
urges professionals to concern themselves with the strategic
points of change or structural forces which can engender
system transformation. To be sure, he recognizes that
planners do not know too well how to identify these points.

But Friedmann does not bemoan the ignorance of planners, neither their lack of a theory of planning nor the reality of the ignorance of experts in the face of mounting social problems in this country and abroad. He sees a dialectic which he hopes will be fruitful. For example, he points out that at long last experts at home are talking to experts abroad, simply because the United States is increasingly similar to developing countries in the sense that planning problems go beyond professional expertise and professional solutions. He also points out that advocacy planning is a new trend in the United States, a trend which reflects Waldo's concern with the normative role of the professions. It implies professional participation in the setting of goals instead of an exclusive concern with optimizing means toward goals that are assumed to be "givens." In short, Friedmann is willing to be optimistic because he expects the professions to respond to the demands placed upon them.

PART III: EDUCATION AND TRAINING

Part III focuses on the education of professionals.

In 1968 the Committee on the Professional School and World Affairs, part of the agency Education and World Affairs, completed a study of the professional school in relation to world affairs.[2] Irwin T. Sanders, Study Director of that committee, elaborates, in Chapter 9, on the committee's work and on the way the professions reacted to the series of studies he had been directing. His account is not devoid of humor; it also immediately suggests some of the resistances to change that one can expect when current practices and dogmas of the profession are questioned.

Gustav F. Papanek draws in part on the extensive work in developing countries of the Development Advisory Service at Harvard University for his review, in Chapter 10, of past experience in training economists. He points out that the reward system of economics as a profession does not encourage economists to undertake field work in practical policy/advisory roles in developing countries. Papanek makes it clear that economists need training in economics, but that

this is not enough. To be effective in developing countries,
they need to familiarize themselves with the problems and
issues which confront advisors in the field. They need a
"clinical" year of practice in diagnosing economic ills in
conditions of uncertainty, handicapped by inadequate data and
forced to deal with complex interrelated issues. They also
need a period of internship. To these ends Papanek stresses
the importance of the team approach, combining experts from
both the host and the aid-giving country and also bringing
together younger men who are starting a career in development economics with experienced practitioners.

Antonio Medina of the University of Puerto Rico, in
Chapter 12, writes directly from his experience with maternal
and child health programs in the Commonwealth. He describes
a university program he has initiated to link the university
directly into an action-oriented service function. This program serves to help the student integrate the more abstract
knowledge imparted in the university and apply it to the
practical realities of work among the medically indigent. Dr.
Medina stresses the need to bring together teaching, research, and service if professional education is to remain
flexible and relevant, a point emphasized by Papanek and
suggested by Wilensky.

Dr. Kenneth R. Hansen, who has had extensive experience in public and private service in this country and abroad,
makes a similar argument, in Chapter 11; he focuses on the
special problems of developing countries. His presentation
is based on a simple insight he succinctly spelled out during
conference discussions:

I believe it is not possible just to say of professionals,
'let them be qualified in their field of discipline and
they will be able to perform any and all professional
functions to the benefit of less developed areas and
people.' There exists a learning and utility curve
starting, it is clear, with the various disciplines, but
extending co-incidentally to familiarity with less developed
regions and cultures and the grasp of detailed knowledge
of specific problems, modes of operation, and indigenous
circumstances. It appears to me that this broad competence can best be systematically mobilized and developed
by research, scholarship, and applied experience

fostered by institutions established for the purpose and
having continuity of function and involvement.

In other words, he argues strongly for the suggestions made
by Dr. Medina.

In Chapter 13, Brian Holmes reiterates in a concise and
elegant fashion the merits of a comparative approach as an
essential element of professional education and research.

Four Major Needs

Summing up, several high points or areas of concern can
be identified:

1.   All participants at the conference were aware of
some need for preparing professionals for service in different
cultures. We will come back to this point. But here it is
useful to note that all professions--engineering, medicine,
education, criminology--seem to have this need. The nature
of the need is not identical in all professions, but it exists.

2.   Having expressed a need for enlarging the scope and
content of professional education, the conference participants
also seemed to agree that they want to stress professional
expertise in a narrow domain of knowledge. This is not
necessarily a conflict in objectives. In a sense they seem to
call for the education of experts who are also generalists, at
least in some problem areas. One point to make here is that
during the discussions, not many supporters for multi-disciplinary
approaches in professional education were heard. We further
discuss these issues, which are, of course, a perennial
problem in professional education, below.

3.   There was considerable discussion of the need for
action-oriented research. Commitment to the study of
emergent problems seemed to be a concern shared generally
across professions. Some participants were quick to point
out that many governments and professionals abroad are tired
of being the subject of endless research, without profit or
results from their point of view. This is a problem which
receives full attention in Part IV of this book. There was

considerable discussion of the need to provide new institutional
structures if professionals in American universities are to
be able to involve themselves in long-term commitments abroad.

4.   The conference discussed the practical problems of
providing opportunities for graduate students in professional
schools to familiarize themselves with the realities of con-
ducting research in developing countries.

Applied Research

Since this conference was a meeting of practitioners, it
not unexpectedly emphasized "applied" or "action-oriented, "
or "policy-oriented" research--the choice of wording is not
too important if the intent is clear.

Indeed, several participants felt very strongly about this.
It seemed to them that American professional schools tend to
over-please the academic market for research. These
schools, or the faculty in these schools, attempt to conduct
a type of fundamental research more appropriate for the
faculties of arts and sciences simply because they are rewarded for such academic work, not because they are particularly talented in such directions. There was therefore
much emphasis given to the need to reward faculty in professional schools for undertaking action-oriented programs,
particularly programs that involve action with research.

But the call for action and relevance, or for commitment
to action and relevance, was not an attack on theory or basic
research. There was continued affirmation of the need for
generating better theories within the professions; particularly
within the social science professions. The call to upgrade the
theoretical basis and therefore the theoretical training of
professionals was argued as part and parcel of the need for
relevance in research.

The significant point made is that professional knowledge
rapidly becomes dated in a changing environment unless the
theories on which it is based evolve from insights that do not
depend heavily on the conventional wisdom of past experience.
In that perspective it is easy to perceive that the ties between
faculties of science and humanities and professional schools
do, out of necessity, become close ties. The professional

schools emphasize both the theoretical development of the
sciences underpinning the professions, and the application of
this knowledge to empirical reality. The faculties of science
emphasize their commitment to the development of their
disciplines.

But relevance implies risk-taking. One participant
pointed out that the present disarray in the bilateral and international aid programs is partially attributable to the
insufficient involvement of universities in policy research.
Persons in universities are not prepared to question the "safe, "
conventional wisdom; therefore, the mistakes of the past are
simply repeated over and over.

Implicit in any notion of involvement, of studying emerging
problems, of doing policy research, is the notion that the
professional schools should take more risks. Action-oriented
research necessarily involves normative elements. At some
point the profession will be saying something about the way
things should be instead of the way they are. The moment a
profession is involved in saying something about the way things
should be, it is clearly taking political risks.

Of course this is the fundamental point which Pusić makes
in his theoretical paper. If coercive power is to become less
important in what he calls "functional" societies, then the
professions need to enlarge the scope of their responsibility,
and therefore continually assume new risks.

But this form of risk-taking is not normal practice in
academic circles, and there is little academic reward for it.
Thus again, the participants emphasized the need to provide
new rewards and incentives for faculty in professional schools
who are willing to be involved in policy research. This means
there is need for new institutional structures.

A strategy of involvement in policy research implies
fundamental changes in the attitudes and prevalent structures
of the professional schools. Rapid turnover of faculty, from
field experience to teaching and research and back to field
experience, would be encouraged. Present career patterns,
emulating those in academic departments, reflect a system
of evaluations and rewards based on academic publication.
This is probably dysfunctional to the growth of policy-oriented

professional schools because the criteria for evaluation are
too narrow. To be sure, academic publication would then remain a basis of evaluation; but policy involvement, field
experience in new situations, institution building and innovation would also provide an important basis for faculty
reward and advancement. Unless the career pattern is modified, faculty members are simply not going to be induced to
enlist.

In addition, the structures need to be adjusted to allow
faculty to serve for longer periods of time in action programs.
It is well known that two-month experts can easily be recruited
from U. S. universities during the summer months; but there
is no structure to allow a faculty member to go to, say, India
for four years and return to his position. Creating employment structures that would allow this type of transfer from
the campus to the field and back to the campus would require
additional financial resources, but this was judged to be only
the second half of the problem. What is lacking primarily at
this time is the conceptualization of the needed innovations.

Some participants underscored the need for supportive
services from the academic community to faculty involved in
action programs. It is not enough to send a faculty member,
or even a larger team, abroad for four years. The team,
whatever its size, needs continued support from the home
base, a need calling for institutional arrangements within or
between professional schools. There has been useful service
of this kind at certain U. S. universities.

Multidisciplinary Approach?

The conference engaged in numerous discussions of the
multidisciplinary team versus the single-searcher or
single-profession approach. The participants recognized
that most faculty members usually prefer to work within the
limits of their own professional knowledge. Multidisciplinary
teams are usually considered a bother, difficult to organize
and to orient to similar objectives. Yet, development problems
are not the prerogative of any one discipline or profession.
One lesson from successful action programs in low-income
areas is that success results from sustained action carried
out consistently over long periods of time at a sufficient level
of intensity on several key aspects of the problem. This lesson

of experience implies the need to create multiprofessional and multidisciplinary structures within universities which would allow and encourage such team endeavors. Some conferees cited the experience of policy-planning research centers or committees serving a number of professional schools and academic departments as constructive attempts to bridge academic barriers.

Yet, while there was a call for cooperation between disciplines and professions, there was little enthusiasm in the group for "multidisciplinary" training in professional schools. Perhaps all, and certainly many, conference participants were concerned with the dichotomy between training generalists and specialists. As a group with considerable experience in developing countries, the conferees tended to emphasize the need for expert knowledge. As the professions begin to rely more and more on the sciences, it is necessary to allow future practitioners a sufficient grounding in at least one scientific discipline to allow for an awareness of the conceptual and logical apparatus which is the basis of expert knowledge. It was argued that in the professional schools based on the social sciences, the tendency toward multidisciplinary approaches can result in students learning jargon, which does not mean they learn how to think about problems.

In other words, there seemed to be a trend to encourage specialization in all the professions. Yet the argument for specialization seems to run against the other argument generated during the meeting: American professionals who intend to work in developing countries cannot expect to be trained to solve exclusively American problems and yet work effectively in different cultures.

One participant coined the term "metadisciplinary approach" to spell out what he thought the conference was trying to express.[3] The metadisciplinary approach has implications for both the training of professionals and the carrying on of research. In regard to training, the meta-disciplinary approach consists in training an expert with a solid grounding in a given area of expertise and with a general knowledge of a problem area. If he is a social planner, he may have a solid grounding in, say, economics or sociology-- but he also becomes sufficiently familiar with and committed to a certain set of problems to which he wishes to apply his expert knowledge. Thus, he becomes a specialist in terms of his expert knowledge and a generalist in terms of a set of problems to which he becomes committed. For example, if he is a social planner, he may be an economist concerned with problems of urbanization in developing countries. If he is a public health expert, he may be concerned with public health problems in the rural areas of developing countries.

How does the metadisciplinary approach affect research in developing countries? It consists essentially in bringing together problem-solvers who have different expert contributions to make, but who are all committed to and thoroughly familiar with a set of development problems. In the meta-disciplinary approach, diverse people gather because they perceive a commonality of interest which is created by their commitment to a problem area. It is the common problem they are interested in which helps them bridge the intellectual barriers of their expert knowledge. This is in contrast to the usual multidisciplinary team, which is often created artificially to attack a problem but in which each expert finds little means of communication with other experts because the problem is unfamiliar and the languages of expertise are also unfamiliar.

The discussion on education, then, can be summed up by two arguments: First, the argument that professional schools need a commitment to both action and theory; second, that professional education needs to be based on both expertise and a commitment to selected development problems.

This point led to the issue of providing practical field experience for the young professionals who will work abroad. On this score, all the Americans attending the meeting were extremely concerned with the problem of financing programs of research and study abroad. Establishing such programs, it was felt, was no longer constrained by the structure and the reward system of American faculties, but was instead a problem made acute by external or internal financial and institution considerations. The financial problem results in part from the failure of the U. S. Congress to provide funds authorized under the International Education Act of 1966 and in part from the rapid shift of funding from research on external to research on internal (that is, American) development problems.

The conference heard many good words on the financial issue, but the group was not large enough to qualify as a pressure group; What was said the reader can well imagine.[4] The reader interested in the training issues will want to read Chapter 11, which provides a succinct resumé of some of the practical problems.

PART IV: COLLABORATION

Part IV of this book examines the issues of building institutions in developing countries and of the past and potential contributions of collaborative international approaches.

All the conference participants were aware that governments in developing countries have in the past few years become increasingly impatient of American or European researchers who take up the time of officials with requests for data and access to confidential documents, who sometimes upset local communities in which they may be mistaken for spies, and who then produce nothing useful. Even though it does not bear any of the direct cost of the research, government still has to accept risks: the findings of the research may publicize the weaknesses of government policy; the researcher may get into trouble with officials or communities from which government has to extricate him; he may gain access to secret information. The potential political embarrassments may be only vaguely foreseen, but they are likely to make the government of a developing country ambivalent toward foreign researchers--welcoming in principle, suspicious in practice. A government is not likely to accept the risks willingly unless it is satisfied that the research workers will provide expert advice and information which it urgently needs. And even if the research is of real interest to the government, the findings are of little use unless they can be communicated before the policy decisions to which they relate have to be taken. A Ph.D. thesis buried in an American university or a scholarly work published five years after a decision is no help at all.

Similar ambivalence can arise in relationships with overseas scholars. They may be suspicious of the ideological motives underlying American research and resentful of the presumption of foreign scholars in tackling problems of their own society without long experience of its culture and language. Neither governments nor overseas institutions can be expected to welcome American research workers if they perceive the research as benefiting only the researchers' professional careers or the standing of their university departments back home.

In Chapter 14, Raúl Devés Jullian, a Chilean engineer, formerly dean of the School of Engineering, is explicit: Developing countries do not need American or Europeans to come and do what local professionals can already do. They need Americans or Europeans to help them do that for which they are not yet prepared. This means collaboration, a mutual effort to work together, to find joint professional goals. His very frank statement should be read with care.

Vernon W. Ruttan, of the University of Minnesota, and P. K. Kelkar, the distinguished director of the India Institute of Technology (I.I.T.)/Kanpur, have specific recommendations to make along the same lines. Ruttan, in Chapter 15, describes the concept of international institutes based on experience in Mexico and the rice institute at Los Baños in the Philippines. In Chapter 16, Kelkar describes the international consortium approach as exemplified by his experience with I.I.T./Kanpur.

Both Ruttan and Kelkar point out that neo-imperialist approaches to professional development are resented. This is also what Adam Curle is saying in Chapter 4, and what Christie is suggesting in Chapter 5. The implications for American training institutions are evident. American professional institutions need to consciously create collaborative arrangements with counterpart institutions abroad. When an American university begins to study a problem at home, it might call on experts from developing countries to come and help; similarly, when an American university sends faculty or students abroad, it can seek to establish common endeavors with local institutions.

SUMMARY

For epilogue an international civil servant, Jack C.
Westoby, who has devoted many years to the international
approach to problem solving, summarizes many of the problems discussed throughout. Westoby is aware, as are many
of the contributors to this book, of the difficulties of the task
at hand. He is aware of the illusions of the fifties and the
sixties. He is aware that development comes from within and
not from outside. His words are crisp: "Technical assistance
is only really successful if it is geared to promoting development from within. It is not simply a question of transferring
skills; these skills have to become firmly rooted, capable of
growth, and attack a wide front." His tone is neither optimistic nor pessimistic, a fitting note of conclusion to a
conference which was also neither entirely one nor entirely
the other.

Indeed, it is difficult to summarize the wide-ranging discussions. But on the last day of the conference, a Sunday
morning in Berkeley at the Faculty Club, all the contributors
to this book sat together and agreed that a portion of the
discussion could be summed up under four general problems:
multi-role adjustment, role articulation, role variables, and
intellectual framework. These are discussed in the notes
Benveniste took on that morning, as follows.

Multi-role Adjustment. The contributors agreed that all
professionals face a problem of role adjustment. This arises
from the complementary aspects of the various non-professional
roles they play in different societies. When the U.S.-trained
engineer builds bridges in Egypt, he is not only an engineer
in the field but also an administrator of the work program--
and administrative practices may differ. The argument is
straightforward. An individual plays many roles; even if the
technical aspects of his professional role are universal, other
roles he is called upon to play do not have such universality.
His professional (universal) role will involve several other
social roles: for example, the host inviting colleagues to his
residence, the parent arranging for schooling for his children,
the husband helping his wife adjust to a new environment. In
short, there will be a multitude of complementary aspects of
his professional role which will differ. If he is not sufficiently

aware of some of these differences, he can spend unnecessary time solving peripheral problems.

Role Articulation. A professional in a developing country may find that his professional role and his other roles in society are articulated differently from what they are at home, with unforeseen consequences to his professional behavior. For example, he may find that politicians have attitudes about and expectations of him different from those usual at home, whether they involve greater or lesser faith in his pronouncements, or variations in what his legitimate area of professional competence is, or other matters. In short, the professional role itself has to be played differently because the environment in which it is played is different. Again, this problem may affect all professions.

Role Variables. A professional may find that although his expertise and knowledge are relevant to a given society, the variables with which he is accustomed to work differ significantly. For example, the economist needs to be aware of the quality and reliability of statistics; the architect needs to familiarize himself with local materials; the educator needs to recognize that different cultural traditions are being transmitted in the schools; the bridge-builder needs to attend to the peculiarities of soil conditions at the building site. To be sure, most professionals are aware of this type of problem; but sometimes the subleties between cultures are not sufficiently taken into account, particularly when the same label is used in different cultures to describe different social activities or conditions.

Intellectual Framework. A more significant problem is that of the models or theories that provide the intellectual framework for professional expertise, particularly for those professions relying on knowledge from the social sciences. What is relevant and useful in one society may not be relevant or useful in other societies. Since the content of professional knowledge is changing, largely as a result of practical testing of theory in the advanced countries, professional schools that limit their scope of interest to U. S.-based problems tend to develop a very parochial knowledge which they assume to be relevant to the whole world. Moreover, professional knowledge tends to become established and respectable; It thus resists the intellectual implications of new conditions, yet practices which fit one set of norms, the values of the past, may not fit emerging norms, the values of the present or of the immediate future.

There is, therefore, a constant problem of adjusting professional practices to the changing social environment, whether the changes be brought about by travel and communication or by internal transformations. Engineers, for example, recognize that some accepted practices of twenty years ago may not be adequate today, if only because a greater value is placed on the social consequences of their action. Greater value is now placed on the esthetics of the environment; power lines, once permissibly visible, are now increasingly placed under ground, engines and motors are not to pollute the atmosphere, oil drilling is not to result in the pollution of beaches, and so forth. Thus, this problem of adjusting to change does not affect all professions in the same way; but none are immune.

NOTES

1.   Seymour M. Lipset and Mildred A. Schwartz, "The Politics of Professionals," in Howard M. Vollmer and Donald L. Mills, eds., Professionalization (Englewood Cliffs, N.J.: Prentice Hall, 1966), pp. 299-309.

2.   Education and World Affairs, The Professional School and World Affairs (Albuquerque, N. M.: University of New Mexico Press, 1968).

3.   Guy Benveniste, "Metadisciplinary or Interdisciplinary: The Experience of the Professional School Committee at Berkeley," International Development Review, XI (1969), pp. 40-42; see also William Alonso, "Beyond the Interdisciplinary Approach to Planning," Berkeley: Center for Planning and Development Research, University of California (August 1968). (Mimeographed.)

4.   See, for example, Irwin T. Sanders and Margie M. Reinhard, A Crisis of Dollars: The Funding Threat to International Affairs in U.S. Higher Education (New York: Education and World Affairs, 1968).

PART I

EXPERTS ABROAD

CHAPTER **2** DILEMMAS OF PRO-
FESSIONALS ABROAD

Warren F. Ilchman
Guy Benveniste

What self-knowledge is necessary for the professional to
understand his role as an agent of change? Perhaps the first
is a recognition that he is an agent of change, whether he
wills it or not. Wittingly or unwittingly, the American professional, especially in low-income countries, affects his
environment in a variety of ways. At the obvious level, he
is an agent of change, for the skill he brings is one thought by
many to make possible some desired objective in the future.
Achieving this objective involves altering existing arrangements in ways which are sometimes appropriately, but often
inappropriately, calculated.

Wittingly professional acts of change are familiar and
already occupy the pages of professional journals. To suggest
some areas and goals, we may recall, for example, that
professionals may want to bring about a more innovative export sector; diversify the markets of a family corporation;
lower infant mortality; invent an increasingly flexible government administration, a more efficient system of tax collection,
a more productive agriculture, a regional plan that coordinates
objectives. But each measure, forecast and possibly implemented by foreign professionals, necessitates further
measures, by those affected, of social and personal preparation, of social and personal repair, a leaving of accustomed
ways and social expectations, a different kind of education,
reorientation of class and caste relationships, new organizational roles, and inevitable tugs and tears in the political
system.

The unwritten annals of professional involvement in other
societies are perhaps just as replete with instances of

unwitting acts as the journals are with witting ones. The list
of professional reports and advices that are never implemented
would probably take years to enumerate. When implementation
of sorts takes place, unforeseen consequences often prevail.
There were, for example, the professionals who suggested a
magnificent export crop scheme for an African country, only
to find that the scheme never succeeded; those who advised
a nation to expand higher education, only to find several years
later that instead of manpower shortages the country faced a
growing pool of unemployed school-leavers. There was a
recommended land reform program that succeeded only in
dispossessing tenant farmers; a tax system that virtually
bankrupted politically the regime which implemented it; a
small-investor scheme that only further entrenched a foreign
minority in the economic life of a country; The examples are
multitudinous, and colleagues in anthropology and sociology
have been highlighting some of them for years.[1] Even less
witting are those results which could never have been planned
for: the revolution in a ministry's hierarchy born of a
foreign professional's refusal to acknowledge "accepted"
channels; the nascent professional association that managed
to survive owing only to a professional's presence; the life
styles that a professional's colleagues adopted by virtue of
his visit; the political implications of the country club life of
many American professionals working abroad; the jealousies
that arise from salary differences among American and host
country professionals.

These effects, witting and unwitting, are possible
irrespective of the professional's formal responsibility
whether he is advising presidents or planning commissions,
foreign industrial groups, or village cooperatives; whether
he is implementing programs for a host country or an American corporation, or assisting through bilateral and multi-
lateral programs. Each professional, regardless of field,
enters upon a situation in which the participants are already
involved in comparatively stable exchange relationships.
Despite continuous attempts to modify these relationships,
the native professionals, the members of host governments,
the country's political participants and citizens have come to
recognize certain rights and obligations as likely.

THE PROFESSIONAL'S RESOURCES

Into existing situations which are different from the
American scene, the American-trained professional brings
with him a set of resources which give him power to affect
the existing exchange relationships. The American-trained
professional is not always aware of all the resources he
brings with him. Regardless of his particular field or of the
task at hand, his resources are not limited to his professional
knowledge (or to folklore). His resources may include the
international status and authority which his profession has in
the eyes of local elites. His status includes his access to
high levels of decision making in the host country, access
sometimes denied his local counterparts. This access to
information and communication in the host country may be
revealed to him and denied to nationals if nationals are considered to be competitors while the foreign expert is considered a short-term ally. The resources may include a
real or imaginary access to foreign economic wealth. It may
be believed that the American-trained professional can formulate and insure foreign loans or other forms of financial aid
or investment. In some instances it may be believed that the
foreign expert can bring coercive power on behalf of certain
objectives his government may be pursuing. In short, the
professional's status as an "expert" or as a citizen of a particular country has more or less value for those who associate
with him. Just as money or exchange credits may be forthcoming on the basis of the professional's presence or advice,
so can they be withdrawn, and so can other coercive action be
taken on his recommendation. Of course, the mix of resources
and of holdings differs among professions and among individuals within a profession. An American agronomist possesses
a mix of resources different from his Indian counterpart's or
an American engineer's. Thus, the professional is not
simply a technician dutifully appraising a situation or efficiently
and neutrally going about his tasks.

Three points are important: First, the American-trained
professional has resources that can mobilize other resources
to implement programs. But quite often the American-trained
professional is not aware that he has these resources, not-
withstanding the fact that wittingly or unwittingly his recommendations may have a very different impact in society other

than in his own. Where he might not be taken seriously at
home, he might be listened to intently by a finance minister
in Asia or Africa. Where he might not have any experience
in policy making at home, he might suddenly find that he is
called upon to advise on broad policy matters abroad.

Second, if he affects existing exchange relationships, the
results of his program or recommendations will often have a
wider impact than anticipated. Calculations based on his
experience in the U. S. scene will not take into account
variables relevant in other societies.

Third, if the American-trained professional is to achieve
the professional objectives he sets out after in developing
countries, he needs to be sensitive to the outcomes of his
objectives and to use his resources to sharpen likelihood;
that is, he needs to become fully and consciously engaged as
an agent of change. For it is our belief that concepts of
optimality as given by professional norms need to be translated to fit the conditions prevailing in different cultures, and,
more importantly, in different political and economic exchange
systems.

Therefore, if the professional is to carry out his responsibilities effectively, he must better understand his roles and
how they determine his modes of perception, system of
causality, and ordering of preferences. These he must understand in order that he see more clearly and choose optimally
in the context of desired professional norms. To see clearly
in this case is to be able to correct for the biases imposed on
his vision by the various roles the professional plays, to see
not only what his professional role prefers him to see, but to
see also the context of choice more fully. Furthermore, to
choose optimally is to select from among strategies and
tactics those which are fruitful, regardless of what is dictated
by professional customs at home. In a perfectly predictable
world, certain choices can be thought of as optimal. If one
saw clearly the possibilities in a less than predictable world,
what might be thought optimal in a professional credo might
be sub-optimizing in the larger social context in which the
profession plays a role.

THE ROLES HE PLAYS

If roles are thought of as sets of norms and understandings that define the way one interacts with others, then it is probably an exaggeration to say that the role of a professional is determinative and exhaustive of the professional's choices. Apart from actions attributable to existential choices, the American professional abroad is pursuing at least four roles:

a.   agent of professional knowledge;

b.   agent of a national culture;

c.   agent of a particular organization or regime;

d.   agent of a superior power in world political stratification.

In some instances these roles are perfectly compatible with each other, though they may mutually keep the professional from seeing clearly and choosing optimally. In other instances, they are incompatible; they may then cost the professional personal conflict and eventually perhaps effectiveness, or else in their incompatibility set up a tension that forces him to view afresh, apart from his roles, the empirical situation in which he finds himself.

Agent of Professional Knowledge

We assume that the role of agent of professional knowledge is the chief determinant of behavior of the professional abroad. The role both facilitates and impedes the professional's ability to see clearly and choose optimally. Education in a relatively coherent theory or an established body of knowledge, socialization through life as part of a relatively self-effacing professional group with a collective ethos and a justification for autonomy, a career in which one's orientations are toward transforming the world rather than interpreting it--all these factors can heighten the feeling of mastery and confidence in problem solving a professional needs. Also, from his professional knowledge and experience, he has the relevant universe simplified in ways to make problem solving easier

and the range of variables more manageable. Implicit in this
definition of the relevant universe is an understanding of a
desired situation toward which action is aimed and a pathologi-
cal status which one avoids or from which one moves.

Each profession advances a system of causation--an "if-
then technology"--that suggests that if a sequence is properly
followed, it will yield an approximation of desired results.
In addition to a fairly commonly held system of causality, professions also often have a commonly held time horizon--a
range of expectations of the time in which changes will normally
follow from certain measures. Finally, in addition to a man-
ageably defined universe and a system of causality and of
expectation, professional knowledge stratifies the world into
persons who take positions toward and materials and processes
that advance or delay desired ends.

The positive functional aspects of professional knowledge
should be clear. By encapsulating a universe in a way that
allows problems to be worked upon, professional knowledge
endows its possessor with the confidence and likely means to
move toward future possibilities and accounts for the activity
and promise of professionals abroad. But there is a dysfunctional side of the coin as well. The manageable universe,
the system of causality and of time horizons, the judgment of
agents and materials all arose in professional training and
experience in relation to the societies in which the profession
developed and has its present concentration of numbers and
power. The training thus reflects how the universe is defined
socially, economically, politically, and technically in those
societies in which the profession began and developed most
substantially. The problems selected, the sequential steps
identified, the agents or materials chosen--all partake of this
experience.

Yet the relevant universe identified by the professional
training and experience may be to narrow a universe when
the professional must solve problems in a low-income
country. An engineer may well need to be a sociologist, a
social worker, or a political analyst in order to include the
variables that are truly relevant to his problem. His education and experience aid him little in understanding this new
and broader universe. Moreover, the desired state--equilibria,
sustained yield, profit maximization, self-sufficiency and

productivity of individuals or families, rational organization--
may be out of the question or irrelevant in relation to resources and the regime's objectives. Either the chosen
agents of change, or the system of causality, or the time
horizon may also be inappropriate in the new setting.

In other words, we are arguing that a profession's
accustomed criteria and approaches can be both facilitating of
problem solving and positively hindering. Owing to the pragmatic presuppositions of professionals, one might shrug one's
shoulders and insist that what we say may be true, but can
be corrected for. To this we reply that there are aspects of
professionalism that make feedback difficult and correction
virtually impossible. First, there is a predisposition of
professionals to elevate the ends of their usual problems and
to conceive of the rest of the universe in terms of the extent
to which it impedes or facilitates these ends. A barrier is
not looked at as a demand to reassess theory or the evaluation of sequences, but as something to be overcome. Seldom
does the professional, when confronting a recalcitrant reality,
feel it necessary to question the adequacy of knowledge or
technique; instead, recalcitrant reality must be transformed
to approximate theory.

Second, professionals tend to accept peer evaluation as
the only legitimate judgment of the quality of their work. This,
of course, differs by professions. Doctors are obviously more
successful in achieving this than architects. But it is an ideal
for many and a reality for some. Not only does this predispose
the professional abroad to refrain from listening to the administrator or the politician; in addition, the number of professionals in most low-income countries is so sparse that the
reality testing provided by countervailing professional opinion
is absent.[2] It might be said that the professional abroad is a
Walter Heller without benefit of a Milton Friedman.

Third, a deeply entrenched anti-political bias is part and
parcel of the ideology of professions, and it is therefore ingrained in the training of professionals. The ideology of a
profession usually juxtaposes the rational criteria advanced
by the profession as the basis for choice "political" criteria
that, presumably, have some non-rational (irrational, anti-
rational) basis. As a result, professionals tend to sharply
limit the relevant universe, even if such an oversimplifica-
tion is clearly dysfunctional to the objectives they pursue.

Agent of a National Culture

From his national culture, as much as from the professional knowledge he possesses, the professional draws his
definitions of the relevant universe for change, his standards
of optimal conditions, his sense of causality and of temporal
expectations, and the heroes and villains in the drama of
change. Indeed, the more his professional knowledge and
his national cultural heritage coincide, the more likely is the
professional to feel that he is pursuing what is "universal"
rather than what is "conventional." An American professional,
perhaps, brings to his choices a belief in the technical solution of problems, an assumption that the private sector is
more efficient than the public sector, a preference for in-
dividualistic authority relations, a capacity for cooperation
in groups, a faith in progressive time and in the importance
of timing, a distrust of personal favors within kin groups, a
strong belief that graft and corruption have no function in a
modern society, and an endorsement of certain forces as
forward-looking and others as reactionary.

These "pre-judgments" need not be thought of as only
dysfunctional; they have certain advantages as well. The
professional who is an agent of American culture is perhaps
able to pass judgment more confidently than those bred in
other cultures. His time horizon may accelerate the otherwise interminable decisions of others. And his preferred
means of group cooperation may contribute to the building
of a productive infrastructure. But, functional or dysfunctional, the role of agent of a national culture is partly
determinate of the capacity of the American professional
abroad to see more clearly and to choose optimally.

Agent of an Organization or Regime

The American professional in a developing country usually
serves a particular organization or regime. He acquires
from this sponsor a set for understanding and norms of behavior. However, these may or may not be congruent with
either the professional norms he espouses or even with the
objectives pursued in the host country.

Of course, this role as agent of an organization is the one the professional plays most consciously, and hence its dysfunctions are most susceptible to correction. For instance, the trade-offs between action as a professional and as an employee of a particular organization or regime are easily recognized. A zone of indifference exists within which a professional will play the role of agent of a particular organization or regime. If the political or program demands of the particular organization exceed this zone, the professional tries to bring about greater congruence; if the conflict between this role and that of agent of professional knowledge becomes acute, the professional resigns. But the result of attempts at congruence will be a narrowing of the universe and of the ends of action in order that problem solving can take place; while, dysfunctionally, this narrowed universe results in too many variables out of the professional's control.

Agent of a Superior Power

The core of the role of agent of a superior world power is confidence that one is right and technically more competent because the political dominance of one's country or regime has as premise the superior ability of its members. The wealth and political influence of the West or the "Modernized" could only come, it is thought, from these manifestly superior qualities.

This can often be seen in the way professionals treat their counterparts in low-income countries. Somehow "the natives never get it right," regardless of the standard of performance. It is often the confidence born of this role that impels the advisor abroad to expand his work to that of planner-cum-political-entrepreneur. Not only does he see his colleagues as less competent than he to exercise the role; he also withholds a measure of responsibility large enough to confirm his initial judgment.

The role is buttressed by a thought-pattern that is widely held among professionals abroad and at home in the university. We shall call it the religion of development.[3] Sharing in the characteristics of religions generally, the religion of development defines the world so completely for its adherents

that change in all varieties, with many causes and outcomes
is obscured. Its devotees find in the religion the direction
for change and the evaluative criteria for choice. As religions
are wont to do, the religion of development places much re-
liance on faith, the undemonstratable, and the metaphysical.
The religion of development is compared with the religions
of Christianity, Communism, and nationalism in schematic
form in Table 1.

Each of the four has its adherents, devotees, and con-
verts; for the religion of development, these include aid-
givers and professionals abroad. To these adherents the
course of change and the agents of change are clear. The
villains and the heroes of the process are identified. There
is even, in "differentiation," an analogue to the ineffable
substance of "grace" that separates the "elect" from others.

The consequences of the religion should be clear. Its
adherents have the answers before the question is asked.
From the devotee's stratification of the world into elect and
heathen, proletariat and capitalists, nationalists and coloni-
alists, or industrialized and unindustrialized derives his
answers, without the hesitancy required for empirical sub-
stantiation. But the debilitating qualities of the religion
come more from its assumptions than from its non-empirical
character. In the religion of development, the first assumption is that the world can be stratified into the "haves" and
the "have-nots" on some criterion of wealth and accompanying complexity. Analysis, once the scholar is committed,
has to be conducted within the stratification. There derives
from this a second assumption, that there is a relation between
the national collective wealth and a nation's institutions and
values. A people "get" what they deserve. Furthermore,
the absence of national collective wealth can be attributed
to the absence of those institutions and values that mark the
"haves." Finally, those nations most closely tutored by
advanced nations are more advanced themselves than are the
untutored.

Thus, the failures of the professional abroad may arise
in large part from his own perceptions of the situation, formed
by virtue of his professional training and experiences; his
successes may arise despite that training and experience.

TABLE 1

Comparative "Religions"

Christianity	Communism	Nationalism	Development
God	Dialectical Materialism	Destiny of the nation	Science and technology
Messiah	Marx	"Father of the Country"	Industrially developed
Elect	Proletariat	Race	Economically underprivileged
Devil; heathen	Capitalists	Colonialists	Backward and feudal classes
Church	Communist Party	Nationalist movement	Planning Commission (AID)
Second Coming	Revolution	Political independence	Economic take-off
Last Judgment	Punishment of capitalists	Punishment of colonialists	Punishment of the idle
Millenium	Communist commonwealth	Autarky	Age of high mass consumption
Grace	Class consciousness	Patriotism	Differentiation

NOTES

1.   See, for example, George M. Foster, Traditional Cultures, and the Impact of Technological Change (New York: Harper, 1962).

2.   Warren F. Ilchman, "Productivity, Administrative Reform, and Anti-Politics: Dilemmas for Developing States, " in Ralph Braibanti, ed., Political and Administrative Development (Durham, N. C.: Duke University Press, 1969).

3.   The concept is further developed in Warren F. Ilchman, "The Unproductive Study of Productivity, " in Warren F. Ilchman et al., eds., Comparative Political Studies (forthcoming).

CHAPTER **3** RELATIVITY IN DEVELOP-
MENT: AN EXAMPLE
FROM CRIMINOLOGY

Nils Christie

My particular experience in comparative criminology
has been concentrated on historical material. I know a good
deal about Norwegian penal history; I know perhaps most
about crime and punishment in the low-income country of
Norway in the eighteenth century. And working with this
material, which is I think closely analogous to conditions in
several low-income countries today, I have often been
struck with the troubles I would have been in if I had been
given the privilege of offering advice, out of my present store
of knowledge, at that time. With all my equipment, and even
with my concrete knowledge of how history has actually gone,
I think I would hesitate before taking up the task of giving advice to my forefathers of 1769.

WHICH CRIMES? TREATED HOW?

First of all, how could I help my forefathers in selecting
which crimes they ought to concentrate on, and what means
they should use?

Two types of crime were dominant at that time, and both
met with what is today considered the utmost of severity.
First and foremost was theft. Stealing was then, as it is now,
one of the basic sins and met with the most severe sanctions.
And I do not feel in a position to blame my great-great-
grandfather, who lived in a society plagued by the most extreme material scarcity and moreover in a gemeinschaft, or
communal, social structure, in which to break a norm was to

break the general thrust of the social contract. I am much
more inclined to blame those of my contemporaries who live
in a high-income gesellschaft, or limited association, social
structure and are yet preoccupied with the crime of theft--a
crime of negligible importance to nearly everyone in an
abundant society.

The other major crime of my forefathers was crime related to sexual behavior. This is in extreme contrast to the
present-day crime picture in Norway, which has rid itself
of much of this sort of crime by abolishing several of the
laws against it. Should I drop some hints to my great-great-
grandfather on how to handle these crimes?

PUNISHMENTS AND SOCIAL INSTITUTIONS

I doubt it. His laws were intimately related to his
society. When he forbade cross-cousin marriage, killed
fathers and brothers for sexual relations with daughters and
sisters, and imprisoned unmarried persons for living together, he was probably engaged in the defense of an institution that both seemed to be and was essential to him.

Of course, by telling him that in two hundred years,
people would only shrug their shoulders at an act for which
he kills, I could perhaps accelerate the process of change.
Granting that some laws are kept more by custom than
functional necessity, we the experts could perhaps speed up
the abolition of inherited non-functional elements. But how
can the expert know what is non-functional? There are always grave risks of destroying institutions that are essential
to a particular society. In 1769 Norway was a colony of
imperial Denmark. The strongest line of Norwegian national
defense was to be found in the independent farmer families.
Anything weakening these families would have strengthened
the foreigners. Institutions are interrelated; that is the
near-to-paralyzing sociological core experience.

But the punishments, were they not cruel, unnecessarily
cruel--those mutilations, brandings on the forehead, killings,
burnings, and lifelong slavery? To me they are and I hope I

would have felt that way had I lived in 1769. But even with
my twentieth-century knowledge, I am not so sure how I
would have acted. Punishing is taking the good things away
from people. A poor man of 1769 owned little indeed that
could be taken away from him except his body or its parts.
And physical suffering, after all, was then more common-
place than it is today. Even slavery could not have been
very effective in an epoch when the condition of those who
were free but poor was not much better than the condition
of the slave in the castle, at least in regard to food, shelter,
and clothing. All in all, I hope I would have advocated
leniency, just as I would today.

In addition to this advocacy, I might have proved useful
to my forefathers by adding to their repertoire of punishments. I could, taking into account the values acceptable
both then and now, suggest penalties that would be perceived
as grave by all parties and yet be preferable in terms of
human suffering to mutilation, slavery, or death. I could,
for example, have argued with some vigor for the use of
deportation. Norway is a very long and narrow country, so
long that it reaches down to Sicily if stretched that way. The
northern parts of the country could have been filled up with
criminals as easily as parts of the United States, Australia,
and Siberia were, and with the same beneficial results. I
see no reason other than lack of imagination for my ancestors
not using that measure more than they actually did.

Hopefully, I would also have made an attempt to feed
some other information into the system. I would have made
some attempts to explain the mechanisms of insanity, to
thereby spare some lives. But again, I would have had to
restrict my advice. Norway then was not well suited to having
madmen rambling around in the valleys, and the country had
few alternatives to penal action. Education without more
humane measures of control might easily prove devastating
to the insane and provoke hate of them. My advice would
have concentrated on alternative means of coping with the
socially most severe cases of insanity.

What of all the modern techniques of criminal policy--
prison reform, probation, parole, treatment, and social
work; could I attempt to introduce these? Certainly I could.
But I hope I would have had the courage not to propose any

of them. I hope I would have had the sociological imagination
to see that these measures were the invention of other types
of societies, and that some of them were of rather dubious
quality. For example, I hope I would have dared to tell my
great-great-grandfather that in 200 years vagrants, particularly alcoholic vagrants, would be handled roughly the same
as in his time, but that procedures would be based on laws
passed by parliament with the pretense of giving treatment
and help. I might even dare to tell him that a new country
called the United States is still more sensitive to discussions
of motive. That country is just now in the middle of a process
of eliminating criminal proceedings for alcoholics altogether
and using the old means of incarceration in completely new
ways called civil commitments. I could continue by telling
my great-great-grandfather about Norway's laws on psycho-
paths and its use of indeterminate sentences, measures of
treatment he also applied in certain cases, but probably
with more guilt feelings, since he rightly believed he did so
out of vengeance and the need to protect society, and not so
much out of the need to treat the unhealthy mind of the criminal.

    I would also tell him about the "Philadelphia" type of
cell prison, a penological fad concept which did not hit Norway until 1814 and was not put into practice before 1850. I
could tell him that Norway regretted the system deeply and
abolished it in the twentieth century. The country has now
returned to the same general pattern as characterized
slavery, one emphasizing a maximum of communal life.
The difference is that the pattern is now imbedded in a society
with a material standard that would have impressed even the
king of Denmark.

    Perhaps this kind of information would have enabled my
ancestors (or the leaders of low-income countries today) to
avoid some mistakes. But I am uneasy at the thought that
they would probably have made other mistakes, simply because they would have been spared those made in high-
income countries today, and that they would not have learned
from the experience. Yet I assume this making of one's own
mistakes to be less of an evil than what results when representatives of generally mistaken social institutions go to
low-income countries to teach them how to repeat the alien
mistakes of the last forty years--when psychiatrists, prison
administrators, and the most accomplished social workers
tour the world with the "message."

Many modern measures are still of unproved effectiveness in the countries where they originate. Their possible
effectiveness in low-income countries is most dubious.
There is, for example, the present practice of undertaking
social work with criminals outside the prison. This is a
good example because it is accepted by experts both in
Western Europe and in the United States as the most hopeful
device for coping with criminals. The few controlled, or at
least ex post facto, experiments that have been conducted
in this whole field seem to give some advantage to social
work with criminals outside the prison over any known form
of incarceration. The best known are the experiments carried
out in Sacramento by Marguerite Wilson and her staff, but
other similar evidence adds to the picture.

But social work is dependent on the total social setting.
To introduce the notion of social work to eighteenth-century
Norwegians, I would have to give a vivid explanation of what
it is a social worker actually does. I would have to explain
that he is a person who listens to people's troubles and to
some of their pleasures, that he gives them advice on daily
matters, that he establishes a warm and close relationship
with them, that he explains--interprets--their behavior to
other people and other people's behavior to them. I hope I
would be so successful in making clear the role of social
worker that my listener would finally exclaim: "Say, boy,
the person you are describing reminds me of someone.
Isn't this actually a sort of paid friend you are talking about?"

He would be right. In his system, the person I am describing is someone who is sophisticated and who is paid
for doing partly what there is no need for doing in his
society, and partly what is done as a matter of course by
friends, or kin, or both. The modern social services are
created, in part to take care of needs created by the peculiar
form of modern society. Perhaps the professional abroad
could give more useful information and better advice to low-
income countries by pointing out such general relationships
and by thinking through, with them, alternative ways of
taking care of problems, ways that would reduce basic
suffering without creating the new plagues of modernized
countries.

THE NATURAL LEVEL OF CRIME

The lesson from these remarks on crime and criminal policy seems to be that much of the exchange of ideas has to take place at a rather high level of abstraction. What sort of system is the professional confronted with? How is control built into the interaction? What part does ideology play? What is perceived as more important: increased private consumption or national independence? Answers to these questions might be useful in deciding on what sort of "crime level" might be established in the particular society.

The idea of "crime level" brings up an area in which professionals in criminology probably could be of some service both to low-income and to high-income countries. Using it, we professionals ought to be able to assist societies to understand the basic mechanisms behind their crime picture and to formulate goals that are attainable.

What I am attempting to do is to re-introduce the old Durkheimian point of view. Taking that point of view seriously, as I think we criminologists ought to, has consequences for our goals with regard to crime. In an extremely oversimplified formulation, we might suggest that societies have a sort of natural level of crime. These levels may differ from society to society, or over time within a society. They seem to be linked up with basic features of each society. One task of criminology is to show how. But even without that knowledge, it seems that we--reasoning from Durkheim's model on the necessity of crime, or from Wilkins on our limited capacity to perceive deviance--might be of some use to societies by plainly telling them that they probably cannot expect very much reduction in the crime level without change in a host of other elements, some perhaps more dear than the crimes are disgusting. We might be helpful by pointing to the possibility that although some crimes may be eliminated, new ones will probably be invented, leaving the crime level unchanged. This knowledge should not be paralyzing, it should not give a feeling that fighting crime is no use. On the contrary; I think this perspective clears the ground by eliminating a distraction, the cry to "reduce crime," with all its inevitable disappointments. The society can then attack the problem of which crimes it prefers to fight, and whether it would prefer to exchange some major problems for new ones. This perspective also leads attention away from crime rates as measures of success and focusses it on a differentiated set of variables, such as human suffering, economic cost, predictability, justice, capability for change, dignity in handling of deviants. Success judged by these variables is probably both more important and realistically more attainable than success judged by the traditional ultimate goal, a crime-free society.[1]

ALTERNATIVES FOR SOCIAL STABILITY

The role of the professions as agents of change in developing countries is, in my view, first and foremost that of saving people from starvation, sickness, or death. But the further the professional departs from this primary task of reducing suffering, that is, the more successful he is, the more it is possible to consider alternative avenues of development. For me it is quite natural to raise questions related to the need for stability; for example, how can professionals preserve certain basic social structures (in low-income countries) while some elements are changed? How can professionals be trained to help keep people alive and reduce suffering, while also promoting the survival of the remaining set of core values of the particular society? How can professionals be used as defenders, expert defenders, of what any society at any time defines as its fundamental values, as the good things worth living for?

ETHICAL DILEMMAS

Professionals working in a foreign culture ought to be more careful in attempts to influence that culture than they usually are at home. Most professionals are showing a good deal of professional imperialism. Where many professions are at work, this imperialism is more easily canceled out than where the professions are few and atypical. Furthermore

(and this is increasingly relevant as more and more professionals work directly with values), the limited boundaries
of today's social research and knowledge means that all advice that has consequences for the social system implies a
substantial amount of risk for that social system. Given this
situation, it seems to me more fair to take risks on behalf
of one's own society than on behalf of someone else's society.
I would feel considerably more at ease working for penal reform that is based on rather meager empirical data in my
own country where I have a sort of fingerspitz-gefühl, an
at-my-fingertips sense, of what is happening and where I
will share any unhappy consequences, than in a culture that
will never be mine and where my children will not grow to
adulthood. Professionals trained abroad and coming home
to their own countries are, of course, in a somewhat different position in this respect.

But we professionals are all on common ground with regard to some other ethical dilemmas, first and foremost
that of whose side we are on. I take it for granted that it will
be on the side of the host country. If I am in Nigeria as a
shipping expert, I will have to do my utmost to develop the
Nigerian merchant marine so that it can compete with the
Norwegian. That is easy, at least in principle. But what
about taking sides with segments within a particular culture:
in struggles between emperor and commoners, between castes,
between parties? What does the communications expert do if
he observes that it is within his talent to transform an in-
efficient despot into an efficient one?

I think these are important questions, and difficult ones.
I think they ought to be analyzed; and I feel that a professional
going abroad on a mission of change-inducing activities can
be a menace, both to the new and to his own society, if he
does not work through a substantial part of these issues.

Finally, a word about research. If my skepticism regarding the blessings of change-inducing activities is to be
persuasive, it should be backed up by research. My question
to researchers is not "How can we professionals change low-
income countries?" but "How can we change parts of a social
system without changing the whole? What strategies of
economic and cultural developments are most easily adapted
to the social structure of low-income countries without
changing other basic institutions?"

Both those longing for change and those longing for stability might benefit from answers.

NOTES

1. I have been very much influenced by an important contribution by Patrick Törnudd, "Teorier og begreps-apparat i kriminologien" ("Theories and concepts in criminology") (paper presented at the Scandinavian Research Seminar in Criminology, Visby, Sweden, 1967).

CHAPTER **4** THE DEVIL'S ADVOCATE
VIEW

Adam Curle

Although I have worked for some time in the Third World,
and have, as a matter of fact, been partly responsible for a
program training others to do likewise, I do have one princi-
pal disqualification for discussing professionals as agents of
change: I am bothered by the concept "agents of change"
itself. I have never been quite able to determine what such
agents are, but I feel a perhaps unreasonable suspicion of
what I imagine they might be. This sounds subjective; it is.
Work in the field of foreign aid is relatively new, and professionals are too inclined to accord it a scientific validity
which it does not yet possess. When opinions are largely
based on personal experience, it is better to say so, and not
try to disguise prejudice as empirical truth by clothing it in
technical jargon.

ADVISORS AS IMPERIALISTS

The concept of advisor entails a built-in condescension.
It is an unspoken statement of superiority; it implies the
survival of intellectual imperialism after political manifesta-
tions have disappeared. In any case, how is the Asian,
African, or Latin American official to know that this stranger
has anything to offer? He is new to the country; how can he
hope to advise on its most intimate and intransigent problems?

The circumstances in which many advisors are appointed
does not help to endear them to the officials with whom they
must work. Sometimes they are foisted onto a particular
ministry because acceptance of them is the condition of

obtaining foreign aid. Sometimes they are arranged for by a
high official with particular interests who is out of office before the elaborate routine of appointment is concluded; his
successor may have different concerns. Some advisors have
been appointed because of the eloquence of an international
agency representative rather than because anyone really
needed them. Sometimes, it is true, advisors are wanted.
But they are wanted on the terms of the local people rather
than on those of the advisor and his agency. The local people
may require particular sorts of technical help, but the advisor may feel that he is qualified to give more general
counsel. It is important to bear in mind that with subjects
like education and social development, the most subtle and
sensitive aspects of a country's character and aspirations
are involved. The goals must be set in terms of local ideology
by local people; the outsider can only comment on the efficiency
of different practical means of reaching these goals. But the
very fact of being appointed an advisor creates a sense of
omnipotence, and many advisors find it hard to limit the
scope of their advice.

ADVISORS AS EDUCATORS

If most host country officials do not want advisors, or
want them for something different from what the advisors
want to give, it is surprising that the relationship ever works
out at all. But the outlook of advisors sometimes changes,
becoming more tolerant and humble. The "advisee" (this is
the only time I shall use the word, and I do so only to draw
attention to its ugliness of sound and of connotation) sometimes comes to like them personally, even to respect their
abilities. After I had spent several months in my first job,
I began to feel very much at ease with some of my local
colleagues, and I think this was reciprocated. My work involved much traveling, and after a couple of years I had
friends in many parts of the country. During this time the
fact that I bore the title of advisor became increasingly
insignificant. I felt that I was engaged with these friends in
a common enterprise. This, of course, raises the question
of the relationship of the advisor with the local people, whom,
presumably, he is to help to do a better job. The group of

advisors to which I was attached was supposed to have a
specifically educative role. We were meant to train our
local counterparts and eventually to work ourselves out of a
job. In a sense this is a logical role, for one might well
say that if the advisor has nothing to impart which is not
already known, he may as well stay at home. There are,
however, two major objections. If, first, one accepts the
advisor's educative capacity as his chief function, he is
immediately placed in an invidious position in relation to the
local people. If he really believes in his role and acts
accordingly, he will find it hard to establish contact. This
need cause no surprise. Many people of the host country are
too well educated and too well informed to find this type of
advisory role either profitable or palatable. And when they
are not so well educated or well informed, they are usually
extremely sensitive to anything which gives off the whiff of
the patronizing, because the patronizing attitude is part of
the pattern of colonialism.

The second reason why the educative role is unsatisfactory
is that it places in false perspective a number of the useful
things the advisor can really do. For example, he can support the views of his local counterpart or even promote them
himself, when it might be embarrassing or difficult (for
political or other reasons) for the local man to do so. He
can perform a useful role by drawing attention to individuals
or publications of significance and by putting his colleagues
in touch with appropriate people and agencies in other
countries. He can perform the same function in identifying
various sources of external aid. He can take some of the
load of work from his colleague: attending meetings and conferences, helping to assemble and analyze data, writing
memoranda, discussing and commenting on a hundred issues
and problems. He can help deal with unforeseen emergencies,
reassure the minister, bolster his colleague's morale, and
attend official functions of all sorts.

His more specifically educative functions will involve
presenting comparative material. His experience in other
countries should enable him to demonstrate what has worked
well and what has not: what has had which consequences;
what problems have been encountered in attempting certain
sorts of development; and so on. In doing so, he leaves to
his local colleague the work of drawing conclusions and

applying the lessons to the home country. To do more would
run the danger of irritating his opposite number by dogmatic
omniscience. In addition, he can carry out studies or write
position papers for the use of his colleague. He can serve as
a commentator and friendly critic of reports, working papers,
and drafts, bringing his different experience and background
to bear without specifically agreeing or disagreeing; he is in
a position to say how he, as an outsider, reacts to them. He
may also be able to point out factual errors and, again as an
outsider, suggest how the wider public might react to the
documents in question. Finally, he may place at the disposal
of his colleague any specialized knowledge of techniques he
may possess.

The role of the advisor as I have experienced it is very
much one of sharing, of "colleagueship," as I have already
indicated by frequent use of the term. I am not greatly in
favor of the word "counterpart," frequently used to describe
the host country officials who work with the advisor, because
it implies a sort of identity, a kind of mirror image. The
strength of the relationship, where it is strong, is that the
two people are different. The advisor and what I prefer to
call his local colleague both bring to bear their separate
skills and experience upon a problem in which they are jointly
concerned. If the relationship works out well, both end up
somewhat wiser than they began.

All this takes time. In order to work effectively as an
advisor, a man has to work through his own preconceptions
of his role; he has to learn enough about the intricacies of
the social situation to operate effectively in it, to break down
the suspicions and reserves of the local people by demon-
strating that he has something to offer; he has to demonstrate
also that he has the good will to offer what he can without
expecting anything in return. In short, it takes as long to
develop a relationship with a local colleague in which one can
act effectively as an advisor as it does to make friends with
him. Only friendship provides the basis of a good reciprocal
relationship in which there is an adequate pooling of knowledge.
This, at least, is one man's interpretation of his own experience.

ADVISORS AS "EDUCATEES"

To the extent that I have been able to share my experience
with a few people in a few developing countries, and to the extent that, as a result, they thought or acted differently, I
suppose I can admit to having been an agent of change. But
their impact on me was considerably greater than mine on
them. I began my tasks with a number of deeply held prejudices, with a strong if unconscious attitude of superiority,
and with no conception of how I would need to develop. Over
the years I have changed considerably in these respects.
What my colleagues may have gained from the relationship
with me was probably not much different from what colleagues
and students have derived from their relationship with me in
the universities (including one in a developing country) where
I have taught. That relationship has been an interchange, a
two-way communication, from which neither party emerges
unchanged.

CHANGING ATTITUDES AND BEHAVIOR

My approach to the problem of what the professional as
agent of change is may seem unduly limited. I have only discussed the professional as advisor, identifying his relationship
with his local colleague as being the area in which he acts
as an agent of change if he so acts at all. In this relationship
the professional is himself changed in the process. It may
be objected that there are many other circumstances in which
technical experts have purposefully set out to change the
attitudes and behavior of, for example, a group of businessmen by stimulating their achievement motivation; or families,
by making them aware of family planning; or farmers, by
breaking down their objections to new methods of cultivation.
To do any of these things would involve a specific use of
social and psychological techniques for achieving change.

I do not doubt that much can be said of the ways in which
attitudes and behavior can be changed and of the modifications
of method demanded by different circumstances, but I am
really doubtful of the relevance of such a discussion in this

context. In the first place to aim at changing attitudes and behavior would be inconsistent with the relationship which one hopes to establish, even if one is sufficiently sure of the nature of the change which should be brought about. Second, and equally important: I doubt whether a foreign technical expert or advisor should be engaged, except in most unusual circumstances, in changing attitudes and behavior. It is certainly legitimate to be engaged with one's local professional equivalent in developing techniques or producing changes in fields which have been specified and sanctioned by local policy. I find it quite another thing, however, for the technical expert to work on such matters by himself.

To me it is axiomatic that the role of the technical assistance expert is to collaborate with people who have the real executive responsibility, hoping that the collaboration may be mutually instructive to the point where assistance is no longer necessary. This type of relationship, between technical or professional equals, is the essence of the work of the agent of change, advisor, consultant (or whatever we choose to call him). It would constitute an act of dangerous arrogance for him to attempt to change the attitudes of a group of people whom, by the nature of things, he cannot know very well. By doing so, moreover, he would fail to achieve the main objective of technical assistance: to bring the need for it to an eventual end. It is perfectly proper for the outsider to work with people who are themselves attempting to bring about change in their own countrymen, but I do not see that this role is greatly different from the one which I have described myself as exercising.

CHANGES IN THE THIRD WORLD

In the early days of technical assistance, many of the developing countries were woefully short of persons with any of the professional qualifications required for development work. Many new nations had fewer graduates than were needed for their first cabinets. This situation is now greatly changed. Although the problems of development persist, the number of highly educated persons in the Third World has increased sharply. Not only have many new institutions of

higher learning been established in these countries, but the
flow of students they are sending to the colleges and universities of Europe and America has become a spate. In
addition, their peoples have shaken loose from the psychological independence upon the European or American which continued even after political independence had been achieved.
In a large number of countries, however low the general level
of development, there are pockets of great sophistication in
planning commissions, scientific and agricultural research
institutions, universities, and so on. Because of these advances, attitudes toward the foreign expert have greatly
changed. In the 1950's he was still greated with a mixture
of deference, resentment, and suspicion; deference because
he was thought to have some piece of knowledge possessed by
none of the local people, resentment because he had this exclusive information, and suspicion because me might be a
fraud, or a colonialist exploiter, or both. Now he is treated
in a much more matter-of-fact fashion. If he has come under
the right auspices it is because he has some skill which can
be put to practical use by the local people, under conditions
which they themselves determine. If his qualifications are
inadequate, the fact will very soon be recognized. If he is
psychologically unsuited to the task of collaboration with his
local colleagues, he will be quietly ignored.

Another tendency should be noted. Technical assistance
is no longer something which flows almost entirely from the
rich nations to the poor ones. The proportion of advisors
and trained technicians from the Third World who work in the
Third World is increasing rapidly. It is no longer true that
only the wealthier countries possess personnel with useful
qualifications, and the fact that one African nation, for
example, can help another has added a new dimension to the
technical assistance relationship.

WORLDWIDE CHANGE

A third change has taken place. There appears to be a
slow but solid drawing together of professional thought and
opinion throughout the world. For example, the network of
intercommunications within the scientific community is more

complex and efficient than ever before and is becoming increasingly comprehensive. Well-trained professionals in
almost any field can communicate easily across national
frontiers. Differences in approach in universities based on
the different national traditions appear to be growing less.
Certainly there are still, for instance, different French and
British styles of university education. Nevertheless, what
is done in specific fields within those institutions is both
mutually comprehensible and mutually valued.

I infer from all these factors that the American or
European who engages in work in the low-income countries
will increasingly find that he is dealing with people whom he
must respect as his technical equals. Moreover, he treats
with them on terms which are much more like those he would
use in his own country than they are like the complex and
ambivalent position of the advisor a few years ago. I see
every chance that this drawing together of the professional
community, so far as its professional role is concerned, will
increase as time goes by. The role of the technical expert
working overseas will then be less that of a missionary coming from a privileged to an underprivileged area, and more
that of a member of a pool of skilled persons which is somewhat larger in the rich countries than the poor ones. His
problems of communication with his local counterparts--
provided that he thinks of them as such, and not as benighted
ignoramuses privileged to be instructed by him--will become
increasingly easy.

There will, of course, be some technological differences;
but these too should be easy to master. To take an illustration
from the field of medicine: Many writers have emphasized
the danger of copying Western medical training, with its
stress on sophisticated techniques of diagnosis and treatment,
when most poor countries need much more emphasis on such
matters as hygiene, nutrition, and health education. Yet the
difference between the former and the latter emphasis is
relatively superficial when modern medicine as a worldwide
phenomen is compared with, for example, the traditional
medical practices of Africa or Asia.

These arguments lead me to suppose that the most
effective training for the technical assistance expert is to be
well grounded in his own professional expertise. Clearly, it

will always be important for him to know something about the
character of any other country or community in which he is
likely to practice his profession. However homogeneous the
international intellectual community, no one should go from
one country to work in another without some knowledge of the
culture, history, and politics of that nation. If, for example,
the professional expert is going to be involved with educational
processes in another country, whether high income or low
income, it will be important for him to learn as much as
possible of the cognitive processes of the people and hence
of their social system, their family structure, and so on. He
should try to learn how to relate the teaching process to the
cognitive map and how to develop the curriculum in some way
meaningful to the life and experience of the people. But
something comparable must be attempted even when working
in different communities in the same country. In any case,
it is perhaps more important to have a general sense of the
combined diversity and interrelatedness of the communities
of the world than to be steeped in the culture of any single
area. In the last resort, it is the individual who can see
himself in a clear relationship to his fellow human beings
who will be able to do the most for his fellows, because he is
able to act with them as an equal.

CHAPTER **5** EXPERTS ABROAD:
PROBLEMS OF THE
APPLICATION OF SOCIAL
SCIENCE TO FOREIGN AID[1]

Harold L. Wilensky

Rich countries like the United States are rich in expertise.
If one assumes that to save themselves, to protect their
national interests, and, on occasion, to do some good, they
will increasingly attempt to export professional and scientific
knowledge and skills to poor countries, one must ask, "What
in modern professional knowledge and doctrine can be applied
to the problems of development of countries with social,
political, and economic structures radically different from
one's own?" I shall argue that much professional skill is
parochial and therefore misleading or irrelevant; and that
the commitments, training, and outlook of the typical product
of an American professional school or graduate school are
inappropriate for practice in low-income countries.

It is easy for a social scientist to say, "We need to inject
more social science into professional school curricula."
But I doubt that in their present state the social sciences
have much to offer the poor countries beyond general orienting
analysis and pessimistic questions. And I think that much
"non-professional" insight and knowledge could and should
be integrated into professional curricula as a supplement to
technical training, wherever there is prospect of practice in
foreign cultures. By examining three success stories--
Israel's technical assistance program, Cornell's Vicos
project in Peru, and the Peace Corps--I have derived leads
for the recruitment and training of professional "change
agents," and will try to specify those parts of our knowledge
industries that are most useful in overcoming the poverty of
nations.

The problem of marketing professional expertise in the
low-income countries is analogous to the problem of rendering
technical assistance in the United States' own urban ghettos
and run-down rural areas. Conversation across national lines
is like conversation across the lines of class, race, religion,
and age in domestic circles. A middle-class social worker
dealing with a Negro school dropout is like an American
community developer turned loose on an isolated village in
Africa. A case worker taking a family history and making
clinical judgments ("defensive hostile personality, weak
superego") in the midst of a riot in Newark is like a Western
economist talking about a ten-year plan for an optimum pattern
of investment and output in the midst of a revolution in Southeast Asia. Both are guided by irrelevant professional doctrine;
both mistakenly assume a more-or-less predictable, stable
environment; to be effective, both would have to overcome
not merely their own doctrinal blindness, but also the for-
midable cultural barriers and political resistance of their
clients.

While one can cite notable successes in the export of
American expertise, the general picture is bleak. The United
States has no great advantage in exporting its ways of life and
thought. Consider the area in which it has clearest technical
superiority--weapons and defense systems. Despite the up-
to-date military establishment and swiftly changing weaponry,
it does not have much success in exporting the arts of war.
It stands astride Southeast Asia, impotent, its political leaders
for several years seized by specious analogies--Vietnam as
Munich, as Greece, as Czechoslovakia; Southeast Asia, with
per capita incomes in the range of $100, become Europe with
incomes 20 to 30 times as large; the 1930's and 1940's become
the 1960's; civil wars accompanied by multiple outside inter-
ventions become simple wars of aggression; unpopular military dictatorships become popular legitimate governments;
wholesale destruction of property and life, and corruption on
a grand scale, are become "saving our allies from Communism" and "maintaining world order." One must remind
oneself that such brittle slogans and doctrines are the product
of professional experts, often men of considerable specialized
knowledge.[2]

Professional and political preconceptions can remain im-
pervious to evidence no less in the peaceful pursuit of

development than in the pursuit of a utopian war. For instance, the United States has no obvious edge in telling the
world how to manage race conflict or how to run a modern
welfare state, [3] although it may have longer experience
running mass education and mass entertainment systems,
and perhaps more know-how in the conduct of big business
enterprise.

Training for humility and modesty, promoting a healthy
skepticism about American omnipotence and an understanding
of its own strength's and weaknesses--these are essential
beginnings in the production of effective change agents.

In short, in considering the cross-cultural application
of American professional practice, Americans can remember
that they have a convenient laboratory for cross-cultural
experience in their heterogeneous cities, where success in
coping with poverty and the urban crisis is as yet limited;
and that if they have an edge over other rich countries in exporting technical assistance, it is confined to a few problems
for which American solutions are at once uniquely successful
at home and adaptable abroad; for instance, the growing of
grain, the taking of censuses, the uses of accounting data,
the organization of a supermarket.

Recognizing these limitations of American ethnocentrism,
one must look more specifically at professional culture. The
problems of exporting technical assistance cannot be grasped
without understanding the organization and ideology of the
professions.

PAROCHIALISM OF PROFESSIONAL CULTURE

Consider first two elements which are common to all
established professions and which are mixed in their consequences for overseas practice: First, the tasks are technical;
Second, the professional man adheres to a set of professional
norms, at the center of which is the service ideal. [4]

The Technical Nature of Professional Tasks

Any occupation wishing to exercise professional authority
must find a technical basis for it, assert an exclusive jurisdiction, link both skill and jurisdiction to standards of training,
and convince the public that its services are uniquely trust-
worthy. Although this traditional model of professionalism,
based mainly on the "free" professions of medicine and law,
misses some aspects of the mixed forms of control now
emerging among salaried professionals, it captures a distinction important for the organization of work and for
public policy. In the minds of both the lay public and professional groups themselves the job of the professional is technical. It is based on systematic knowledge or doctrine
acquired only through lengthy prescribed training.

To say "technical" is not to say "scientific." For example, contrast two of the oldest professions--medicine and
the ministry. Medicine has emphasized its roots in the
physical and natural sciences along with high, rigorously
defined, and enforced standards of training designed to impart
that body of knowledge. Among the dominant denominations
in the ministry, rigorous standards of training are also
stressed, and competing doctrines are well codified and
systematized, providing a diverse technical base for practice--
a base less secure than the widely accepted dogma of medicine, but still within the scope of the definition. Similarly,
the legal profession is based on moral doctrines only slightly
modified by systematic empirical research. In a sense social
work has vacillated between the ministry (doctrine-oriented
social reform) and medicine (science-oriented clinical practice) as models for the professional thurst. Public administration, too, has moved between doctrine-oriented civic
reform and science-oriented theories of organization.

If technical tasks are not necessarily scientific, they are
nonetheless inaccessible to the layman. Professional knowledge, like all knowledge, is to some extent tacit; and it is
this that gives the established professions their auro of
mystery. As Michael Polanyi reminds us, "there are things
that we know but cannot tell";[5] the doctor's recognition of
the characteristic appearance of a disease, the taxonomist's
recognition of the specimen of a species--these are like our

everyday recognition of the identity of a person, the mood of a face, acts of understanding complex entities which we cannot fully report.

The expert may be defined as a man who knows so much that he can communicate only a small part of it. This element of tacit knowledge in the sciences and professions helps explain their achievement of exclusive jurisdiction; it also helps explain their traditionalism. The client public sees a mystery in the tasks to be performed, a mystery which is not given to the ordinary man to acquire. Since tacit knowledge is relatively inaccessible, it is also less subject to direct criticism and quick change. The tacit component of their knowledge base is a seldom recognized cause of the tenacious conservatism of the established professions.

The tradition of professionalism in the modern West-- the accent on technical task as a justification for exclusive jurisdiction--is pursued by hundreds of occupations in the rich countries; and indigenous experts in the underdeveloped nations have themselves been trained in schools drawing on this tradition. The typical professional man--the export product under discussion here--thus suffers from the familiar limitations of the expert: a "trained incapacity," an intensity of focus that blinds the vision; he is likely to be unaware of the contributions of other experts (not to mention non-experts) and to be inflexible when he must apply his skills to new situations and strange places. So far, specialization, conservatism, and the device of the mystery combine to make the professional man irrelevant to the urgent tasks of development in poor countries.

But the same technical training that makes the typical expert inflexible may on occasion have the reverse effect. While the professional push for autonomy can take the form of an unattractive struggle for exclusive jurisdiction, it is also the basis for an independence of judgment that counters bureaucratic pathologies and fosters flexibility in a crisis. Two studies provide suggestive evidence.

After intensive observation and interviewing of twelve employment interviewers in two sections of a department of a state employment agency, Peter M. Blau noted that one section showed a readiness to adapt the formal rules of

performance evaluation, workload, and the like to the
mission of the agency, which was matching job seekers to
employers' requests. Interviewers in the "least professional"
section avoided operations that did not show in their performance records, which emphasized number of placements.
They minimized job counseling, interviewed job applicants
superficially, and did not share information about job open-
ings or likely employees with fellow interviewers but instead
hid the slips under their desk blotters or in the files until
they could make the placement themselves. They also wasted
time on operations that did show in the record (for example,
they made out job orders for placing employees who were on
temporary layoff and really had jobs). In contrast, interviewers in the "more professional" section (indicated loosely
by common training in counseling and interviewing, by more
job security based on permanent civil service status, and
by the presence of such persons as a former social worker
and a prospective clinical psychologist) adapted agency procedures to client and agency goals. Professional security
and autonomy enhanced teamwork, increased section productivity, and lessened the need to seek security in fixed rules.[6]

Similarly, a study of ten medium-sized private hospitals
found that the larger the proportion of registered nurses
(as against practical nurses) who had five years or more of
service at the hospital (again a loose index of professionalism),
the more the nursing service resisted change in the daily
conduct of work, but the more flexibility it displayed in crisis
situations. Confronted with a stream of serious injuries from
a four-alarm fire, the more professional nurses proved more
willing to take initiative and assume authority.[7] A hint that
professionalism can advance even routine innovations comes
from Arthur Stinchcombe in data on three pairs of firms in
three industries (textiles, machinery, electric power).
"Those firms with more professionals [and technical staff]
innovate more rapidly than those with fewer, within the
same industry. And those firms which innovate more rapidly
create more positions for professionals."[8] This suggests
that the presence of many technical experts sets in motion a
circular reinforcement of institutionalized innovation.[9]
Stinchcombe wisely warns against extending the finding too
far: universities epitomize high ratios of professionals to
officials, but have slow rates of innovation in teaching and
administration, and many German and Russian firms with

weak staffing nevertheless grow faster than their counterparts in other countries rich in expertise. Knowledge of the relations between professionalism and innovation remains primitive.

In short, the "technical" side of professionalism is a double-edged sword: it is training for rigidity and a parochial conservatism; at the same time it is training for initiative and the exercise of independent judgment. The practical problem of selection and training for overseas practice is how to produce an expert who knows something but is not blinded by what he knows--a skilled man who is flexible and non-doctrinaire. Little research tells us the conditions under which that blend develops. Perhaps American professionals who go abroad--that is, who try something different--are already self-selected or trained for a bit more flexibility and intellectual breadth. But the professionals in the host country like the typical American expert who stays in the conventional domestic career, may accent the routine performance of his specialized duty.

The Service Ideal

The second major element in the culture of professionalism, the service ideal, is also mixed in its consequences for practice in low-income countries. The norms of the established professions dictate not only that the practitioner do technically competent, high-quality work, but that he adhere to a service ideal--devotion to the client's interests should guide decisions more than personal or commercial profit should, when the two are in conflict.

Although I am as cynical as the next fellow, I believe that the norm of selflessness is more than lip service. It is probably acted out in the established professions at a somewhat higher rate than in other occupations. Among the reasons are the following: (1) The belief that the professions offer a superior opportunity for service is widespread; it is one of the motives accounting for the excess of aspirants over entrants to these occupations--and there may be a self-selection of the service-motivated. (2) The client is peculiarly vulnerable; he is both in trouble and ignorant of

how to help himself out of it. If he did not believe that the
service ideal were operative, if he thought that the income
of the professional were a commanding motive, he would be
forced to approach the professional as he does a car dealer--
demanding a specific result in a specific time and a guarantee
of restitution should mistakes be made. He would also refuse
to give confidences or reveal potentially embarrassing facts.
The service ideal is the pivot around which the moral claim
to professional status revolves.

Supporting the service norm are several additional ideas
which influence relations with clients and colleagues but which
distinguish professional occupations in only minor degree.
For instance, norms covering client relations dictate that the
professional be impersonal and objective (limit the relationship to the technical task at hand, avoid emotional involvement)
and impartial (do not discriminate, give equal service regardless of personal sentiment).

In the area of colleague relations, two norms seem especially well developed in established professions: (1) "Do
what you can to maintain professional standards of work"
(for example, professionals tend to honor the technical competence of the formally qualified, avoid criticism of colleagues
in public, condemn unqualified practitioners, avoid too much
or too little work if it lowers standards); (2) "Be aware of the
limited competence of your own specialty within the profession, honor the claims of other specialties, and be ready to
refer clients to a more competent colleague."[10] Both norms
can be viewed as essential conditions for the maintenance of
the master norm--the technical service ideal.

In short, the degree of professionalization is measured
not just by the degree of success in the claim to exclusive
technical competence, but also by the degree of adherence to
the service ideal and its supporting norms of professional
conduct. Of interest in this connection is the question of
which occupations have gone how far in professionalizing.
Established solidly since the late Middle Ages have been law,
the clergy, university teaching (although the church did
dominate universities, medieval faculty were by no means
all clergy), and to some extent medicine (especially in Italy).
During the Renaissance and after, the military provided
professional careers for a dispossessed aristocracy.

Officer cadres in the standing armies of Europe from the
sixteenth to the nineteenth centuries developed a professionalism
based on a sense of brotherhood in a self-regulating fraternity
dedicated to codes of honor and service. Dentistry, architecture, and some areas of engineering (for example, civil
engineering) were professionalized by the early 1900's;
certified public accounting and several scientific and engineering fields came along more recently. Some are still in
the process of professionalizing: social work, correctional
work, veterinary medicine, and perhaps city planning and
various managerial jobs for nonprofit organizations--school
superintendents, foundation executives, administrators of
social agencies and hospitals. There are many borderline
cases, such as school teaching, librarianship, nursing,
pharmacy, optometry. Finally, many occupations will assert
claims to professional status and find that the claims are
honored by no one but themselves. I am inclined to place here
occupations in which a market orientation is overwhelming--
public relations, advertising, and funeral directing.

Implications for Agents of Change

If the accent on professional autonomy leads not to trained
incapacity, a fixed oblivion to the aims and claims of others,
but to flexibility in crises, then the technical man should
flourish in the unstable environment of modernizing low-income
countries. Further, a touch of selfless devotion is the mark
of a successful agent of change; insofar as professional schools
recruit and train men committed to service, and insofar as
the recruits express the service ideal in commitment to the
people in need, the schools produce an exportable product.
But insofar as the supporting norms of professional conduct
foster a type who stands on professional ceremony, who
accents the maintenance of exclusive jurisdiction and a rigid
adherence to standards appropriate only to a country rich in
professional resources, then professional neutrality and
objectivity is another phrase for political insensitivity, and
these norms may subvert effective international practice.

BROADENING THE KNOWLEDGE BASE:
SOCIAL SCIENCE?

When professional schools become interested in the tasks
of development and look to the social sciences for educational
materials and inspiration, what can they find? What are the
uses and limits of social science in this enterprise?

I see social science as a source of two broad types of
intelligence needed for the tasks of development, the "technical" and the "social-political-ideological." Technical
intelligence consists of scientific data, records, and arguments; it is mainly economic in content. Schools of engineering, agriculture, and public health (in its narrowest,
vaccine-injecting aspects) are especially attuned to this type
of intelligence. Social-political-ideological intelligence
consists of facts about, and techniques of changing, the
thoughts, feelings, and conduct of men; its content is mainly
doctrines and data on social action, community development,
and modernization. Schools of social welfare, public administration, and planning are especially attuned to this type
of intelligence.

Technical Knowledge and Skills

The first criticism of the "technical" knowledge base is
that the economic bias is naive. Gunnar Myrdal recently
elaborated this theme in his encyclopedic Asian Drama. A
quotation captures the main idea:

> In the Western World an analysis [of growth] in 'economic'
> terms--markets and prices, employment and unemploy-
> ment, consumption and savings, investment and output--
> [an analysis] that abstracts from modes and levels of
> living, from attitudes, institutions and culture may make
> sense. [But] an analogous procedure plainly does not
> [apply] in underdeveloped countries,

where economic and non-economic spheres are so closely
meshed. There one must deal with attitudes and institutions
and take account of very low levels of living. [11]

Whatever the merit of this general criticism, I think that many experts abroad--economists and non-economists alike-- have been misled by rather narrow economic biases and a related concentration on efficiency criteria. These experts evidence no sense of the conflict between efficiency and such values as equality, security, and political order. If one maximizes the rate of technological change, one cannot maximize equality of income distribution. Or if an efficiency socialist wants to eliminate unemployment and generally over- come the waste of capitalism, Fabian style (via nationaliza- tion, central planning, manpower controls, and so on), he cannot then greatly enhance workers' participation in industry. Similarly, industrial peace and harmony for the sake of economic efficiency are incompatible with great freedom of association, a free labor movement, and strikes.

Economically-biased experts are sometimes oblivious to the conflicts between hierarchical order and equality: if for efficiency's sake one enhances the authority of administrative leaders in politics and industry, one is unlikely to increase participation by the masses in important decisions. Such ex- perts also understate the conflicts between rapid rates of growth and social and psychological security: if one increases mobility, self-reliance, and entrepreneurial spirit, one will find it difficult to assure high stable levels of employment, a tolerable technology in the workplace, job security through wage and work guarantees, lifetime tenure, and other job rights. Above all, the philosophers of efficiency tend to underestimate the effects of rapid economic growth on political order; if in order to increase the efficiency of land use, one introduces large, mechanized commercial farms requiring few workers, then one may increase underemployment, force migration into overpopulated cities, and exacerbate political instability. Development theory, if not combined with broader social science, is thin.

Irony, Paradox: Paralysis?

Now suppose, as is increasingly the case, that develop- ment theory is combined with extensive social science training. Then it produces a sense of irony, an awareness of para- doxes, and often the conviction that the social and political environment is unyielding.

At the most elementary level--the level of freshman anthropology or sociology--the student acquires the notion of "tradition" or "cultural values" as obstacles to development. Aside from the empirical fact that on occasion tradition is overcome and radical changes in values occur, there is a logical problem. Explanations of backwardness in terms of "traditional values" are tautological. The values are inferred from behavior and then used to explain behavior: Fertility continues to be high because the group has high fertility values. Or, "tradition prevents change"; but "tradition" is just another name for the absence of change and thus explains nothing. [12]

George Foster provides a marvelous example of the limits of such explanations, an example which also underscores the the error of singleminded devotion to technical efficiency:

> In village India, cooking is traditionally done over an open dung fire in the kitchen. There is no chimney, and there are few windows, so the room fills with choking smoke which gradually filters through the thatch roof. Cooking is unpleasant under such conditions, and respiratory and eye ailments are common. The Community Development Programme has recognized this situation as a serious threat to health, and has developed an inexpensive pottery stove, a "smokeless chula," which maximizes the efficiency of fuel and draws smoke off through a chimney. It is sold at very low cost to villagers. Yet the smokeless chula has had limited success. In much of India wood-boring white ants infest roofs and if they are not suppressed they ruin a roof in a very short time. The continual presence of smoke in the roof accomplishes this end. If smoke is eliminated roofs must be replaced far more often, and the expense is greater than farmers are able to support. So the problem of introducing the smokeless chula--at least in many areas--lies not in the villager's addiction to smoke-irritated eyes, nor in his love of tradition, nor in his inability to understand the cooking advantages of the new stove, nor in the direct cost of the stove itself. He has simply added up the total cost and found that the disadvantages of the new stove outweigh the advantages. In this case the critical area of resistance has nothing to do with cooking at all. [13]

A leading student of Apache culture provides further
illustration of common hazards in the use of "traditional
values" as explanations of patterns of social behavior. A
basic value in Apache culture, says Morris Opler, is that
"sustained physical effort for productive ends is most praise-
worthy." It crosscuts all life areas, all social groups and
categories and determines behavior. The most important
deities are pictured as incessant workers; many myths have
the moral, "Beware of sloth" (there once was a lazy fellow,
a glutton; danger comes, his legs won't take him away, and
he's done for); ideals of beauty--short, squat, roundfaced,
and strong--boil down to sturdiness; property cannot be
inherited, it is destroyed at death, for the young must make
their own way up; in the legitimation of leadership the chief
is not a wise old sage, a person apart--his tenure must
instead be validated by constant activity; and so on. [14]

This analysis illustrates three typical traps: First, Opler
observes the instances of "physical effort" (Apache practices
and attitudes), infers the value from these instances, and
then postulates the value as a cause of Apache behavior
patterns, when the value is itself part of the action to be ex-
plained. Second, the analysis lacks the specificity that comes
from asking, "Values in the service of what functions, values
instituted in what roles?" Finally, it lacks the caution that
comes from systematic comparison of societies. With
respect to specificity and comparison, Opler confuses hardihood as an aspect of bravery, on the one hand, and industriousness, the willingness to submit oneself to unremitting
toil, on the other hand. Societies based on hunting, raiding,
or a pastoral economy must train their "workers" to muster
great speed in order to avoid or combat predators, human
or animal. For instance, the Navaho, who used to engage
in large-scale raiding and small-scale gathering, had many
precepts about laziness. "Lazy" for them meant the inability
to produce bursts of energy when on the warpath. The in-
dustrious Pueblo Indians might look lazy to the hardy Navaho.
Further comparison would show that in general, raiders
make good pastoralists. Chasing lions and leopards away
from cows, or chasing wolves and hostile cowboys away from
sheep, requires the same skills and values as fighting. The
Navaho in fact eventually moved from raiding to sheep herd-
ing; the value of hardihood, which originated in the service
of warfare, continued in the service of a pastoral economy.

If a society lacks the technology and social organization to
subjugate others or to move fast as a group, its members
will value individual hardihood, Wild West style. As for industriousness, that is a value common to all societies in
which a surplus is accumulated for non-subsistence purposes.
And to label various expressions of industriousness is not to
explain them.

More useful but still limited is the cultural relativism of
Margaret Mead or Ruth Benedict. [15] Students exposed to
work like their come away with a sense that the world is
wondrously diversified: piety is central in the Buddhist countries; firmness and self-discipline, among Greek peasants;
family responsibility, among middle-class and upper-class
East Indians; masculinity, among Latin American males.
All this, perhaps, makes the student more tolerant and humane,
but as a guide for work in low-income countries it is rather
vague.

At more sophisticated levels, development theory based
on social science inspires pessimism. The paradoxes of
economic growth are laid bare. Consider two typical hypotheses [16] about the counteracting changes that result from
economic growth.

1.   Technological change and investment in education,
transportation, and communication bring marked benefits
in increased output, a rise in standards of living. But these
in turn bring costly increases in aspirations (Duesenberry's
"demonstration effect")--the appetite for more is whetted,
but rewards do not keep pace. The end product is increased
opposition to civil authority--an efflorescence of secessionist
groups, mobs of urban unemployed, radical political and
religious sects, hostile labor movements.

One cannot even assume that education will inevitable pay
off. If educational policy does not prevent the newly educated
from adopting the attitude that they are too good to get their
hands dirty, the highly publicized "investment in human capital" can dampen economic growth, as well as increase the
political distance between elite and masses. [17] "An intelligentsia left in idleness and largely unemployable can be a
source of reactionary, rather than economic, activity; young
people brought up to despise manual work can reinforce the

resistance to development; education that draws off talent from the land reinforces the stagnation of the villages; an excess of would-be bureaucrats seeking civil service employment aggravates the shortage of technologists."[18] Even more uncertain is the political impact of foreign aid that produces an abundance of educated and employable young people: if the same aid creates jobs for them in an already overblown government bureaucracy, then they are eliminated as a source of serious pressure for necessary reforms in administration, land tenure, and taxation. If, on the other hand, aid does not create jobs for the educated, if they are not brought into government, they may become a source of political extremism and instability. Obviously what counts for development is which types of education are combined with what other measures.

2. The problem of gauging the optimal mix of central planning and direct controls with free market mechanisms: too much state planning creates corruption; too little fosters failure in national integration. If planners recommend quantitative controls on licensing, whether of foreign exchange, imports, materials, building sites, or bank loans, they provoke an enormous demand for corruption, Saigon style. Corruption increases fear that the government, or the section of it one has bribed, is unstable. That provokes a fear of personal ruin, which, in turn, inspires more corruption. If planners instead rely on indirect controls and free markets, then long-run development goals, inspiring national images of the future--the kind of great aspirations captured in a well-publicized central plan--are lost to view. And the nation is not built.

The optimal mix is difficult to gauge. Since almost all of the rulers of poor countries are so strongly committed to extensive central planning and government action for the kind of development they want, the paradoxes are almost academic.

The development literature is vast, and major controversies are not settled by a weight of evidence. For instance, there is the old Marxian controversy. Do technological and economic changes precede non-economic changes, is the economic sphere in some sense dominant? The question is not purely academic, for the answer guides the mix of investment (capital goods vs. education and the welfare state) and

types of experts (economists, accountants, engineers vs.
sociologists and experts in fertility control or community
development).

I think that at lower levels of development, and for the
very long run, some general predictions may be made on the
premise that changes in economic conditions or in technology
determine changes in the social order more than the reverse.
Take the Tanala, once a stable primitive tribe with a subsistence economy and communal ownership of land. The
initiating change was an exhaustion of jungle that compelled
a change in technique of rice cultivation. They had to give
up the dry-rice for the wet-rice method. There followed a
mad scramble for the few fertile valleys. According to
Abram Kardiner, this shift in method of cultivation caused
dramatic social changes: (1) the extended family system was
broken up (irrigated rice fields could be tended by one family,
so why share the product?); (2) property became important
as a measure of prestige, and land could not be inherited;
(3) tribal democracy was replaced by a king with absolute
power and a feudal hierarchy with permanent land tenure;
(4) slaves--of no economic importance in the old setup--
became assets both as workers and as sources of revenue by
ransom; (5) the new fears of poverty and oppression stimu-
lated the hoarding of wealth, an increase of crime and homo-
sexuality, and the introduction of concepts denoting "evil
spirits." Lauriston Sharp similarly traces the social and
cultural effects of a shift from the stone ax to the steel ax
among the Yir Yoront, an Australian aboriginal group. The
introduction of the steel ax weakened values based on a reli-
ance on nature, on the prestige of masculinity and age, and
on various kinship relations; it also increased anxiety and
introduced the new crimes of stealing and trespassing. [19]
The limiting or determining effect of technological change is
plain.

With higher levels of surplus energy, however, the limits
of existing technology, while still fateful, leave more choices
open for both elites and the rank-and-file citizen. Although
the distinction between "primitive" and "complex" obscures
considerable cultural diversity among the primitives, although
the astonishing sophistication and interdependence of modern
technology makes errors more costly and increases dependence on its continued use (so that many modern men have the

oppressive sense that technology is king), nevertheless the range of cultural and political possibilities accompanying a complex technology is greater; there is more chance to act out diverse values and beliefs and to adopt various styles of life. Hence, insofar as technological and economic changes determine modern social life, predictions of the specific consequences of technological change are less possible. One can say, for instance, that advancing industrialism requires increasing elaboration of organizational forms. But techno-logical determinism will not explain why one political system is democratic while another is totalitarian, or the vast varieties of each. Nor will it explain the accent on private vs. public welfare services in the United States; the greater equalitarian tendencies of American culture as compared with that of Britain; or Britain's stronger tradition of civil liberties. In short, many of the most important variations that have arisen in the last fifty or one hundred years between rich countries demand that one take account of values and beliefs as well as technology.

Myrdal seems to take an opposite view. He implies that at low levels of development, technology is seldom as crucial as values and beliefs (nor as crucial as non-economic attri-butes of social structure), but at high levels of development, technology is the dominant engine of change. He argues that technological or economic change in low-income countries is unlikely unless there are prior, radical changes in the social or institutional structure,[20] that important social changes will not follow in the wake of economic change (the new middle classes, once they are large and rich enough, will not over-throw corrupt governments; fertility will not be adequately controlled when aspirations rise; and so on).

I offer these examples, hinting at the state of one of many controversies, to make one point only: development theory enriched by social science has little direct application to modernization planning. The political leader, the top planner, the professional expert given a heavy dose of this literature is apt to find himself paralyzed by the paradoxes and the disputes.

That is not to say that the social science of development is not intellectually exciting, or even that it gives no useful orientation to the man of action. There is some hope of small

increments of rationality: areas of genuine ignorance can be
reduced. Some consensus exists, for instance on the proposition that sustained development does not typically occur
without a "big push," a critical minimum effort of great size
and speed. Poor countries cannot rely on too gradual an
approach.

Six Variables of Change

One can also derive a list of variables whose interrelations are important in promoting or impeding development
and which must somehow be taken into account. Existing research does not permit confident assertions about their connections; neither do good measures and reliable data exist
for discovering their relative importance for development.
Myrdal provides a convenient list of these variables; they
describe the focal points of change in poor countries:[21]

Output and Incomes. Low average labor productivity and low
per capita income. (Myrdal does not equate this with development, which he says is "the movement of the whole social
system upward.")

Conditions of Production. Small industrial sector. In agriculture, crafts, and traditional industries, techniques are
primitive, capital intensity low. Savings meager. Little
enterprise, especially long-term. Overhead capital (roads,
ports, communications facilities) inadequate. Labor utilization poor.

Levels of Living. Insufficient food intake, bad housing, bad
provisions for hygiene and medical care, few facilities for
vocational training at any level, weak cultural and educational
facilities.

Attitudes Toward Life and Work (the realm of values and
beliefs). Low levels of work discipline, punctuality, and
orderliness. Population is superstitious, unambitious, un-
adaptable, uncooperative, resistant to change, submissive
to authority and exploitation, has low standards of personal
hygiene, and does not believe in birth control.

Socio-political Institutions. Land tenure system blocking
agricultural advance (those who work the land neither own it

nor have secure tenure on it); undeveloped social arrangements for enterprise, employment, trade, and credit; weak
mechanisms for national integration; ineffective government
agencies and low standards of integrity and efficiency in public administration; unstable national politics; weak local
self-government; weak infrastructure of voluntary associations. "At the root of all these institutional debilities is a
low degree of popular participation and a rigid, inegalitarian
social stratification."[22]

Public Policies. Policies applied to conditions 2-5 designed
to speed up development; plans for change. (Myrdal argues
that 4 and 5 are the proper priorities for direct attack and
that it is futile to rely on the indirect effects of changes in
1, 2, and 3.)

Despite some consensus in the social science of development, despite the lists of dilemmas and variables one must
think about, the main story is one of vigorous intellectual
debate with little direct application.

Social-Political-Ideological Knowledge

More directly relevant, more immediately helpful than
theories of development is a fund of information and experience in social action and political organization, guided by
broad ideologies of modernization, community development,
and self-help. Linked with social science (especially
sociology, anthropology, political science, and what used to
be called institutional economics), these political insights
can lead to effective action for development. Such linkage of
social science and social action has been expressed in
promising poverty programs in the United States: the various
neighborhood and city-wide "opportunity mobilizations"
sponsored by the President's Committee on Delinquency and
Youth Crime; the Ford Foundation "gray areas" projects;
and some of the newer anti-poverty programs. All recognize
that social problems are rooted in social structure; all accent
political skills and the use of "indigenous non-professionals"
to break cultural barriers between helping agents and the poor;
all involve the efforts of public as well as private agencies;
and all assume that substantial change will not occur unless

the target people themselves are involved in the action.
Ironically, these ideas have been acted out more boldly elsewhere. In the United States of the late 1960's, in the atmosphere of a racial and welfare backlash, with the Vietnam war
draining political energies and polarizing the people, such
programs are barely launched before they are shot down in a
cloud of complaint about cost, coordination, and control, amid
cries of "welfare scandal. " The nation has been unwilling to
fund alternative approaches at a high enough level for a long
enough time to allow evaluation.

Three Success Stories

Fortunately I can turn to three successes in "technical
assistance" abroad, inspired by similar ideas and funded for
many years. They involve Cornell University's Vicos project
in Peru, the Peace Corps youngsters abroad, and Israeli experts everywhere. I chose these success tales casually; I
do not claim that they represent the universe of successes.
But they do involve a great range of technical tasks, from
highest to lowest; a great variety of disciplines, professions,
and types of change agents; and vastly different settings.
Although I draw on systematic studies of these cases, I am
prepared to discount some of their claims as self-promoting
propaganda, and my report remains impressionistic. Read-
ing accounts of these development efforts, however, I was
struck with the similarity of the forces said to cause success.
The formula seems to be: Invest heavily on many fronts in
an integrated effort; draw on teams of zealous change agents
who are strongly committed both to their work and to the
larger mission of development and who possess relevant attitudes and skills; go in only where the receiving government
or community and the exporting government or institution are
serious about the program.

Vicos: Peasant Society in Transition.

Vicos is perhaps the most spectacular crash program in
peaceful cultural change in history, and systematic evidence
of its success is solid.[23] Until 1952 Vicos was a large public
estate covering about 40, 000 acres in a valley in Peru about
250 miles north of Lima. The population of about 1, 700

Indians had been bound to the land as serfs or peons since
early colonial times. It was run by absentee renters and
administrators, whites or Mestizos, who reserved the most
fertile land for commercial exploitation. The peasants
worked without pay on manor land for several days a week.
They also had to supply free services to the manor as cooks,
grooms, swineherds, watchmen, servants. Finally, they
paid a labor tax for the privilege of working small family
plots. Their land had lost its fertility, seed had degenerated,
and the main crops and animals were stunted and diseased.
The usual malnutrition, endemic and epidemic diseases
were common; for instance, 80 per cent of the population was
infected with harmful parasites.

The political system was traditional, hierarchical, and
repressive. The Mestizo patron appointed eight Indian straw
bosses to supervise the labor force in the fields. In matters
not directly affecting the manor--marriage and religion,
public works, disputes over land and animals--a political-
religious hierarchy of elders, some seventeen Indian officials,
ruled. Sanctions ranged from brute force to the impounding
of peon property. All protest movements had been squelched
by a coalition of landlords, clergy, and police.

In 1952, after a two-year survey of the Vicos social
system by a Peruvian anthropologist, and in collaboration
with the Peruvian Institute of Indigenous Affairs, the Peru
Project of Cornell University subleased Vicos and its serfs.
The previous renter had gone bankrupt; Cornell anthropologists seized the opportunity to conduct an experiment in
modernization. The intervention was massive. During a
period of twelve years, using skills ranging fron anthropology
to sewing, 75 Cornell experts, 15 Peace Corps volunteers,
and several local artisans carried out a revolution in Vicos.
The outsiders ended free services to the patron, wiped out
peonage, began to pay for labor, carried out land reform,
introduced modern farming methods (fertilizer, good seed,
pesticides, proper row spacing) and gradually turned over
power to the peasants. An integrated program of institutional
and economic change included communal workshops, a credit
cooperative, a hotel, a forestation program, new schools,
health programs, and the teaching of skills in language, self-
government, agriculture, and crafts.

Rapid and successful modernization is evident in a new leadership operating a new community government, in rising agricultural productivity and commercial ventures, a higher standard of living (better housing and clothing, improved nutrition, the introduction of household appliances), all of which has brought the return migration of many departed Vicosinos. Old men who once ruled in family and community alike today consult their educated grandsons before making decisions. The young men who learned Spanish in school or in adult literacy classes or who glimpsed the wider world when they served in the Peruvian army, together with skilled artisans and farmers of all ages, have come into their own. Community leaders and the young, who once displayed attitudes of despair and apathy, now show optimism, even enthusiasm. In short, there is enhanced dignity among these peasants, a new enlightenment among the young, and a new respect for the Vicosinos in surrounding communities, although the traditional Mestizos view them as increasingly aggressive and insubordinate. Symbol of the democratization of social relations is the reaction of one Vicosino to a visiting dignitary, a Peruvian Congressman on an "inspection" tour of Vicos. The Congressman remarked that he was surprised to see that many Vicosinos still had the dirty habit of chewing coca. The Vicosino peasant, in an exquisite riposte, asked why the Congressman was smoking a cigarette when he certainly must know that Reader's Digest had recently reported the connection with cancer.

The only clear failure in this decade of development is the limited effect of health programs; the death rate actually climbed. Further, a mental health survey has uncovered signs of an increased level of anxiety--a cost, perhaps, of modernization everywhere.

In 1957, Cornell relinquished control; in 1962, ten years after the experiment began, the Peruvian government was able to execute a decree of expropriation and sell the property to the Vicosinos. The community is now independent and flourishing; Cornell plays only a research and consultant role, supplementing a continuing government program of development.

Israel's Program

From 1958 to 1966, 1,700 Israeli experts, organized in 489 missions, served in 62 countries abroad. In 1966, 406 were in Africa, 112 in the Mediterranean area, 70 in Latin America and the Caribbean, 52 in Asia--a total of 640 experts abroad. Most of them build pioneer and youth movements and engage in agriculture and irrigation, rural planning, medicine, academic and vocational education, rural planning, and community development. Two in three concentrate on agriculture and youth leadership programs. Much of this work is based on Israeli experience in comprehensive regional planning and rural settlement, using as a prototype the Lachish Development Region, in which immigrant settlers, for the most part strangers to agriculture, settled virgin land and eventually built a regional town of 18,000 residents plus 7,000 settlers dispersed among ten villages and three rural centers. Israeli teams have helped introduce variations on this scheme in Venezuela and Nepal, among other places. There is further a steady interchange of personnel between Israel and poorer countries; over 9,000 students from under-developed areas have studied development methods in Israel.[24]

In all this there are specific claims of achievement in raised output and income, new or revitalized communities, new social structures based on land reform, effective credit and distribution systems, and the like. But the most impressive signs of success are that tiny Israel exports a large number of experts--in relation to its population, more than any other developed nation except France, and that the governments and international organizations receiving Israeli experts ask for more, despite strong Arab pressures on the African and Mediterranean countries to break the tie.

The Peace Corps

In contrast to the experienced Israeli experts and the action-researchers of Cornell, the Peace Corps is a collection of youthful amateurs. It constituted well over half of America's total technical assistance personnel abroad in 1968, when there were over 11,000 Peace Corpsmen overseas. The Corpsmen are, typically, unspecialized B.A.'s, who go through only about 13 weeks of very elementary training, usually covering job assignments, area studies, American studies, world affairs, health and hygiene, sensitivity training, physical training, Corps orientation, and five hours a day of language training. Most volunteers engage in teaching; the next largest category of activity is community development, a loose phrase to describe efforts to promote self-help projects in local villages.

One cannot yet judge the long-run impact of the Peace Corps; followup studies are limited, community projects and community consciousness alike may collapse after the Corpsman leaves. Peace Corps volunteers who have written about their experience are much less optimistic than their elders, who accent the salutary effects on both the returned Corpsman and the community he lived in, and the favorable image of the United States the Corps creates abroad. But aside from general support in this country and host countries, aside from the fact that successive waves of Corpsmen routinely enter poor countries and survive, some systematic evaluations of tangible achievements are available.

Carefully evaluating a rural development program in Colombia after the first group of volunteers had completed their two-year tour of duty, Morris Stein found the following results.[25]

1. The volunteers initiated, participated in, or completed 44 rural schools (55 more were started); 29 rural roads (53 started); 27 aqueducts (29 started); and 4 health centers (13 started), staffed by 14 doctors 11 nurses. They built well over 1,000 latrines and 100 sports fields, and established 21 sports leagues, 26 cooperatives, and a great many juntas of Accion Communal, sports clubs, women's groups and other organizations.

2. Opinions of a sample of Colombians (N = 343 adults, 122 children) were taken. The sample included those who participated and those who stayed out of volunteers' projects; leaders and non-leaders; Colombians at "difficult" sites and less difficult sites. Opinions were favorable but not uncritical. (For example, volunteers were perceived as important stimulators or catalysts in the establishment or rejuvenation of juntas. Well over nine of each ten adults and children displayed generally positive attitudes both toward the Corps and toward the specific volunteers they had known. The few

critics mentioned lack of material aid or said that the volunteers should have known the culture and language of the people
better. Anecdotes were consistent with interviews.

3.   Ratings and observations by Peace Corps supervisors
were consistent with the opinions of the Colombians and the
local anecdotes.

Four Sources of Success

What these three success tales have in common, what
accounts for their achievements are four factors: large investment of resources, some personal qualities of the agents
of change, the commitment and competence of the host government, and the commitment of the donor.

Large Investment of Resources.

Many resources, including diversified semi-technical
and political skills must be invested for success. The rich
countries cannot go about the world renting haciendas and
putting in 1 expert for every 170 natives--roughly the case
in Vicos. Yet, consistent with the idea of the "big push,"
the intervention must be serious and sustained, be directed
to several inter-related problems, and tap both professional
and non-professional skills. In Vicos, Cornell used university-
trained agronomists and experienced farmers and building
tradesmen as well as Peace Corps amateurs. Israel draws
on a history of nation building; it concentrates on settling new
areas, building new communities, agricultural instruction,
youth work. In selecting experts to go overseas, Israel
emphasizes experience rather than university training,
although a combination of the two is common. For instance,
many of the Israeli experts were instructors either in the
Nahal, a special section of the army which conducts intensive
military training and builds border settlements, or in Gadna,
a major youth organization which conducts paramilitary
training, accents the pioneer virtues, and indoctrinates youth
in national goals. That may sound alien to American ears,
but it is relevant to the problem of forging unity among a
loose collection of rival tribes, clans, villages, and regions
in an African state. The Young Pioneers Movement in the

Central African Republic--based on the Israeli <u>Nahal</u> program--
was developed by the native government to "'condition' the
unemployed youth of the towns ...to form a spearhead of
progress in the rural areas...from model modern cooperative
villages which are expected to have a salutary influence on the
neighboring tribal villages."[26] Israeli experts work within
a framework established by the native government. "The staff
of the movement were initially trained in Israel...they are now
trained at the Kolongo School, near Bangui, with the help of
about 20 Israeli experts...for the first year the responsible
posts were to be filled by Israelis with a national counterpart
working alongside them, while in the second year the responsibilities were to be turned over to the counterparts, who would
be aided by Israeli technical advisors."[27]

The Peace Corps typically recruits "B.A. generalists"
on the assumption that middle level, semi-technical tasks can
quickly be learned by a strongly motivated, well educated
youngster. The American accent is on professional expertise,
taking as the national symbol of efficiency a systems analyst
in the Pentagon calculating the cost effectiveness of a billion-
dollar B-52 wing vs. half a dozen Polaris submarines; one
tends to forget the expertise of Everyman. A rich country
has experienced a general upgrading of its entire population;
it can tap a fund of basic knowledge learned in an atmosphere
of machines and literacy. Before he tries for his first job,
the typical American can read, write, drive a car, tinker
with motors, use tools. That is why the armed forces and
industry can train most Americans for most jobs so quickly.
And that is why the Vicos investigators remark that advising
Vicosinos on how to raise potatoes did not require farming
experience[28] and conclude that much of the innovation in Vicos
was simply the store of ideas and skills drawn from Western
civilization that any member of the Cornell project could
command, whatever his specialty.

Incidentally: in technical assistance, the semi-professional
handyman is the fastest growing category of personnel.[29] He
is usually used in collaboration with more technical types, who
are in shorter supply.

<u>Personal Qualities of Professionals</u>

The most successful change agents are strongly committed
to modernization goals, or to international practice of their

skills, or to both; they are receptive to teamwork in a context of communal or government sponsorship; they are aware of non-economic consequences of economic action; they are self-reliant, flexible, and egalitarian.

Patterns of Motivation and Commitment. Cornell's project teams in Vicos were motivated by the opportunity to do anthropological research and thereby further their own academic reputation and careers at home, and by an ideology of participatory democracy (the belief that suppressed peasant populations, once freed, given encouragement and help, can and ought to control their own destinies through local organizations). Israeli experts combine a similar missionary zeal with princely salaries. Israel views technical assistance as crucial for its political position, helpful for its African markets, and satisfying for its self-image. ("Until a few years ago, " said the Director of the African Department of the Israeli foreign office, "every mission was...a mission of request...(for) support, arms, manpower. Now we give and take.")[30] Israel therefore pays its experts as much as two to three times what they could earn in the public sector at home. From the large pool of manpower available, the most experienced and committed experts can be selected. The Peace Corps with pay at close to subsistence levels, achieves the same result by an elaborate selection and selection-in-training program and by tapping a large, previously unrecognized pool of youthful idealism. Although volunteers have a variety of complex and overlapping motives, one study shows that 93 per cent reported a "desire to give" as the basis for applying, and only 65 per cent a "desire to gain."[31] An evaluation study shows that trainees who are accepted for overseas assignment in Colombia, compared to the rejects, are generally more involved in social interaction, more self-confident, and more humanistically inclined. Conversely, "action-oriented" Corpsmen, who were "impatient" and "controlling" in their efforts to get a particular construction project completed, were less successful than "socially oriented" or "people oriented" types.[32] The volunteers sent to Ghana in 1961 who earned the highest performance ratings (based on personal interviews with psychologists in the field) accented either constructive personal relationships with a wide variety of Africans, together with wide-ranging interest in Africa, or a more narrow focus in which there was a strong commitment to teaching--both involving close contact with the people and identification with African development goals.[33]

Obviously, in all three cases, the change agents were internationally-minded and sympathetic to the aspirations of poor people and national independence. If the Peace Corps volunteers are not that way at the outset, they become so. Stein reports that before their Peace Corps experience, 53 per cent of his 51 volunteers in Colombia indicated career choices in government or international affairs; twelve months after their return, the figure was 80 per cent, with major shifts toward international affairs with a social science base. Political activism also increased. [34]

Teamwork in a Context of Communal or State Control. The annals of technical assistance are full of atrocity tales about the over-specialized expert who successfully does his "thing" and thereby destroys some other more essential factor: the engineer who builds his dam provides a breeding ground for disease in the basin below; or the soil he irrigates turns out to be inhospitable to the crops that can be grown in that climate; or his labor-saving device increases debilitating idleness in a labor-rich community. The three programs I have described, in contrast, encourage the change agent to accept teamwork in a framework of local participation and government planning. The Peace Corps is self-consciously anti-professional; this is so partly because it wants to avoid becoming a junior to the Agency for International Development (AID), but also because it thinks that professionalism inhibits the collaboration necessary to do the job. Cornell organized a great range of skills in project teams. The Israeli experts like to work with their hands, and with local people; they are accustomed to cooperative effort by agronomists, sociologists, agricultural economists, and engineers, and work well with men of different levels of sophistication.

The watchword for all is "improvise": adapt the tools and techniques to the limited resources of men and material on hand; do not wait for conventional possibilities; invent an organizational form and a practical technique that works. For instance, Israeli resettlement projects make future ownership of land contingent on adoption of new techniques of farming. For other projects, for example construction, the Israelis create joint-stock companies in which host governments have majority ownership; Israeli experts keep management in their own hands until natives can be trained to take over. Similarly, in order to encourage the Vicosinos to

cultivate blight-free potatoes, the Cornell innovators set up
a credit system whereby the local people could get the seed,
insecticides, and other necessary materials, then pay off the
loan with a share of the crop at the end of the season. The
first-year success of the few who tried this system inspired
its rapid spread and within six years Vicos, as the largest
potato producer of the region, was selling surplus on the
Lima market.

Finally, the aggressively communal spirit of Israel, its
experience with the kibbutz and other forms of cooperation;
the ideology of participatory democracy of applied anthropology; the Peace Corps involvement with local communities--
all mesh with the facts of political life in poor countries
struggling to be modern. Government planning is taken for
granted; collective or public forms of economic enterprise
are typical; mobilization of the population for self-help is
necessary if development is to be self-sustaining. The American professional expert does not always find such a collecti-
vistic environment congenial.

Awareness of the Social and Political Effects of Action.
Awareness of noneconomic consequences is related to the
accent on teamwork. For instance, the Israeli mission to
Iran advised the government to avoid large commercial farms
that would force people into the cities. Working through a
traditional village social structure, and emphasizing cooperation and a government policy of land redistribution, Israeli
agronomists, economists, and sociologists were able to
motivate and train people to manage small farms. In Vicos,
awareness of the interdependence of economic and social
structures was central to the design of the entire project.
Vicos' economic life could not be altered without taking
account of several socio-political contexts: the national
government, represented by the Indian Institute; the Mestizo
merchants in nearby trading towns, represented by a coordi-
nating body involving numerous government entities; and
publicity through the mass media. Despite the temptation to
get on with the job and bypass the former straw bosses, all
old and respected men, the Cornell action-researchers worked
through these bosses until they could be retired and replaced
by younger, more modernization-oriented men. After a few
years, control passed to a ten-man council elected annually.

Self-Reliance, Flexibility, Egalitarianism. In a world of
meager resources, self-reliance and flexibility count. In a
world where everyone wants to be more equal than everyone
else, informality and a genuine commitment to equality help.
And in a world of fanatical faiths in nation and race, cross-
cultural experience is useful.

Plainly, the recruits to the three programs under discussion meet the bill. Anthropologists by custom earn their
union card and pay their dues by living with a strange people.
The first Vicos investigator, Mario C. Vazquez, stunned the
community, especially the Mestizos in nearby cities, by
declining to adopt a posture of superiority toward the Indians;
he and the North Americans who followed him lived with
Vicos families. Quite aside from their humanitarian and
equalitarian values, the anthropologists had to do this in order
to win the confidence and cooperation of Vicosinos in their
field work.

Israelis generally, especially those born in Israel, play
down status and class differences; they are also anti-isolationist
and anti-colonial. The experts sent abroad not only share this
equalitarian stance, but they have, typically, also had experience working with various ethnic groups, for example in settlement programs for new immigrants to Israel from low-income
countries. All of this carries over in their contacts with
natives and provides a sharp contrast with the behavior of
European and American experts abroad. Israeli experts
typically avoid capitals, do not stay in the best hotels. They
often rough it, living in close contact with natives, including
native experts. The aims are to demonstrate that manual
labor has dignity, to secure local participation, and to transfer expertise.

The Peace Corps ideology is, of course, radically egalitarian. Although criteria for selection-in-training vary from
program to program, they typically include dedication to service based on evidence of consideration for others, variety of
contact with ethnic and socio-economic groups, and active
participation in community organizations; self-sufficiency,
including evidence of emancipation from family, outdoor experience, and adeptness with tools; concern with domestic and
international affairs.[35] There is also a "Transition Training"
program, in which some volunteers complete their training at

sites that approximate the living conditions of their host country.[36] For instance, the University of Hawaii runs a program for practice in living in an Asian village, and the Corps training camp in Puerto Rico sends trainees out to find a Puerto Rican family with whom they can live for a time. Similarly, a recent Berkeley project to train Corpsmen bound for Peru used a wide range of field trips designed to simulate the village experience: trainees visited nearby Oakland slums repeatedly until they improved their powers of observation regarding life styles different from their own (sooner or later they notice that there are no mail boxes, no covers on garbage cans, no Volkswagens) and learned to overcome their fears about knocking on doors of strangers in unstructured situations. They received a few dollars to go to small cities in northern California for two or three days, with instructions to live within a poverty budget (for example, to sleep in a sleazy hotel or flophouse); where possible, they tried out their Spanish. They returned with answers to a series of questions about city life (how do you get a liquor license, who are the most powerful men in town, name the heads of major voluntary associations and describe their functions, is there a poverty program, are there signs of its success). The Peace Corps director in Peru was enthusiastic about the self-confidence and realism of the products.

On the job the volunteers mix socially: cars are prohibited, the living allowance is kept low, and the volunteer may be the only white man in a black village. Sentiment is thus reinforced by necessity; they have to fraternize. Even where U. S. relations with the host were deteriorating, as in Ghana, the Corpsmen became good friends with natives.[37]

In sum: if professional schools are to recruit and train effective change agents, they must search for men and women who are internationally minded, committed to modernization goals, and receptive to teamwork under government or communal control. On the cognitive side, they should understand the social and political as well as the economic consequences of action. Perhaps the social science literature on development, with appropriate tolerance for its ambiguity, can help here. In personality and orientation, they should be self-reliant and self-confident, patient, flexible, and egalitarian. Their biographies should include cross-cultural experience.

Commitment and Competence of the Host Government

Israel has an advantage in overcoming the suspicions of
the leaders of poor countries because it is a new nation with
no past record as a colonial power. My impression is that
the most successful Israeli projects are those with strong
support from the central government of the host country.
Trying to implement a program of land reform and rural
redevelopment, Iran permitted Israeli experts to go over
the heads of middle-level bureaucrats and obstructionists.
Cornell was allowed to rent the Vicos hacienda, and the
Peruvian government fought for transfer of title to the peasants
for five years against strong opposition.

Projects imported as window-dressing, those ten-year
development plans destined from the beginning only for a
dusty file, are useless. Further, the host governments
sometimes see community developers such as Peace Corps
volunteers as stirring up the masses, as pushing their
equalitarian political ideals too hard. Occasionally, military
or special forces personnel from the guest government work
at cross purposes with civilian aid personnel. Such short
circuits can alienate the host government--a risk built into
any serious effort to guide social change in an atmosphere of
small wars and cold wars.

Not so obvious is what level of administrative and political
competence of the host government is necessary for the fruitful use of aid and, given severe limitations of competence,
whether anything can be done. If the aid is massive and is
rendered within a context of a "big push" for development, the
level of competence must be very high; if the aid is small
and scattered and quite limited in aspiration, success does
not rest so heavily on the state of administration, but neither
does the aid count much for long-run development.

The case of aid to the small kingdom of Nepal in 1951-62
illustrates this relationship between competence and the size
of the aid effort. In the twelve years following the 1950 revolution, foreign powers and agencies, including the United
States, India, China, the Soviet Union, Israel, Switzerland,
West Germany, Japan, Australia, New Zealand, the UN, and
the Ford Foundation, put $90,000,000 of aid into Nepal, with
generally adverse effects. Nepal lacked elementary

administrative competence and political will; repeated civil
service purges made continuity of plans and action impossible;
but aid did bloat an already over-inflated bureaucracy, paralyzing further the capacity to change. Less dramatic than the
futility of massive American intervention in Vietnam, the more
peaceful humanitarian effort in Nepal proved equally futile and
is at least as well documented. [38]

That an attempt by American and Nepalese personnel to
build 70 foot-bridges in two years resulted in the completion
of only 1 bridge in five years is a measure of failure characteristic of practically all of the big-nation projects in Nepal.
The paternalism and condescension of the Indians was expressed
in their habit of giving the Nepalese virtually no responsibilities
in the execution of Indian aid projects. Equally ineffective was
the American practice of launching ambitious national projects
with meager financing and little provision for training Nepalese,
coupled with the democratic urge to turn over authority to the
untrained. The Soviet Union record was no better. The
Swiss, however, circumvented the Nepalese bureaucracy,
recognized the shortage of elementary skills, and started
cautiously with Swiss-managed dairy and cheese plants, taking their time in a long-run effort to train Nepalese successors.
Using the techniques of cooperation and community development already described, the Israelis were equally successful
in their modest efforts in resettlement, construction, and
training. The multiplicity of these smaller, well-publicized
aid programs, however, created the illusion of great activity--
spreading the false impression that development was going
ahead without basic reforms in taxation, administration, and
land tenure.

The lesson of Nepal is that to the extent that host officials
and civil servants are incompetent and the donor governments
do not train them, large-scale aid is futile and small-scale
aid yields puny results.

Commitment of the Donor Government or Institution

Without strong funding and support, no foreign aid program will have lasting effect. That the United States has in
past years had fewer technical assistance personnel abroad
in absolute number, including the Peace Corps, than the
United Kingdom and France, and that in proportion to size,

Belgium and Israel have far exceeded the U. S. investment,
may be only a mild scandal. [39] For the opponents of aid can
argue that increased American effort is not justified by the
results so far, that it would merely increase the dependence
of host governments on external financing, involve American
experts in the internal politics of other countries, and suck
the country further into an international scramble to help
countries in a position to traffic in big-power hostilities.
(In the late 1960's the United States was phasing out AID and
increasing Peace Corps budgets, apparently on the premise
that it was enough to spread goodwill in the relatively non-
controversial area of village development.)

If such arguments against increased effort by the United
States are overriding, there are still several alternatives for
a greatly expanded effort. First, the country can put more
emphasis on training natives in the United States and can develop a bigger capacity for the task. Second, to remove the
onus of the "Ugly American" or the "Imperialist American, "
the country can put a greater share of effort into cooperative
projects in which it provides the financing, the smaller, less
"aligned" countries (Israel, Switzerland, Sweden) provide the
technical expertise, and the host governments provide the
trainees. Finally, and most important, the United States can
funnel a larger fraction of personnel and money through international organizations--the numerous agencies of the UN, the
International Labor Organization, the Organization for Economic
Cooperation and Development, the International Bank for Reconstruction and Development, and the International Development Association. The merits of combining cooperative
projects with international sponsorship are evident in Nepal.
As part of that dismal picture, the American campaign in the
1950's to eradicate malaria over a large area in a short time,
using government personnel with limited American technical
support, failed. When the American effort merged with that
of the World Health Organization (WHO) in a combination of
American money, WHO technicians, and Nepalese assistance,
however, it succeeded. The combined operation assured
competent administration for a long enough period for Nepalese officials to take over, at the same time that it kept the
project out of the shifting political winds. Also possible is
merging the entire Peace Corps with the UN--a symbol of
goodwill that might be as effective as the American enterprise now going.

REFASHIONING THE MODEL

The traditional model of professionalism more or less fits the reality in rich countries, but it is in many ways irrelevant to the problems of poor countries. Nevertheless, it provides some elements of hope. Professional culture is a double-edged sword; on the one hand, its accent on technical tasks as a basis for exclusive jurisdiction fosters training for rigidity, inflexibility. On the other hand, its accent on autonomy in the exercise of professional skill--the rendering of objective, impartial, independent advice and judgment-- fosters a bit of flexibility and self-reliance. And insofar as the service ideal can be harnessed for international work, it is a favorable force for success in technical assistance.

The Peace Corps generalist, the anthropological action researcher, the Israeli expert are successful abroad in part because they are not bound by professionalism. Indeed, here in the United States, the best specialist in depth--even some- one so technical as an engineer--is one who begins with a liberal arts education, a common core permitting quick re- freshing and retraining. The problem for the professional school is how to select and train experts who know something (the Peace Corps does not use people with high-level skills), who at the same time are tolerant of the aims and claims of rival specialists and less skilled personnel, and who are dedicated enough and sensitive enough to perform flexibly and effectively abroad.

In producing such people the professions can look to different models for different levels of foreign aid. The model to set before a new recruit who wants to become an elite adviser is that of the "program professional"--a policy- oriented expert with a sense of long-run goals and possibili- ties. In the United States this type is evident in many a corner of the bureaucratic machinery--the specialist in depth (e.g., experts in social insurance, rehabilitation, public assistance, public finance, housing, race relations, labor disputes settlement) whose professional competence and commitment are beyond question, but whose commitment to particular programs and policies (for example, health insurance) is just as strong. By virtue of his technical prowess, he makes himself indispensable as a policy adviser.

In his job moves--between government and private agencies,
civic organizations, foundations, universities--he follows the
programs to which both his skills and his social philosophy
are bound. [40] His counterpart is found among lawyers working
for minority defense agencies and civil liberties organizations;
social scientists working for government agencies, political
parties, and congressional committees; and labor staff experts
striving to keep labor Left. End products of broad movements
of social reform, these men combine professional standards
of work with programmatic sense and constitute an important
link between professional culture and civil culture, the man of
knowledge and the man of power. I sense that schools of
planning, public administration, and some departments of social
science are beginning to produce these men.

At middle and lower levels of foreign aid, the Peace
Corpsman provides a good model.

Meanwhile the United States can be more deliberate and
systematic in producing professionals for practice abroad.
With respect to training, the professional school in a great
metropolis can design practicums and field units for work in
the ghettos analagous to Peace Corps training and the Israeli
experience. I realize that the ghetto is developing a resistance
to invasion by hit-and-run social scientists. With the large
number of "street workers, " reporters, clergymen, and
caseworkers approaching them for off-the-record confidential
stories, the leaders of ghetto groups, including delinquent
gangs, have developed by now a considerable sophistication
in the public relations line. They sometimes view the graduate
student who invades their territory as just another snooper
who can be "put on" or kicked out. Nevertheless, if developed
with caution and good sense, these supplementary practicum
experiences would help any professional school recruit to
overcome his natural parochialism and ease the reality shock
when he goes abroad.

With respect to recruitment, the professional school can
look to a growing manpower pool--young people whose experience and orientation are appropriate for foreign aid programs.
The ideologies of American economic individualism--the great
accent on free markets, private property, and minimum
government--are in many ways incongruent with the ideological
mixes of planning, socialism, democracy, and modernization

that prevail in poor countries. An increasing fraction of
young Americans reject the core ideology of American society;
they are more in tune with the doctrines of community development and planning; they can be recruited for work
abroad. Easier to locate is the pool of returned Peace Corpsmen (now more than 25,000) and international-minded under-
graduates who have studied for a year abroad. With that
resource growing steadily, a little aggressive recruitment
could increase the fraction of professionals ready to move
when the U. S. government begins to do its development duty
and the social science of development improves.

NOTES

1.   I am grateful to Eugene A. Hammel, Arthur L.
Stinchcombe, and Guy Benveniste for critical readings and
to J. Malcolm Walker and Lillian Rubin for research
assistance.

2.   Harold L. Wilensky, Organizational Intelligence:
Knowledge and Policy in Government and Industry (New York:
Basic Books, 1967), pp. 24 ff, 182-191.

3.   Harold L. Wilensky and Charles N. Lebeaux, Industrial Society and Social Welfare (New York: The Free
Press, 1965), pp. v-lii.

4.   This section is based partly on Harold L. Wilensky,
"The Professionalization of Everyone?", American Journal
of Sociology, 70 (September, 1964), pp. 137-158, and the
citations therein.

5.   "Tacit Knowing: Its Bearing on Some Problems of
Philosophy," Reviews of Modern Physics, 34 (October, 1962),
p. 601.

6.   Peter M. Blau, The Dynamics of Bureaucracy
(Chicago: University of Chicago Press, 1955), pp. 49-67,
82-96, 207-210.

7.   Paul E. Mott, "Sources of Adaptation and Flexibility in Large Organizations" (unpublished Ph.D. dissertation, University of Michigan, 1960).

8.   Arthur L. Stinchcombe, "The Sociology of Organization and the Theory of the Firm," Pacific Sociological Review, No. 3 (Fall, 1960), p. 81.

9.   Cf. Joseph A. Schumpeter, Capitalism, Socialism, and Democracy (2d ed.; New York: Harper, 1947), pp. 131 ff., passim.

10.   Wilensky and Lebeaux, op. cit., pp. 303-308.

11.   Gunnar Myrdal, Asian Drama: An Inquiry into the Poverty of Nations (Pantheon paperback ed.; New York: Random House, 1968), p. 19.

12.   Cf. Kingsley Davis, The Theory of Change and Response in Modern Demographic History (Berkeley: Institute of International Studies, University of California, Reprint 123).

13.   George M. Foster, Traditional Cultures, and the Impact of Technological Change (New York: Harper, 1962), pp. 80-81.

14.   Morris E. Opler, "Cultural Anthropology: An Application of Themes in Culture," Journal of the Washington Academy of Sciences, 36 (May, 1946), pp. 137-166.

15.   Margaret Mead, From the South Seas (New York: William Morrow, 1939) and Ruth Benedict, Patterns of Culture (Boston: Houghton Mifflin, 1934).

16.   I develop these from Myrdal, op. cit.; Ronald G. Ridker, "Discontent and Economic Growth," Economic Development and Cultural Change, II (October, 1962), pp. 1-15; W. Arthur Lewis, The Theory of Economic Growth (London: George Allen and Unwin, 1955); Charles Wolf, Jr., Foreign Aid: Theory and Practice in Southern Asia (Princeton: Princeton University Press, 1960), pp. 299-351, an empirical attempt to relate level of living, economic aspirations and expectations, and political extremism;

and Eugene B. Mihaly, Foreign Aid and Politics in Nepal
(London: Oxford University Press, 1965), a detailed analysis
of the relative effects, mostly bad, of several nations'
attempts to aid Nepal. Among scores of general books that
represent the sophisticated modernization literature, see
Wilbert E. Moore and Arnold S. Feldman, eds. Labor Commitment and Social Change in Developing Areas (New York:
Social Science Research Council, 1960).

17. Cf. Myrdal, op. cit., p. 1877.

18. Ibid., p. 1960.

19. Abram Kardiner, The Psychological Frontiers of
Society (New York: Columbia University Press, 1945), pp.
418 ff., and Ralph Linton, "The Tanala of Madagascar,"
in Abram Kardiner, The Individual and His Society (New
York: Columbia University Press, 1939), pp. 251-290;
Lauriston Sharp, "Steel Axes for Stone-Age Australians,"
Human Organization, 11 (Summer, 1952), pp. 17-22.

20. Myrdal, op. cit., p. 26.

21. Ibid., pp. 1859-1878.

22. Ibid., p. 1863.

23. "The Vicos Case: Peasant Society in Transition,"
special issue of The American Behavioral Scientist, No. 8
(March, 1965); and Allan R. Holmberg, "Changing Community
Attitudes and Values in Peru: A Case Study in Guided Change,"
in Richard N. Adams, ed., Social Change in Latin America
Today (New York: Harper, 1960), pp. 63-107.

24. Sources: Israel, Ministry of Foreign Affairs,
Israel's Programme of International Cooperation (Jerusalem:
Israel Government Printer, 1967); Mordechai E. Kreinin,
Israel and Africa: A Study in Technical Cooperation (New
York: Praeger, 1964); "Economic and Social Work for Young
People During Defence Service: The Israeli Formula,"
International Labour Review, No. 93 (January, 1966), 66-79;
Angus Maddison, Foreign Skills and Technical Assistance in
Economic Development (Paris: Organisation for Economic
Cooperation and Development, Development Centre, 1965);

"The Young Pioneers Movement in the Central African Republic, " International Labour Review, 93 (January, 1966), 19-28; "Civic Service and Community Works in Mali, " International Labour Review, 93 (January, 1966), 50-65; and Mihaly, Foreign Aid and Politics in Nepal, op. cit., pp. 164 ff.; I am grateful to Eliezer Rosenstein, sociologist, and Pinhas Zusman, agricultural economist, both former participants in Israel's technical assistance efforts, for further information.

25.   Morris L. Stein, Volunteers for Peace (New York: John Wiley and Sons, 1966).

26.   "The Young Pioneers..." op. cit., p. 20.

27.   Ibid., pp. 22-23.

28.   "The Vicos Case...," op. cit., p. 24.

29.   Maddison, op. cit., p. 22.

30.   N. Lorch in A. Malkin and Z. Goldberg, Israel's Relationships with the Developing Countries ("Petach" series; Israel: Berl Katzenelson Institute, 1963), p. 8. (In Hebrew)

31.   Joseph G. Colman, "A Discovery of Commitment, " The Annals, 365 (May, 1966), p. 15.

32.   Stein, op. cit., p. 71, p. 191.

33.   M. Brewster Smith, "Explorations in Competence: A Study of Peace Corps Teachers in Ghana, " American Psychologist, 21 (June, 1966), pp. 559-560.

34.   Stein, op. cit., p. 228.

35.   Smith, op. cit.

36.   Thomas Maretzki, "Transition Training: A Theoretical Approach, " Human Organization, 24 (Summer, 1965), pp. 128-134.

37.   Arnold and Marion Zeitlin, "The Peace Corps Isn't Doing Its Job, " Saturday Evening Post, 293 (January 1, 1966), pp. 7-8.

38.   Mihaly, Foreign Aid and Politics in Nepal, op. cit.

39.   For 1963 figures: Maddison, op. cit., p. 21.
Current figures for the U. S. are available in Agency for
International Development, annual Report to the Congress,
(Washington, D. C.: U. S. Government Printing Office);
figures for other countries are available in Monthly Summary
of Peace Corps Volunteers and Trainees (Washington, D. C.:
Office of Volunteer Support and Special Studies, Peace Corps).

40.   Harold L. Wilensky, Intellectuals in Labor Unions:
Organizational Pressures on Professional Roles (New York:
The Free Press, 1956), pp. 129-143.

PART II

THINKING ANEW ABOUT PROFESSIONS AND CHANGE

CHAPTER

6

A THEORETICAL MODEL OF
THE ROLE OF PROFESSIONALS
IN COMPLEX DEVELOPMENT
SITUATIONS

Eugen Pusić

Social development in any society can be understood as a
complex process of interaction between what I will call "total
societal productivity" and the prevailing system of relationships which determines the availability, as well as the modes
of apperception, interpretation, and utilization, of information.
By "productivity" I mean the total creativity of people making
up a society, that part of its total potential which is actually
put to use, in all fields, from economics to morals, from
science to religion, from arts to political organization. All
the fields are interacting, and which one is more "important"
for the total effect has to be decided in each case. Though it
is probable that under conditions of scarcity the sector of
economic production and distribution of goods and services
will assume paramount importance, that does not mean that
the same will hold in a society of abundance.

TECHNIQUES AND INTERESTS

Structures defining the use of information in a society
have two aspects. One is the technical possibility of utilizing
information for the achievement of results. The other is the
question of whose interests are served by these results. Techniques and interests are the two poles around which a society
and its informational capabilities are structured. The possibility of understanding and applying information needed for
the performance of tasks, and the way information is handled
to choose between interest alternatives and standardize

behavior in interest conflicts, interact with each other and are
often so intertwined that it is only possible to separate them
through an abstract analysis.

The total productivity and the complexity of information-
structures tend to increase in response to the pressure of
relevant uncertainty impinging upon man from his natural and
social environment.

Increase in one variable depends on an increase in the
other. Potential creativity can be realized only through existing information-structures. (These are distinct from the
information-code of heredity; "culture is not a biologically
transmitted complex."[1]) The greater the complexity of these
information-structures the greater their capability for absorbing and utilizing information. Each level of social productivity
has, as it were, a corresponding level of structural complexity
satisfying the requirement of "requisite variety." Also, the
more complex structures demand a constant and more abundant
inflow of energy, which implies a higher average of continuously
realized productivity, because the more complex structures
consume a greater amount of social energy in the internal processes of linkage and coordination. The term "energy" is used
here in a figurative sense, only alliteratively similar to John
T. Dorsey's "information-energy model." Dorsey speaks about
energy in the literal sense of calories or megawatts and relates
the energy-level a society is able to extract and utilize to the
amount of technical information this energy-conversion requires.[2]

The change in information-structures, the increase in
their complexity proceeds along several dimensions, corresponding to two main aspects: techniques and interests. Increases in the span of social division of labor correspond to
the increasing complexity of structures for the productive use
of technical information. The increasing dispersion of interests
reflects a greater possibility of satisfying basic material needs,
with a concomitant wider span of interests and greater number
of interest-circles in which each individual can participate.
Individual interest-preferences become, on the average, less
compelling; the tendency of people in a community to split into
interest groups with clearly defined positions and borderlines
tends to decrease.

Most importantly, the role which <u>power</u> plays in society changes as structures become increasingly complex, and so does rationality. The nature of rules regulating behavior in a society, their categorical or hypothetical character, becomes different, as does the transparency of given social situations for those who participate in them. It is interesting to consider in this context the relationship between the prevailing span of social division of labor and the pressure towards uniformity, postulated by Durkheim. His notion of "pressure towards uniformity" can be interpreted as an expression of power relationships aiming at the restriction of the free flow of information, in its technical aspect as well as in its interest aspect. [3]

THREE STAGES OF SOCIAL DEVELOPMENT

Societies can be classified into three stages.

Stage 1: Group Society

In the first phase, of relative helplessness, man is on the defensive. The very heavy pressure of uncertainty coming from the social as well as from the natural environment creates a sort of defensive solidarity within comparatively small groups with simple structure and without bridges between them. Absolute loyalty to the group corresponds to irreconcilable opposition among groups; a small span of division of labor, to a high concentration of interests upon a few objectives; great transparency within the group, to almost complete opacity in relation to the environment. Though the rules regulating behavior are mostly categorical, there is relatively little emphasis on systematic and society-wide application of power. Existing structures are too simple for this task. External pressures supply the binding element holding the community together.

Stage 2: Power Society

In the next phase, greater social productivity permits
more complex structures which serve mainly to check uncertainty arising from the social environment. Comparatively
small and isolated groups are integrated into larger structures
through the systematic application of power at the level of the
community. The institutions of power -- from property to
political sovereignty -- make the social environment more
amenable to control and so more predictable. But this gain
is bought at the price of significantly greater tensions within
communities because power operates mainly as an instrument
of domination in potential or actual conflicts of interests.
Power-holders and power-subjects tend to become the main
opposed interest groups, power being at the same time the
main binding agent and the chief divisive force. In this second
phase, the span of division of labor is increasing slowly. There
is comparatively little dispersion of interests. All possible
interest-orientations of the individual are still subordinated to
the satisfaction of basic existential needs. A minority able to
satisfy these needs more amply than the mass has to concentrate on upholding the power structure guaranteeing their pre-
ferential position. Rationality is narrowly circumscribed to
those areas where technological expertness has developed.
Thus in social relations rationality is more widespread among
the rulers than among the ruled. Transparency increases but
is inhibited in social relations by the rulers who need to rely
on secrecy and misrepresentation of social reality as an instrument of power.

Stage 3: Functional Society

In the third phase of his social development, man perfects
instruments which permit him to control a significant proportion
of the uncertainty stemming from natural causes, chief among
them material scarcity. The common denominator of the technological and social revolutions implied in this change is the
transformation of existing structures into structures of a considerably higher degree of complexity. The new patterns have
to accommodate, on the one hand, the rising flood of technological information -- in the widest sense of the term -- and

on the other to permit the socially meaningful expression of
a widening span of interests by an increasing number of people.

This more intricate system of relationships exists only on
the condition that the flow of productivity in a society has been
stabilized on consistently higher levels. The production, handling,
and use of information claim more and more of the available
social energy. This is the reason why large-scale bureaucracy
as a specialized information-handling structure is a relative
late-comer in the development of a culture. And the same re-
flection lends weight to Max Weber's contention that "monocratic-
bureaucratic administration" is a product of comparatively recent history.

The greater equality in chances of interest-satisfaction is
possible only if these chances are realistic for a very large
majority of the population, meaning more abundantly available
means of gratification. The complexity of structures is expressed in a wider span of division of labor, as well as in
greater dispersion of interests. Potential interest conflicts
become more numerous but individually less compelling as
motives for behavior because their preference ordering is less
general and less absolute and because more and more conflicts
are intra-personal. There is less motivation for favoring the
method of interest-domination over all other possible solutions
of conflict situations. This has important consequences for the
application of power-as-coercion on a society-wide basis. The
reason for establishing a monopoly of the means of physical
constraint as a social institution, that is, the domination of a
given aggregate of interests in all conflicts over time, is losing
its urgency.

A decrease in uncertainty permits a greater prevalence of
rationality as the underlying mental attitude of the individual.
Categorical rules as means of regulating behavior are displaced
by hypothetical prescriptions of the "if...then" type. Increasing transparency of social situations is paralleled by a "com-
partmentalized transparency" of the technological information
flow.

At present, the world is in transition from stage two to
stage three. The new structures permitting a wider flow of
technical information and implying greater equality of chances
in the expression and realization of interests are already in

existence. But they are limited to narrow areas of high productivity or confined to a shallow upper layer where the structures are shared on a worldwide basis. But the unity of the
world, even if it is at present only communicational, influences
significantly the development process in each individual country
The transformation, the seeming overlapping of stages, are
characteristic of the situation we professionals have to cope
with.

PROFESSIONALS AS RELATED TO THE STAGE

People form the central element of the information-
structures in any society, as well as the main source of its
productivity.[4] Professionals are people in a special social
role. In order to analyze their possible impact on development, one must understand how their role is related to a stage
in the development of the productivity and information-structure
of a society.

Some of the characteristics of the professional role seem
to be fairly universally accepted. In most parts of the world,
it is agreed that professionals are people who: (a) perform an
activity on the basis of specialized training and, usually, higher
education; (b) work full-time for (c) a remuneration which is
their main source of income. Professionals subscribe to some
sort of ethical code or value-scheme, but the content of these
values may be different in different cultures. The same can be
said about the trait of professional solidarity, which receives
various interpretations and limits in different cultures.

There is, however, a list of characteristics considered
essential for the role of the professional in some societies but
not in others. The term "professional" is sometimes used
restrictively for people performing their high specialized
activity under conditions of relative independence, who "work
for themselves" and not in an organization or for an entre-
preneur. Often the activity of the professional is understood
as the application of knowledge, not its creation. Thus the
teacher in an art school falls into the category of professional
but the creative artist does not; the doctor in a hospital does,
but not the scientist in fundamental biology. Or the relationship

of the professional to the client for his professional services
is stressed and interpreted as a relation of dependence and
trust on the part of the client. Or, more generally, the orientation of the professional towards the performance of service is
considered essential. (It is possible, however, to observe a
service orientation in given activities even at pre-professional
stages, as with the cameralist bureaucracy in Germany and
Austria in the seventeenth and eighteenth centuries.)

Some of these characteristics are defined by the prevailing
span of the social division of labor and the corresponding level
of productivity. People cannot work full-time at an activity
which is not immediately productive and live from it, without
using coercion, before a certain general level of productivity
is reached permitting the span of division of labor to extend to
pursuits which contribute to survival only in an indirect way.

Specialized training and higher education require an even
more advanced stage of development in which complex technological information is available and can be used for practical
purposes. Other aspects might be expressions either of a given
level of general development or of a stage in the transformation
of a special culture.

The list of existing professions is lengthening, and they
almost defy classification. Some are related most directly to
material production, among them engineering, agricultural
economics, architecture, forestry management. Others combine the production aim with an integrative function; among
these are urban planning and the consulting systems specialty.
Still others are mainly integrative; for example, the law, public
administration, business administration, applied sociology.
Another group combines integrative purposes with a mediative
role, such as education, or social mediation with a restorative
effect, for instance, social work. There is a group of professions, for example medicine or criminology, in which the
accent is chiefly on restoration of impaired productive capacity
and structural integration.

Like any other social institution, the role of the professional is a product of social development. It is a part of it
and, to a certain extent, also the contributing cause of development. By following the tangled links between these two concepts we can attempt to better understand the whole phenomenon.

The Professional: Transitional

On the whole, the professional seems to be characteristic
of the transition from stage 2 to stage 3 in the development of
social productivity and the corresponding information-structures.
Professionalism tends towards the expansion of the intellectual,
informational element.

Even in the older professions such as the army and the
crafts, * despite the great manual skill required, the tendency
is toward greater expertise, meaning a more important informational content. In this sense the crafts were clearly a
progressive, propulsive sector of social development, particularly at the beginning of the industrial era.

In his famous "Parable, " Henri de Saint-Simon includes
the craftsmen among the constructive, valuable, essential
population of France:

Let us assume that France should lose unexpectedly
fifty of its foremost physicists, fifty of its first physiolo-
gists... fifty of its first joiners, fifty of its first wood-
workers, that is about three thousand foremost scientists,
artists and craftsmen of France.

As these are the Frenchmen who are productive in
the most essential sense... really the bloom of French
society, those without whom the nation cannot live, the
nation would become a body without a soul; losing them
it could not exist, it would perish. [5]

*Both were certainly considered to be professions at cer-
tain times and in certain places: The mercenaries and their
leaders, the condottieri, had all the characteristics of professionals in Italy and other parts of Europe in the Renaissance,
and craftsmen in the German-speaking countries of Central
Europe were, even at the beginning of the twentieth century,
called "die Professionisten. "

Similarly, today the military in developing countries has also
a progressive aspect. It has been pointed out particularly
that: (a) the armed forces include technical experts; (b) they
play an important role in the process of socialization; (c) they
increase stability; (d) they represent, on the whole, a rational
approach; (e) they contribute to development by building roads
and railways and undertaking other useful investment projects. [6]

The proliferation of professions in developed countries
in our times is an expression of the "information explosion, "
the vast increase of the importance of information for productivity and the significant growth in the capability for information-handling. In this sense the professions increase
their social influence by creating higher levels of productivity
and more complex information-structures.

On the other hand, the technological profile of the professions themselves changes under the impact of further developments of the social division of labor. As the span of
division grows, there is less possibility for any socially
meaningful activity to be performed by an individual working
in technological isolation. The group, the team, the collective setting replaces the individual as the smallest technically meaningful unit of work. Without reducing expertness,
these developments are transforming the doctor, the architect,
the social worker into a member of a team; there are other
professionals, for instance the administrator, the planner, the
systems specialist, -- who could never conceive of their work
otherwise.

The social context in which the professions first emerged
was one of power institutions. Normally, the older professions
-- administration, the law, the church, education, the army --
were born as instruments of an existing social power center.
At first the professional's orientation is toward the support
of the established order, a subservience to power which goes
beyond personal attitudes into the realm of ideology, communication, and organization. Professionals depend on the
power elites and, sometimes, are members of these elites.
But even in this early phase, the professionals bring a certain
rationality to the exercise of power, a reasonableness and
systematic approach which in itself limits the essentially ar-
bitrary nature of power.

And from the beginning there is another side to this
picture. There are the would-be professionals, the intellectuals who for one reason or another are not employed in
the professional roles to which, by their education, they
aspire. These are persons with intellectual training but without professional commitment, with the capacity to understand
the reality of social relationships but without the economic
position and security the social system provides those who are
professionals. This intelligentsia belongs, more often than
not, to the disaffected part of a power-society, highly critical
of the established order, producing the prophets of new ideologies and providing the kernel of movements for social
change. Educated elites are in fact sometimes thought to induce social change by their very existence. "There seems to
be general agreement that groups which have wider orientation
in terms of education or travel are often focal points in efforts
at induced change." [7]

Professionals as Propulsion for Change

As development goes on, however, the professions themselves evolve a critical attitude toward things-as-they-are.
Social welfare workers, applied sociologists, planners, public
health specialists are naturally let to look for the underlying
causes of the problems they have to cope with. If they find
them, as often they do, in the existing power system, changing
this system -- however gently and gradually -- will tend to
become part of their broader professional goals, and the corresponding behavior will receive a positive evaluation in the
professional code.

This professional goal of social action towards change
tends to overshadow the original stress on professional expertise. But this shift is not easy, and it leads to the question;
Is it permissible for a profession to overstep the limits of its
technical knowledge and yet remain a profession? The problem appears in highly developed countries as well. "Social
work in America faces the alternative of confining itself to
well-defined areas where its technical knowledge and skill are
well established and respected, or of varying its single standard of preparation and extending its efforts to new problem
areas where it has special concern and commitment, but where
it cannot at this moment assert superior knowledge and skill." [8]

Professions by their very existence tend to work, in a certain sense, for equality. They confront the established ascriptive criteria of social status with new and prestigious achievement standards and so loosen the old patterns of inequality. Also, the majority of professions tend to incorporate the ideal of equality into the codes governing their relations with the users of their services. This attitude is reinforced by the increasingly collective character of professional performance, its dependence on work-groups, laboratories, and other auxiliary units. It is enhanced by more impersonal methods of financing the professional services. It is sanctioned by spreading democratic ideologies. [9]

In the course of the emergency of industrial society, the work performed by the professions has the very important characteristic, and indeed the privilege, of not being amenable to the prevailing industrial method of dividing the work-process itself into progressively smaller and simpler particles. The work of the professional remains whole, even when the profession itself subdivides into new and more narrowly circumscribed special fields. The cardiologist is not related in the same way to the general practitioner as the mechanic on the conveyor-belt is to his general supervisor. In an era of technological alienation the professions gain the added attractiveness of un-alienated, "complete" work. In this they are the precursors of a work-situation of the individual which tends to become more general as automation and new control techniques tend to shift repetitive routine operations from man to machine. Even in an organizational and collective setting the professional retains the personal independence which flows from the necessary inner completeness of his professional work. Professionals tend to be less affected by the stereotype of the "Organization Man" even in a time when the power of organizations is at its maximum. As "cosmopolitans, "[10] professionals always retain a part of their personal independence and, in a way, prepare the way for a greater independence for all.

Technically, the professions are a source of progress in productivity. They do require higher levels of general productivity in a society, but they also tend to produce such levels by performing in the more complex productive processes, by creating the necessary orderliness in the general environment and building the system of the productive undertakings themselves, and above all by being the carriers of the growing pool of information on which the modern expansion of productivity is built.

But politically, the professions are the most promising new institution for the integration of a society not based on coercive power. Their influence is derived from knowledge and tends toward functional specialization, not toward overall domination. Their political claim is for participation, not technocracy; in terms of David Apter's classification of claims for participation into "popular," "functional," and "interest" claims, the claim of the professionals belongs definitely to the "functional" category. [11] The professions can be integrated only in a collaborative setting, and their total social influence depends on the recognition of equality among information-sources. By becoming conscious of this situation, the professions as a whole can develop movements for social action. David French has noted, for example, that "social workers . . . have to accept the fact that at this point in history social work is closer to the 'social movement' and of the continuum than to the 'professional' end, and act accordingly. American social work was a social movement long before it was a profession. "[12]

PROSPECTS

What is the perspective for the future? The burst of technological productivity in the developed parts of the world is so powerful that it represents a potential source of change for the whole world. As these changes begin to interact more intensively with each other, the stages I have abstracted from history will probably be less applicable than they are to the past. Parts of the world which are still at stage 1, "group society," or in transition from stage 1 to stage 2, "power society," will necessarily be affected by other parts which are already on the threshold of stage 3, "functional society. "

It is possible to imagine that the stages will be accelerated and even be telescoped into one in each society. Thus, in any case, at some point in the future the world as a whole will certainly present a single picture of development. It is in this sense only that one can speak of the world as one.

The decisive front-line on this strategic map of development is the advance from power society to functional society.
This seems to be our most realistic chance to avoid a cata-
clysmic clash between the existing power systems. But this
advance depends today on the total situation in the world. The
weight of all the world's societies still in transition toward integration into power systems is holding back progress in the
most forward sections. These countries, with their necessarily positive attitude toward coercive power -- which to them
must appear as the specific condition for leaving their own dismal past behind -- are natural allies of the conservative forces
in the developed power systems which are opposing and counteracting their transformation into functional information-structures
corresponding to the levels of productivity already reached in
these societies.

It seems, therefore, crucial to establish a world-wide
network of institutions and social processes which could make
more effective the oneness of the world and which would be, in
its operations, as independent as possible of the existing political power systems. To try to by-pass governments seems,
at least today, to offer better possibilities than to strive for a
world government. Some first steps have been made already.
One of the most urgent tasks in this context would be to integrate the less developed countries into the world's development without necessarily strengthening and solidifying their
internal political power systems.

Within this broad perspective the potential role of the professions is important.

The professions, though very significant as a part of a
community's total social productivity, are unlikely to emerge
by spontaneous process during the early stages of development.
If the professions are a useful contributing factor in raising productivity and influencing structural development in the direction of functional instead of power relationships, then a prin-
cipal professional contribution to countries below a certain
level of productivity will have to come from the outside.

The present levels of effort along these lines are plainly
inadequate, not only because far too little is done in quantitative
terms, but more fundamentally because the role of adviser entails responsibilities and raises expectations which the average
professional cannot satisfy.

To "advise" implies knowing better, and this, in the majority of instances, is simply not the case. The advantage in professional knowledge and technical skill which the adviser has, possibly, over the people he works with is more than balanced by the disadvantage of not knowing or misunderstanding a practically unlimited number of specific and topical factors essential for the accomplishment of the task. This relationship is, probably, particularly unfavorable for professions in which the existing technical knowledge and skill is not much more than a theoretical generalization from everyday experience in a given cultural setting, as in social work or public administration. The stories of "experts" stumbling over blocks which are obvious to every child in the country are assuming the proportions of a literature. The social problems of advisers -- becoming discouraged, apathetic, opinionated, or aggressive, or retiring into a personal limbo as a result of lack of recognition or success -- tend to get as serious as the problems they are sent to help solve.

Advisers are frequently put into a position where they must go beyond their field of expertise. The narrower span of division of labor in the developing country draws the adviser, willy-nilly, into contiguous fields; the expectations of the host induces him to make proposals for broad policies and plans which transcend not only what he knows but also what can be properly called technical advice. These broad plans are, as often as not, rather naive and utopian speculations of the adviser which he himself would see differently in his own country. Measures which, at home, he would perceive clearly as matters of political struggle and conflict of interests are presented to his hosts as technical problems, with technical solutions which he draws from his superior expertness and which can be implemented simply on the condition that this knowledge be acknowledged and acquired. So advisers blithely advise centralization or decentralization, the introduction of a merit system, of social insurance schemes, of land reforms, of equality for women and other far-reaching transformations of the institutional and social system of a country as if the transformation were only a matter of know-how. This is certainly not to say that advisers are superficial and irresponsible people. On the contrary, the more thorough and responsible they are, the harder they will try to fulfill the obligations of a role which is beyond the scope of the professional as specialist.

The people of the country with whom the advisers are
working have from the beginning a highly ambivalent attitude
toward them. On the one hand, the adviser is for them a
person embodying all they know or assume about the superior
achievements of the country he comes from. They are prepared to vastly exaggerate his knowledge and importance and
expect from him more than any average good professional can
give. Moreover, they are equally prepared to resent being
put in the position of people receiving advice or assistance.
They will watch for the first mistakes the adviser cannot help
making, or for the first signs of his disorientation, and sometimes they will be unable to suppress their glee. This means
that the more ambitious programs of advising will almost certainly foster movements toward all kinds of isolationism; they
will strengthen tendencies to "go our own way" even in matters where it would be manifestly more profitable not to do so.
This has been observed even in settings where strong ideological
bonds of solidarity bound together the advisers and the people
they were advising. The collaboration of professionals across
national boundaries is easier where the difference between the
professional's home country and his host country is less pro-
nounced. But with the decrease of the difference, resentment
at accepting "advice" will tend to increase.

This does not mean that advice is not needed and should
not be given. But advice should grow out of a massive long-
term program of professionals working in other countries at
tasks with in their special field of competence. The fundamental approach should be not to advise, but to do. And instead of the present trickle, there should be a steady stream
directed to the strategic points of development. Out of these
larger numbers the successful advisers would be selected by
a largely automatic process. These would be people who happen to have the necessary capabilities for understanding and
empathy, who for one reason or another fit better in the new
milieu, who are more easily accepted, and who have in the
course of their activities in the other country developed ideas
which can be useful and seem convincing to the people of the
host country. To give any kind of useful advice the professional has first to learn much himself about the host country.
And he can only learn by working and living there for a time,
not as an adviser from the beginning, but as a professional
expected to do a professional job. He will teach more by
being successful at his profession than by any number of reports, suggestions, or conclusions.

In this operational role the largely neutral attitude of the outside professional toward those conflicts of interests and emotional tensions that move the nationals of the country would be an asset, instead of the liability it is in the role of adviser. He would demonstrate by his own behavior the possibility of professional objectivity, which is one of the important conditions of success in most professions.

Also, in action it would be easier for the professional to adjust to the more restricted span of specialization than it is in giving general advice. A case worker or a specialist in community organization will adjust with less difficulty to the practical task of including the administration of a children's home in his weekly round of work than he will to abstract talk and writing about institutional care. The organization-and-methods specialist will be able to perform without further preparation simple personnel work or elementary financial administration. My main argument is that one must think in new ways. The concept of advisers does not work well. New institutional mechanisms must be created to allow professionals from one society to be integrated into the working structure of the institutions where they are expected to function; to set them apart and provide them with a "counterpart" reduces by 50 per cent their chances of achieving anything. Their integration can, of course, never be complete. And it should not be. Just by being outsiders they can perform the stimulating and innovating role of "marginal men," in the sense introduced by Stonequist. But they should not be artifically isolated. Of course, world-wide programs of professional inter-country mobility will also have to overcome the well-known practical problems, such as language difficulties and differences of basic habits and standards of living. But these problems are not new. And they were and are tackled successfully by a number of agencies and organizations when it was, or is, in their economic or political interest to do so. There is no doubt that it can be done on a more massive scale when it is in the fundamental interest of the world.

These programs would have to be planned in such a way that they could be reduced parallel with the growth of professional capabilities in the developing countries. This raises the important problem known under the journalistic nickname of "brain-drain." A great share of the effort at training professionals in developing countries is lost for their country of origin by their emigration to countries with a higher standard of living, where better opportunities exist to apply their professional expertise with all the auxiliary and supporting services they were taught to consider indispensable. A report by the UN also that "lack of professional freedom, a feeling that there is insufficient esteem for the work performed, and the paucity of contacts with persons in similar specialties may be contributory factors."13

It is essential to understand that for a considerable time to come this process is unavoidable and should be accepted. But one of the reasons a massive movement of professionals to developing countries is necessary is precisely to offset the "brain-drain" and organize the migration of professionals as a two-way street. The attraction of working in a location which is novel and exotic, without ultimate loss of the standard of living available in the home country, would be as great for professionals from developed countries as is, today, the hope of newly trained professionals from developing countries of bettering their lot by going to the richer parts of the world.

Equally important as supplying professionals for developing countries is the need to improve the informational microstructure of the professions in all countries. Today, in the most developed countries (economically speaking) the influence of the professions in creating functional institutions and relationships can make itself felt. But it is in these countries also that the professions still carry with them past traditions of serving power systems and still have an orientation toward material gain as a primary goal. Changing these sometimes deeply ingrained attitudes is a precondition if the professions are to grow into their ultimate social role and become important structural elements of the functional society of tomorrow.

NOTES

1.   Ruth Benedict, Patterns of Culture (New York: Penguin Books, 1934) p. 13.

2.   John T. Dorsey, Jr., "The Information-Energy Model," in Ferrel Heady and Sybil Stokes, eds., Papers in

Comparative Public Administration (Ann Arbor: University of Michigan Press, 1962), pp. 37-57.

3. Erik Allardt, "Emil Durkheim - Sein Beitrag zur politischen Soziologie, " Kölner Zeitschrift für Soziologie und Sozialpsychologie, No. 1 (März, 1968), p. 3.

4. See Bertram M. Gross, "Social Systems Accounting, " in Raymond H. Bauer, ed., Social Indicators (Cambridge: MIT Press, 1966).

5. Henri de Saint-Simon, L'Organisateur, Vol. IV, p. 17; quoted by Georges Gurvitch in "Les fondateurs francais de la sociologie contemporaine: Saint-Simon et P. J. Proudhon, " Les Cours de Sorbonne (Paris, 1955), p. 32.

6. See H. Daalder, The Role of the Military in the Emerging Countries (The Hague: Mouton & Co., 1962), pp. 18-20.

7. United Nations, 1965 Report on the World Social Situation (New York: United Nations, 1966), p. 6.

8. David G. French, Objectives of the Profession of Social Work (Bangkok: United Nations Economic Commission for Asia and the Far East, 1967), p. 17.

9. Higher education has been found to be correlated with more egalitarian attitudes (lowest education has also, but not the middle level). Cf. Charles C. Moskos, Jr., and Wendell Bell, "Some Implications of Equality for Political, Economic and Social Development, " International Review of Community Development, 13-14 (1965), p. 230.

10. Alvin W. Gouldner, "Cosmopolitans and Locals: Toward an Analysis of Latent Social Roles, " Administrative Science Quarterly, No. 2 (1957-58), pp. 281-480.

11. David E. Apter, "Political Systems and Development Change, " Proceedings of the International Political Science Association 7th World Congress (Brussels, 1967), p. 6.

12. David G. French, op. cit. , p. 18.

13. United Nations, 1965 Report on the World Social Situation op. cit. , p. 62.

CHAPTER 7   PUBLIC ADMINISTRATION
AND CHANGE: TERRA
PAENA INCOGNITA

C. Dwight Waldo

Public administration is not now, nor is it likely to become in the proximate future, a profession in any strict sense,
though paradoxically and maddeningly in a general sense its
practitioners have many of the qualities of professionals. To
put it negatively, public administrators are not (for example)
peasants, unskilled laborers, or businessmen; positively,
they do have trained skills, habits of work, codes of conduct,
and so forth that fit in general the descriptions of professionalism. Part of the problem relates of course to the great
diversity of the public service altogether; is it "a" profession
of government (to use Brian Chapman's terminology) or a
cluster of professions more or less related but also more or
less separate? In any event, public administration is clearly
far from the situation of medicine and law, in which (to gloss
over complications) there is a single professional degree of
long standing, and general recognition of a unitary profession.
In public administration at present time, both sides, the academic and the governmental are confusing, problematic, controversial. It is difficult to define and separate the career or
careers for which students are ostensibly educated; and those
in the academy dispute whether public administration is most
usefully defined as a subdiscipline of political science, an
independent discipline, or a congeries of disciplines brought
together and given focus and meaning by a professional orientation and intention.

Obviously a different sort of problem is posed in this case
than in the case of the "genuine" (recognized) professions; or,
if the problem is the same, it is certainly of a different order

of magnitude. The public administrationist has not only to adjust his profession to an unfamiliar environment, taking for
granted professionally given goals and the general validity and
usefulness of his science or technology; but he starts with the
serious handicap of a problem of professional identity and
recognition, unclear goals, and a science and technology which
has a highly problematic relationship to the foreign environment.

Of the many pertinent questions relating to the foregoing,
I note only an irony: whereas most professionals who go abroad
regard themselves (I should guess) first of all as professionals
and only secondarily as agents of change, the public administrator who goes abroad is quite conscious of the fact that he
is supposed to be an agent of change, but that his professional
status is quite uncertain.

IMPLICATIONS OF INSTRUMENTALISM

What has come to impress me as peculiar and paradoxical
is that though American public administration generally has been
a major agent of change in American life; though social, economic, even political change is the raison d'être of many administrative agencies; and though American administrative
agencies exist in a milieu of swift and sweeping change, never-
the less American public administration has no consciously articulated philosophy of change and no generally accepted theory
of change. That is, it has neither a normative nor a causal
theory about change which is well rationalized, well articulated,
and generally accepted.

Origins as Context

How did this situation come about? By exploring what happened one arrives at a clearer understanding of how the traditional value-neutral, instrumentalist posture and ideology
of public administration came about and what it implies.

First of all, self-conscious American public administration was not imported nor invented to act as an agent of change
in a stagnant, traditional society. Rather, public administration came to self-consciousness, "professionalization," and
increasingly rapid growth in an extraordinarily dynamic, rapidly changing milieu. America imported the advanced science
and technology of Europe, but left behind the rigid class structure and feudally derived institutions that set restraining brakes
in Europe. A steady stream of vigorous and resourceful immigrants, an ever more productive agriculture, and a vigorous
and sometimes rapacious capitalism were developing -- sometimes ravaging -- a new continent.

Second, in the late nineteenth century, Jeffersonian-
Jacksonian ideas of popular government became diluted and
debased. The public services were progressively less technically competent to perform at the level that increasing complexity demanded; they were increasingly the complaisant
or corrupted tools of a ruthless capitalism; and through abuse
of the spoils system they were perceived as a threat to the integrity and even continued existence of republican institutions.

Third, although waves of reform started to sweep the
country in the period in which public administration was reaching self-consciousness, and although the reforms were closely
related to the development of both administrative "ideology"
and administrative institutions, the changes were indeed reform,
not revolution. The country was, remained, and is a pre-
dominantly business-oriented, middle-class country. To the
dictum of Jefferson that that government is best which governs
least was added that of a later President, that the business of
the United States is business.

Fourth, not only was ceaseless and massive change characteristic of the milieu; this change was given meaning by a
widely and deeply accepted national ideology. Change was
seen as development, as progress, progress toward the realization of the goods that have been the goals of history: release
from the bonds of poverty, increasing well-being and comfort,
expanding freedoms. In late nineteenth and early twentieth
century America, the idea of progress reached one of its most
effulgent flowerings. And its mechanism as well as its goal
was conceived to be the "free individual" -- who came often
to be identified with something called "free enterprise."

American public administration developed functions and ideology appropriate to the historical situation. Its most general function was to maintain the ring within which the economic struggle took place: to enforce the basic legal rules, protect against invasion and insurrection, maintain a monetary-financial mechanism, and preserve law and order. So far as it had a promotional, stimulating function, as in agriculture, this was by sector, selectively, depending on the vagaries of politics and history. Often and increasingly its function was regulatory: to restrain and correct the causes of free enterprise, increasingly those of organized and usually big business. Thus arose at the federal level the several independent regulatory agencies and the scores, perhaps hundreds, of regulatory functions in the departments. Still another function was that of special help to or salvage of groups perceived as needful and deserving: children, working women, the disabled, the Indian.

This basic pattern continues today. The upheavals of the New Deal did not so much disturb it as extend it. Of the two developments of Roosevelt's presidency most important for public administration, one, the National Resources Planning Board, did not survive; and the other, the Tennessee Valley Authority, survived only with the understanding that it would stay at home and behave itself, not proselytize for a national network of like bodies. World War II and the "Fair Deal" and "Great Society" programs have in various ways extended and complicated the original patterns without basically altering them, adding (for example) a special promotional-regulatory regimen for atomic energy, a special "mission" agency in the National Aeronautics and Space Administration, and special programs and agencies to renew the central cities and help the poor escape their poverty.

The ideology of public administration when it was established was thus appropriate to the situation. Moreover, it conceived of itself as non-partisan. This became a virtue, given the partisan abuses against which it was posed, though perhaps it had virtue thrust upon it as much as it actively sought to be "good. " More, it conceived of itself as not simply non-partisan, but neutral. Its neutrality, however, must be seen through the lens that J. D. Kingsley used in viewing "representative bureaucracy" in Britain; that is, it is neutral only in the sense that it accords with, and so thoroughly reflects,

the middle-class ethos in which it developed. [1] American
public service had a situational, middle-class neutrality given
tone by the ideal of efficiency, tempered and molded by professional training, sectoral and program commitment, and
shifting winds of politics.

Ambivalence toward Change

    The moral of the tale is that American public administra-
tion did not develop any general idea of change or development
rationalized with respect to its own role and function.   Change
in general did not need to be sought out; rather, it was a
spectacular and often overwhelming fact.   Nor did change in
general have to be rationalized: the ethos of the day gave
assurance that change is development and progress.   Neither
did the government have to act in general to cause change and
progress; the engine was outside of government, and government needed only to correct abuses, spur lagging sectors,
and rescue and aid those who were, unfortunately, not able to
keep up with the march into a brighter future.   American
public service, which has perhaps been more "engaged" with
change (affected and effecting it, created by and creating it)
than any in history, has served a governmental system that
has no official philosophy or theory of change; and neither has
this public service had a general philosophy or theory of change
of its own (apart from that breathed from the air along with all
citizens).   It has not been aware of the need for theory, or
even of its absence.   The only exception or qualification of
these generalizations concerns Keynesian economic doctrines,
which in a general but diluted way have come to serve as a
theory to justify, guide, and stimulate specifically economic
development.   Keynesian economic ideas are now more or less
received doctrine in public administration, and they have a
clear relationship to a number of administrative developments.

    The academic sector of public administration shares this
remarkable ambivalence toward change; this acceptance of it
as a fact and as (on the whole) good, together with a low level
of conscious concern for the mechanisms, direction, and implications of general or large-scale change.   This is my impression, and I have confirmed it by an extensive review of
the literature of the past generation.   Of concern within public

administration there has been much, to be sure (reform, improvement, reorganization, and even the "management of change" in organizations); but of concern for change produced by public administration there has been until recently very little. One of the things that has moved the field in this direction recently has been, in fact, concern with overseas affairs, manifested in the growing literature on comparative and development administration.

UNIVERSALITY AND EFFICIENCY:
CONUNDRUMS

Two related conundrums (or two ways of stating the same conundrum) have intrigued and baffled me through the years. One is the extent to which the "classic" theory and technology of organization and administration is related to a specific environment; whether, to what extent, and in what ways, it can be universalized; whether it is true, as L. D. White asserted in 1936, that "a principle, considered as a tested hypothesis and applied in the light of its appropriate frame of reference, is as useful a guide to action in the public administration of Russia as of Great Britain, or Irak as of the United States."[2] The other is whether bureaucracy, as ideal-typically delineated by Max Weber, is the all-purpose instrument of efficient goal achievement that he thought. Is it, as he said, "from a purely technical point of view, capable of attaining the most rational known means of carrying out imperative control over human beings.... [and] superior to any other form in precision, stability, in the stringency of its discipline, and in its reliability"?[3]

What now strikes me as a deeper insight, a fresh view, is that both these theories view the world from the here and now, looking from "modern" societies to the primitive or traditional; that they both lack a dynamic, an explanation or theory of how to get from the primitive or traditional to the modern; and that the view of things that both give is, for some purposes, skewed or irrelevant. Both have an "other things being equal" proviso, implicit or explicit (White's "applied in the light of its appropriate frame of reference"). But other things are not equal, nor does either theory deal with the

central problem of how to make them equal. Both theories
imply that a certain administrative apparatus would not work
as well in a low-income country as in a high-income country,
and would not enable the former to become the latter. But
neither makes this assertion outright, and certainly neither
explains it. Neither theory specifies what "adjustments" of
the apparatus to make to adapt it to a low-income environment, or how to use the apparatus to transform a low-income
environment into a high-income environment.

No doubt there is more disposition to grant my argument
with respect to the classic theory and technology of organization and administration than with respect to Weber's bureaucracy. Weber did, after all, have a reach extending back into
antiquity and as far away as China. He pointed out significant
correlations between bureaucracy and such factors as the development of law and pecuniary economies. He was certainly
interested in finding causal relationships, and indeed his monu-
mental work can be interpreted as a search for causal relations among such large and protean matters as religion, science,
economic system, and class structure. But however suggestive
and seminal his hypotheses or theories, they are far indeed
from a set of close-knit and demonstrated propositions on how
to achieve a bureaucratic apparatus functioning in a modern
context.

It is essentially correct, I think, to say that Weber -- and
others who have written about European bureaucracy -- have
been in somewhat the same situation as we in the United States
are, and have reacted rather similarly. Here, as noted above,
change has been a "given, " and there has been no call to develop a theory of change through the agency of governmental
administration. In Western Europe the role of government as
agent of development has (on the whole) been greater; but the
development has taken place over a long period of time, much
of it long ago, and what took place is still subject to conflicting interpretations. Bureaucratic theory "rationalizes"
what took place after the event; it does not explain, as a tested
scientific theory would.

Through the years I have had a recurring difference of
opinion with students from low-income countries concerning
Robert A. Dahl and Charles E. Lindblom's Politics, Economics and Welfare. [4] I have thought this one of the major works

in social science of my generation. It seemed to me to map
accurately the large terrain of society; to delineate insight-
fully the interrelations of the social, the political, the economic; to explain fairly the interrelations of the various parts
and principles in realizing the goals of individuals and of
society. It seemed to me to be both a true map and a universal
map. But students from low-income countries have asserted,
repeatedly and forcefully, that it is not universal, that it may
be an accurate map of the world of Dahl and Lindblom but that
it is not an accurate map of other worlds. I was at first inclined to put this contention down to ignorance, perversity,
or ideological bias; finally, however, I think I understand.
Perhaps I too have had my distorting lens.

ADMINISTRATION IN AN
AGE OF REVOLUTIONS

Whether or not the United States is in some senses
"overdeveloped, " it indisputably is a high-income country. As
such, it has problems related to its affluence, as well as
problems related to its underdevelopment and its development.
The "mix" itself poses not just problems, but threats --
revolutionary threats to continuing development, even to political stability.

A large literature on the multitude of "revolutions" of
the twentieth century attests to what surrounds us in the United
States on all sides. These revolutions are of many kinds of
differing magnitudes, and of varying speeds. Some are more
or less independent, even antagonistic; but some blend into
and reinforce eath other. Among them are the scientific-
technological revolution, the anti-scientific-technological
revolution, the revolution of rising expectations, the revolution in morals, the generational revolt, the student revolt,
the racial revolution, the poor people's revolt, the urban
revolution.

Patently, these revolutions are related to the fact and to
the idea of development. Some are instruments and causes
of development; some are reflections or "measures" of development; some are reactions against development -- or

revolts in favor of a new direction of development, according
to claim or interpretation. A country that is developing but
also is in some respects both underdeveloped and overdeveloped has a full complement of revolutionary forces with
which it must reckon. By definition, it cannot be other than
complex and troubled. The United States may be so defined
and certainly fits the description.

This way of putting things may or may not be useful or
congenial; but in any case I believe the country is heading into
a Time of Troubles. The revolutionary forces are capable of
reinforcing each other under certain circumstances, and these
circumstances are likely to occur. The mood of the day is to
a disturbing degree one of anxiety, alienation, frustration,
anger, and violence. Such events as severe rioting, a sharp
military defeat, or even devaluation of the dollar are unpredict-
able in their synergistic effect on a complicated and precarious
situation. I do not anticipate overthrow of the government by
force; but I expect a period of disturbances of a magnitude
great enough to make some alterations in our ways of govern-
ance.

Public administration needs to be aware of the revolutions
and consciously, diligently address itself to them. We administrators bear some responsibility, one way or another,
for their genesis, and certainly we will be deeply affected by
them. Of course, to some extent, we are already consciously
engaged: in line of legal duty some are promoting a revolution,
some are dealing with the effects of a revolution, some are
trying to prevent a revolution. But what I argue for is a higher
level of consciousness and a greater, more imaginative and
constructive response on the part of the public service. This
would appear to be a common prudence, if not plain duty.

If I am even roughly correct, what is indicated is that
American public administration is entering into a period of
rapid, stressful change without adequate theories of change
and adequate tools to deal with change. The problems of international relations and warfare, urban decay and violence,
poverty and racial inequality are hardly the sole responsibility of public administration. But public administration is
the central instrument of society for dealing with them. And
how many, in or out of public service, are happy about the
record so far? Present administrative ideas and institutions

are tragically inadequate to the need for remedial and preventive action.

I conclude that one problem illumines the other. When one
carefully examines the problem of bettering the performance
of the American public administrator as an agent of change in
low-income countries he works his way back to the realization that -- paradoxically -- the public administrator is without an adequate theory and technology of change even at home.
Likewise, when one examines the characteristic and increasingly urgent problems of public administration at home, he
works back to the realization that there are not adequate theories and technologies for dealing with change in a period in
which rapid change is patently inevitable and potentially dis-
astrous. Further, neither abroad nor at home is the public
administrator likely to be aware of his lack. He senses, if
at all perceptive, that something is missing. But many factors
have combined to make it difficult for him to understand what
this is and how it might be supplied.

I conclude further that attention to the matter of achieving
a higher level of consciousness of and knowledge about change
is a first order of professional business; that to the extent
that administrators are successful in achieving sharpened
awareness of and increased knowledge about change they will
improve their effectiveness both abroad and at home; and that
to the extent they are successful they will also have moved a
considerable distance toward solving some of their problems
of identity and mission.

STEPS TOWARD A THEORY

Of course, to need something is one thing; to be able to
get it something else. To achieve what I have been glibly
calling a theory and technology of change certainly will not
be easy. In the immediate future, it is in fact impossible in
any rounded sense. On the other hand, the problem sensed
and the need identified, public administrators certainly can
do better than they now do. I have some comments on the
nature of the problem-solving task, and some steps to suggest
for consideration in moving toward solution in public administration.

Public administration is in a position like that of an
agnostic who is in trouble; who in a certain situation would
like to use science but cannot find any, or enough; who then
decides that what he needs is a religious faith, because it
would at least give him strength and hope; and who then sets
out rationally to shop the market for one. Perhaps this is
not a good analogy, but it will serve in making some points.

The first point, assuming that public administration is
in trouble, is that it does not have enough science. This is
not just a matter of a lack in an academic-professional enterprise called public administration. It is a lack in each of the
social sciences and in all of them globally. To be sure there
are in the literature a profusion of theories of change and development: micro, macro, and middle-range. But they are a
jumble, or perhaps a jungle. They are not agreed upon,
ordered and classified, ready to be used with a high order of
confidence. Economics is the most advanced of the social
sciences with respect to theories of change; but even in economics such theories are far from being sorted out and ready
to use.

In any case, to "develop" a country or culture requires
theories and technologies of social science that bridge across
and interrelate what have come to be thought of as separate
social sciences. For in the real world there are no divisions
between social sciences, only bafflingly complex interrelations
between phenomena.

The second point is that until and unless much more
science is achieved, acts of faith are going to be required. No
doubt it is well to emphasize caution before the act of faith.
Even elementary prudence, it seems to me, should be enough
to keep public administration from attempting some of the
"development" projects, large and small, in which it finds itself engaged. But after examining what science is available
and exercising what prudence is necessary, acts of faith will
be necessary. The field can, if it wishes, find a scientific
faith of a type: use the framework and terminology of pragmatism, and speak of testing social science by using it ex-
perimentally. This will not be dishonest or ridiculous. But
it will still be an act of faith, from my present viewpoint.

The third point is that if through some unexpected good
fortune the field were to achieve a scientifically respectable
mastery of cause and effect in developing a low-income country
into a high-income country, the field will still have need of
acts of faith of another kind.   Basically and simply, administrators shall have to believe that the human situation in the
high-income countries, with their industrialization, science
and technology, urbanization, and so forth, is better than in
the low-income countries.   To many this is a self-evident
proposition.   And I myself often quote Sophie Tucker's "I've
been poor and I've been rich, and believe me, rich is better."
However, it is not a scientifically demonstrable proposition,
even in principle, according to the fashionable philosophy of
recent times.   There are now not simply individual skeptics
a la Thoreau, but deadly serious and more or less effective revolts being mounted against the characteristic style, techniques,
and artifacts of high-income societies; and these revolts are
mounted, it may be asserted, to recover a human dimension
that low-income societies are perceived (rightly or wrongly)
as having.   Any professional who goes abroad with the intent of
acting as an agent of change will have to believe!   A highway
engineer must believe in transportation, a sanitary engineer
in sanitation, and a public administrator in the beneficence
and efficacy of governmental administrative action.   To the
extent to which there is erosion of belief in the blessings of
modernity, the act of faith at any level will become more
difficult.

Although some professionals abroad may be motivated
simply by pecuniary gain or a sense of adventure, typically
their engagement in and justification for an assignment as a
change agent is related at some level to religious or ideological beliefs, most commonly to some combination of the two.
I shall not try to develop the implications of this.   I merely re-
iterate that I think it is an important aspect of the matter, and
one that professionals are likely to overlook, approaching the
problem of change as a professional, scientific, and educational problem.   Religion, especially, may be regarded by the
formally secular as something relevant only as providing data
to be included at some level in the calculations, perhaps as an
impediment.   But even ideology may not be perceived in its
faith-giving role in the development process.

I must state a personal point of view which no doubt has shaped my analysis of the subject, but which also has been shaped and refined by the analysis.

In the United States, public administration presents a picture of mingled strengths and weaknesses, or perhaps of many strengths but over-all weakness. As for the strengths: one could compile a long list of important advances during recent years. These would include advances in conceptual sophistication, techniques developed or borrowed and adapted, new legislation to improve the public services, new university programs to train for public administration, and recovery of the American Society of Public Administration from the anemia of the fifties.

The weaknesses include an inability to find a successful resolution to the crisis of identity which arose when the public administration of the twenties and thirties was deeply shaken by events and ideas in the forties; a continuing inability to find successful solutions to problems posed by the general (but not complete) rejection of the politics-administration dichotomy with its accompanying stance of value-neutrality for public administration; a growing sense in and out of the public service that received ideas and present administrative techniques -- for all they offer -- are not adequate for meeting present and pressing problems and certainly will not suffice for a future that threatens increasing turbulence.

I do not catalog here the strengths and weaknesses of American public administration in its overseas technical assistance role; suffice it to say that there are some instances of seeming success and some of seeming failure, but that in the majority of instances one cannot pass judgment because so many factors (including future events) are so relevant to a fair and informed judgment that the mind first hesitates, then boggles. What is clear, however, is that when one goes overseas in the technical assistance role he discovers that American public administration has, despite its historic claim of value-neutrality and technical universality, a culture-related quality and even a unique "Americanness" that makes it difficult to transplant and to relate to a different milieu; that the technical assistance experience to date has revealed severe problems not just on the technical side -- though these are severe enough -- but also on the side of human values and political goals; and

that the probing and development of ideas and research that
has proceeded under the heading of Comparative Public Administration both emphasizes and illuminates what experience
demonstrates.

It is my opinion that the weaknesses and problems of
public administration relate importantly to its inability to arrive at agreement on a conception of role and mission to take
the place of that destroyed and abandoned in the forties and
fifties.   That it has not done so is quite understandable, easily
forgivable, given the extremely difficult problems posed by
the institutional and intellectual context within which the answers had perforce to be sought.   Still, the problem remains,
and is urgent.   I hesitate to use the locution "philosophy" because it is at once so indefinite in meaning and so trite, but
what public administration as a self-conscious enterprise
and public administrationists as individuals stand in urgent
need of is indeed a philosophy.   They need a set of well-
rationalized and well-articulated beliefs that will give meaning,
provide focus, and release energies.

To arrive at these will of course not be easy, and I do not
assert that they can only or necessarily be achieved by con-
templation of what is meant by "development."   I do assert,
however, that to address the questions that are raised by juxta-
posing the problems of "change" overseas and at home is one
way, and a promising way, to move toward better answers
than we so far have found.   To speak of change is to speak of
development, and to speak of development is to raise all the
problems of goal-related behavior and of the relationship of
means to ends.   The better we professionals do with this
tangle of problems -- insoluble except as we must solve them
provisionally, proximately -- the better the public administration professional will do both in low-income countries and
in high-income countries.

NOTES

1.   The reference is to Kingsley's Representative
Bureaucracy; An interpretation of the British Civil Service
(Yellow Springs, Ohio, 1944).

2.   L. D. White, "The Meaning of Principles in Public Administration, " in John M. Gaus et al. eds. , Frontiers of Public Administration, (New York: Russell, 1936), p. 17.

3.   Max Weber, The Theory of Social and Economic Organization, translated by A. M. Henderson and Talcott Parsons (New York: Oxford University Press, 1947), p. 337.

4.   Robert A. Dahl and Charles E. Lindblom, Politics, Economics and Welfare (New York: Harper and Row).

CHAPTER **8** THE CONCEPT OF
INNOVATIVE PLANNING

John Friedmann

A plan results in a more or less "balanced" allocation of
resources, but institutional development is an instance of
innovative planning for key areas of change within a complex
system. [1] A rudimentary plan can be drafted in a matter of
months; institutional development often takes years of patient
effort. The Guayana project in Venezuela, involving professors from both the Massachusetts Institute of Technology
and Harvard University, and the Chilean Program in Urban
and Regional Development managed by the Ford Foundation
are examples of continuing involvement over many years.
These projects are exceptions to the usual consulting arrangements. Their results will have to be measured in terms of the
institutional capabilities created to carry on the job of dealing
with varieties of ever-changing problems. This calls for
greater subtlety of measurement and new criteria of institutional performance. [2]

GOALS AND METHODS: THE TAO

The goals and methods of innovative planning are completely different from those of planning for the allocation of
resources. Innovative planners must learn to practice what I
call the Tao of planning. And the Tao says: "Truly, a great
cutter does not cut. " This counsel is even more appropriate
where the innovator is a foreign technical advisor. What does
it mean?

The Sense of Time

Every national culture has its own rhythm of life, its
own sense of time.   America's is the sequential, driving
rhythm of linear time.   John G. Gunnell writes:

> Development as a mode of thought involves the emer-
> gence of an orientation toward time and change which has
> found its paradigmatic expression in modern Western
> society.   In general this means a focus where society as
> well as the life of the individual is perceived as moving
> along a unilinear plane from the past, through the pres-
> ent and toward the future, and where the future is under-
> stood not only as a dimension of existence and a boundary
> of life, but as an object of intentional action which can
> be anticipated, appropriated, controlled, and made to
> conform to goals devised in the present.   Here the future
> is something to be planned and actualized by consciously
> innovative and creative action. [3]

As yet very little is known about rhythm and time con-
ceptions in the newly industrializing societies.   We sense
that they are different from our own.   Professionals often believe that if a society adopts development as its over-riding
objective, it must also adopt the Western, unilinear conception of time. [4]   But this belief may well be ethnocentric.
When a foreign expert acts according to the time of Western
man, he will almost surely meet with nagging frustrations of
delay, misunderstanding, and inability to reach the other man.
These frustrations may be largely avoided if the planner can
learn to follow the rhythm that is native to the country where
he works.

"Tao invariably does nothing, and yet there is nothing
that is not done. "   This famous quotation from the Tao-te
Ching sounds as paradoxical to Western man as does the
following: "The most yielding of things outruns the most unyielding. "   There is a brutal driving force in the posture of
many foreign advisors who wish to replace as quickly as
possible what they consider to be outmoded patterns with their
own inventions.   But their environment acts rather like a
rubber wall: it yields to impact only to spring back to its
original position as soon as pressure is relaxed.   To achieve

a permanent change, there must be time, the right time to
let initiatives float up to the surface from below, the right time
for consensus to emerge, the right time for resistance to wear
down. [5] The innovation must be fitted into the structure of
things; it cannot be artifically maintained for very long.
Professional support of this thesis among approximately 750
foreign and national experts working in the area of induced
social change in developing countries indicates that 78 per
cent of the foreign experts and 80 per cent of the nationals
"believe that proceeding at a slow pace of action generally
has the greater chance of success in the face of traditional
ways; only 15 per cent of the foreign and 17 per cent of the
national experts favour fast action. This overwhelming support of a slow tempo appears in every region and sphere of
activity." As one expert in Africa commented, "It was found
the pace of development could not be forced. Things moved
somewhat slower than one is accustomed to in Europe and
any attempt to accelerate this resulted in resentment, enemies
-- and frustration. To go slowly, then, is more than a slogan.
It represents considered advice."[5]

Limits of Knowledge and Effort

The technical expert must also know the limits of his
knowledge. He must be humble enough to learn from others,
know when to draw back, and learn to listen with attention.
If he listens long enough and carefully, his own thoughts may
be given back to him as the ideas of others. As the Tao-te
Ching expresses it: "To give life, but not to own, to achieve
but not to cherish, to lead but not be master -- this is the
Mystic Virtue."

The purpose of innovative planning is to accomplish the
structural transformation of a system. But, according to Lao
Tzu, "all things go through their own transformations." The
art is to accomplish things without apparent effort. If the
innovative effort is concentrated at the critical points of transformation, so that a small change will produce large adjustments in many other parts of the system, this is possible.
Even a minor shift in the position of the fulcrum tips a see-saw
to one side. The direction of change is usually predictable and,
if the Tao is followed, the change can be accomplished with an
economy of means.

Tao is the wisdom of non-action. But innovative planning calls for building up new institutional devices.[6] To this end, leadership must be selected and developed, long-term financing must be assured, clientele groups must be carefully nurtured, the costs and benefits of innovation must be calculated for different groups with power to destroy or seriously impede the new organization, and the change objectives must be accepted as legitimate by wider publics.

Very little is known of the requirements of successful innovative planning, but these conditions seem essential as an absolute minimum.

American city planners are not taught the skills of innovation nor the difficult art of advice. In fact, the dominant professional ideology tends to reject these skills, because in the American environment, innovation has always been accepted as a matter of course: the need was seen to lie in balancing the multiple innovations that, in conjunction, generate the transformations of society. With the social revolution under way, America has for the first time created a climate propitious to the acceptance of innovative planning; harmony and consensus tend to be rejected and conflict is more readily accepted as a condition of social advance. But professional ideology is slow to adapt itself. It may be years before system innovation is accepted as a central task of urban planning. Whether this judgment is too pessimistic, I do not know. For instance, a seminar on innovative planning was offered in the Department of City and Regional Planning of the University of Toronto during the Spring Term of 1968 by Professor Gerald Hodge. Yet I have been challenged on the assertion that skills in innovation and advice can be acquired by academic study. It is my impression, however, that the relevant literature is accumulating.[7]

THE CITY AS AGENT OF CHANGE

One condition of innovative planning is to know the pressure points of the society and precisely where within the social system to apply creative energy. To make this determination, it is necessary not only to arrive at a deep and comprehensive

understanding of the structure and internal dynamics of a
given social system, but also to define the ends of system
transformation. Since the important ends are bound to vary
between the developing and the post-industrial societies, the
major focal points of change are also likely to be different.
I argue that urbanization is one of these critical areas of inter-
section for newly developing societies and that the study of
innovative planning out, therefore, to concentrate on clarifying
the relationships among the forces operating in this area and
on projecting possible outcomes for system change of different
"settings" of policy variables.

Over thirty years ago, Karl Mannheim suggested that
planners concentrate on what he called the principia media
which operate in a specific historical situation. [8] In the con-
temporary language of social science, they would be called
structural forces. The elements of social systems are organized by these major lines of interacting force somewhat
as are particles within a moving magnetic field. But the
changes set up in this field, either by self-generated forces
or by forces impinging on the field from the outside, eventually
produce new structural arrangements to which the old principia
media must yield. Mannheim believed that any process of
social change is the result of contending interacting forces of
different strength, some emergent, others dominant, and still
others declining. Together, they contain within themselves a
number of potentially different societal outcomes. The task
for planning, then, he said, is to discover the principia media
operating in a society as multiple possibilities and, by en-
couraging some (while suppressing others), to lend a helping
hand to history. For Mannheim, planning was a form of guided
social change on a large scale.

If this idea is followed through, innovative planning would
concentrate on certain sensitive intersections of societal forces
which, from a purely instrumental viewpoint, could be considered as the major points of system transformation. In developing societies, one of these principia media is the process
of urbanization, considered both in its demographic-ecological
dimension (the concentration of population in urban clusters
of cities) and in its socio-cultural dimension (the adoption of
urban living patterns, or "modernization"). [9] By engender-
ing urbanization in these two senses, a national social system
is eventually transformed. If this interpretation is accepted,

the city may be regarded primarily as an agent of change, as a
major force for national development, instead of as a set of
social and economic problems. [10] As William Mangin has said
in reference to squatter settlements in Latin America, the
problem appears in itself as the solution. [11]

Urbanization occurs as an inevitable accompaniment of
national development. It is also a process capable of being
guided through a scientific-technical intelligence. This formulation permits one to see a functional linkage between planning
for urban and for economic development. Both variables are
partially independent of each other. Urban development can
occur without a commensurate development of the economy;
policies for economic development may have different outcomes for urbanization. But economic development and urbanization are also partially contingent on each other. What
happens in urban development is not without effect on the behavior of the national economy. The first requirement is therefore to determine national policies for urban development and
to learn the use of instruments for carrying them out. [12]

This interpretation of the city as an agent of social change
is different from the prevailing concept in American city
planning which sees urbanization as resulting only in local
problems -- blight, smog, crime, and congestion -- and the
city, therefore, as an obstacle to economic change. "Regardless of the future, " writes William McCord, "it seems beyond
dispute that the developing nations are already over-urbanized,
burdened with festering cities beyond their capacity to support. "[13] And he goes on to say:

> However false the tinsel of these cities, their image of
> luxury continues to inveigle the peasant into immigration.
> At first, when the ex-villager enters the city, he must
> be overwhelmed by the glory of New Delhi's Secretariat,
> Mexico's Reforma Boulevard, Accra's government build-
> ings, or by the Paris-like magnificence of Cairo along
> the Nile. But soon he has to face the physical realities
> of city life -- the barriada, or favela, or bidonville which
> are the rotten cores within the apple. Unless he has un-
> usual training, he quickly discovers that no one wants his
> labor. [14]

For McCord, at least, the city occupies the "outer edge of civilization. "[15]

Perhaps the naked facts are the same, but interpretations may differ. One of the main problems for urban and regional development in the newly industrializing countries is how to generate and capture innovative impulses at certain favored points within the system and stimulate migration toward "core regions" and "social development poles" rather than turn the migrants back from the outer "edges of civilization" towards the heartland or rural utopia. [16]

The other major problem is how to maintain the national system undergoing accelerated urbanization in equilibrium and to achieve the progressive integration of the national economy in its territorial dimension through a balanced system of cities.

Both functions of urban development planning -- that of using cities as innovating, transforming elements in a national society and of achieving social, political, and economic integration across regional space -- drop out of view in American city planning practice because in the United States these problems have been largely solved. In the underdeveloped areas of the world, however, the process of urbanization still acts as a major structural force in national development and, as such, suggests a need for formulating national policies which will be capable of guiding this critical process as a whole toward socially desired ends. [17]

But the pragmatic character of American city planning has worked against the search for an adequate theory of urbanization. Courses on the theory of the city have generally held to the study of ecological and related physical patterns. Recently, this study has been broadened to include also non-North-American patterns. [18] But ecological theory is not the most appropriate one for innovative planning. We as planners have scarcely begun to work on a theoretical formulation of the relationship between the process of urbanization as a principium medium and national development in an historical context. [19] The American-trained planner needs something more than practical experience overseas to become competent. He requires a theory that will prepare him to ask the proper questions and to study the dynamic relationships in

the process of urbanization as a basis for his policy prescriptions. This theory is not likely to grow out of American
experience alone, though it will certainly have relevance for
it. It has to be formulated by careful study of the role of
urbanization at earlier stages in the evolution of many national
societies. [20]

The American city planning profession is passing through
a crisis as the demands made on it exceed its traditional competence. Just as in the developing countries, planners in the
United States are being asked to deal with social problems
arising from poverty and the physical segregation in central
cities of migrants with a different cultural inheritance from
that of the dominant society. There is also a growing acceptance of the idea of innovation and experiment with urban problems that is reflected in the proposal for "advocacy planning, "
according to which planners work for special interest groups
competing with each other. [21] Many instances of advocacy
planning -- such as for the disadvantaged urban Negro communities -- could be called innovative. They are forcing a
change in the accepted rules of the game of the larger society.
From this, there has resulted a sharp turn in planning education toward the social sciences from physical planning and
design, accompanied by a tendency toward greater professional
specialization. These changes facilitate communication across
national boundaries; despite its immense national power, the
United States is, in some ways, becoming more like an underdeveloped country, which is to say, more like the rest of the
world. In relation to the problems to be solved, the social
ignorance would seem to be nearly as great. Revolutionary
changes are occurring in the culture. Militarism is pervasive.
The traditional bases of social and political consensus are
breaking down. Violence in the streets is becoming a familiar
sight. A sense of impotence is spreading. [22] On a more positive side, perhaps, convergence is occurring as the result of
a trend toward systematic approaches to urban development in
the United States, especially in the housing and transportation
sectors and in social policy and services. [23] Both the United
States and many of the underdeveloped countries are beginning
to look at questions of urban development from a national perspective and to create the institutional basis by which such a
perspective may foster effective action at the local level.

Under these conditions, it may be for the first time possible to sustain a meaningful dialogue between American experts and those of the developing world. The planning specialists of any nation may have more in common than planning generalists, and consequently more to talk about. United States poverty planners may have significant things to say to the poor countries, but planners from poor countries may also have important contributions to make to the national development of our own society. There is apparently a growing area of compatible knowledge throughout the world. Comparative study and collaborative planning efforts in this growing area can bring substantial benefits to all the groups concerned, American no less than foreign.

NOTES

1.   John Friedmann, "Planning as Innovation: the Chilean Case, " Journal of the American Institute of Planners, XXXII, No. 4 (July, 1966), pp. 194-203; "A Conceptual Model for the Analysis of Planning Behavior, " Administrative Science Quarterly, XII, No. 2 (September, 1967), pp. 225-252; and (with Walter Stohr), "The Uses of Regional Science: Policy Planning in Chile, " Regional Science Association, Papers: European Congress, Vienna, 1966, XVIII (1967), pp. 207-222.

2.   Professor John W. Hanson suggests the following criteria of successful institution-building (see Milton J. Esman, The Institution-Building Concepts: an Interim Appraisal. [Pittsburgh: Inter-University Research Program in Institution Building, University of Pittsburgh, Graduate School of Public and International Affairs, March 1967], pp. 28-29):

"1. Use of services: the extent to which programs are willingly used or requested by publics the organization is designed to serve.

"2. Survival: The maintenance (and presumably also the expansion) of values and distinctive identity. These apply both to the institution itself and to its norms and include the concept of 'innovation transferral' -- innovations pioneered by the organization which have been transferred to other organizations which might more appropriately perform them...

"3. Support: The extent to which capital resources...
are providing for initiating, maintaining, and expanding programs, and the extent to which other organizations mobilize
influence behind the subject organization's leadership and
programs.

"4. Respect and Approval: The extent to which the programs and the personnel of the organization are judged to be
serving accepted or emergent goals well or as being qualified
to serve such goals well.

"5. Normative Spread: The extent to which action and
belief patterns incorporated in the organization have become
normative both within the organization and for other social
units or related to its sphere of operation.

"6. Autonomy: The degree of freedom of an organization to set and implement goals.

"7. Innovative Thrust: The capacity of the organization
to continue to innovate. "

3.   John G. Gunnell, "Time and the Concept of Develop-
ment, " in CAG Occasional Papers (Bloomington, Ind. , April,
1966), pp. 35-36; other relevant papers are Alfred Diamant,
"The Temporal Dimension in Models of Administration and
Organization, " in CAG Occasional Papers (April, 1966), and
especially Hahn-Been Lee, "Developmentalist Time and
Leadership in Developing Countries, " in CAG Occasional
Papers (February, 1967).

4.   This viewpoint is defended by Warren F. Ilchman,
"New Time in Old Clocks: Productivity, Development, and
Comparative Public Administration, " in CAG Occasional
Papers (Bloomington, Ind. , February 1967).

5.   Herbert H. Hyman, Gene N. Levine, and Charles R.
Wright, Inducing Social Change in Developing Countries: An
International Survey of Expert Advice (Geneva: United Nations
Research Institute for Social Development, 1967), pp. 70-73,
p. 109; for a general discussion of alternatives in establishing
a pace of change (and priorities in development programming),
see Wilbert E. Moore, "Problems in Timing, Balance, and
Priorities in Development Measures, " Economic Development

and Cultural Change, II, No. 4, pp. 239-248; a very competent handling of the various roles of the foreign expert in
an unfamiliar cultural environment is provided by Sune Carl-
son, Development Economics and Administration (Bonniers:
Svenska Bok for Laget, 1964); particularly descriptive is what
Suneson calls the "second month depression, " when "the
transport and office facilities are not what he expected, he
does not get the information he needs, he has no one to work
with, and there is no one who wants to listen to him. Only
time will solve these problems. " (Emphasis mine).

6.   Esman, The Institution-Building Concepts: an Interim Appraisal, op. cit. , p. 36 ff.

7.   In addition to Milton Esman's study cited above, and
the works referred to therein, Bertram Gross, The Managing
of Organizations (New York: The Free Press of Glencoe, 1964)
may be considered basic; although not directly pertinent to the
issue, it does provide the intellectual foundations for an analysis of innovative efforts (and advice); other relevant works
include W. A. Johr and H. W. Singer, The Role of the Economist as Official Advisor (London: Allen and Unwin, 1954);
Lyman Bryce, "Notes on Theory of Advice, " Political Science
Quarterly, LXVI (1951), pp. 321-339; an interesting case study
of an attempted institutional reform that failed is described by
Roderick T. Groves, "Administrative Reform and the Politics
of Reform, " Public Administration Review, XXVII, No. 5
(December 1967), pp. 436-445; case studies of this sort need
to be built up to develop both a descriptive and normative theory
of innovative planning.

8.   Karl Mannheim, Man and Society in an Age of Reconstruction (New York: Harcourt, Brace, and Co. , 1949),
pp. 174-196.

9.   David Popenoe, "On the Meaning of 'Urban' in Urban
Studies, " Urban Affairs Quarterly, I, No. 1 (September 1965),
pp. 17-34; John Friedmann, "Two Concepts of Urbanization:
A Comment. " Urban Affairs Quarterly, I, No. 4 (June 1966),
pp. 78-84.

10.   John Friedmann, "The Role of Cities in National Development" (paper prepared for the Seminar on Urbanization
and National Development, Jahuel, Chile, April 22-25, 1968).
(Mimeographed.)

11. William Mangin, "Latin American Squatter Settlements: A Problem and a Solution," Latin American Research Review, II, No. 3 (1967), pp. 65-98.

12. John Friedmann, "The Urban-Regional Frame for National Development," International Development Review, VII, No. 3 (September 1966), pp. 9-14.

13. William McCord, "Portrait of Transitional Man," in Irving Louis Horowitz, The New Sociology. Essays in Social Science and Social Theory of Honor of C. Wright Mills (New York, Oxford University Press, 1964), p. 430.

14. Ibid., p. 431.

15. Ibid., p. 437.

16. John Friedmann, "A strategy of Deliberate Urbanization," Journal of the American Institute of Planners, (forthcoming).

17. John Friedmann and Tomas Lackington, "Hyperurbanization and National Development in Chile: Some Hypotheses," Urban Affairs Quarterly, II, No. 4 (1967), pp. 3-29; and Francine F. Rabinovitz, "Urban Development and Political Development in Latin America," in CAG Occasional Papers (Bloomington, Ind., October 1967).

18. Leo F. Schnore, "On the Spatial Structure of the Two Americas," in Philip M. Hauser and Leo F. Schnore, ed., The Study of Urbanization (New York: John Wiley and Sons, 1965), ch. 10.

19. Leonard Reissman, The Urban Process (New York: The Free Press of Glencoe, 1964), ch. 7 and 8; see also John Friedmann, "A General Theory of Polarized Development" (Santiago, Chile: The Ford Foundation Program in Urban and Regional Development Assistance, 1968). (Mimeographed.)

20. An excellent example of such a study is Allen Pred, The Spatial Dynamic of U.S. Urban-Industrial Growth, 1800-1914 (Cambridge: M.I.T. Press, 1966).

21. Paul Davidoff, "Advocacy and Pluralism in Planning, " Journal of the American Institute of Planning. Vol. XXXI (November 1965), pp. 331-338.

22. An editorial in Life, Vol. LVIV, No. 8 (February 23, 1968), is characteristic of the changes occurring; its title: "Wherever We Look, Something's Wrong".

23. See, for example, Bertram M. Gross, "The State of the Nation; Social Systems Accounting, " in Raymond A. Bauer, ed., Social Indicators (Cambridge: M. I. T. Press, 1966); and Brian J. L. Berry, Strategies, Models, and Economic Theories of Development in Rural Regions (Washington, D. C.: U. S. Department of Agriculture, Economic Research Service, Agricultural Economic Report No. 127, December, 1967).

PART III

PROFESSIONAL EDUCATION
FOR WORLD RESPONSIBILITY

CHAPTER **9** THE EXPERIENCE
TO DATE

Irwin T. Sanders

As social values change and new expectations arise there is
a redefinition of many of the social roles in a society. Professional people are in the thick of such redefinition. They often
find it hard to determine their role because they find no clear
national goals providing direction. George J. Maslach, Dean of
the Engineering School at Berkeley, has stated the problem in
this way:

> A hundred years ago, in a time of great crisis --
> our Civil War -- the United States embarked upon a
> program to become an industrial nation. In a very few
> years, the wartime growth of industry was turned to
> the export of manufactured products with surprisingly
> good results. One hundred years later, a great major-
> ity of the U. S. working force are industrially oriented,
> and less than 8 percent earn their livelihood on farms.
> With our new affluence growing out of these economic
> developments, more than 50 percent of our labor force
> are providing services.
>
> As a nation, we are today searching for new goals.
> Included in these are such diverse programs as putting
> a man on the moon and a containing action in Vietnam,
> expenditures for which are large compared to the expend-
> itures for the Peace Corps program and the Office of
> Economic Opportunity program. If educational institu-
> tions are asked to provide personnel educated and dedi-
> cated to these goals, they have a rather perplexing
> problem, for these goals are quite different from those
> that we have just passed through, such as the education
> of a large number of engineers for the development of
> wartime products in the defense of the nation -- a goal
> of our society back in the late 30's and early 40's.

153

NEW GOALS, NEW ROLES

Some of the emerging goals closest to professional services
are those of social justice, broader economic opportunity and
improvement of living space. To the extent that these goals
become realized in behavior, two major shifts occur: first, benefits which were originally thought of as a privilege for which an
individual paid will now be regarded as a right of citizenship (for
which one will also have to pay). In medicine, for instance, the
disadvantaged no longer seek free medical care provided gratui-
tously by the physicians as an obligation to society; the disadvantaged are demanding that good health care is their right as
American citizens and not because they are poor. In social
welfare, the lowest income groups are not content to go to social
workers for categorical aid of various kinds, but demand a guar-
anteed annual income as members of the affluent American
society. The right of an ordinary person to the services of a
lawyer is being reaffirmed every day, so that now the legal profession is being forced to consider the problem of the distribution
of legal services just as the doctor worries about the distribution
of health services. These new demands call for new social
mechanisms which American society does not yet use exten-
sively. Either the professionals will help devise and guide these
mechanisms or, if they do not, political leaders and others will
set them up with little regard to some of the features which the
professionals would stress.

There is a second shift implied in any movement American
society makes toward achieving the goals of social justice,
improvement in living conditions, and the like. That is the
requirement that a professional person be trained to think
beyond the immediate needs of client or patient -- which will
always be the professional's chief concern -- to the added needs
of society. "Society" will, of course, be defined differently in
keepingwith the problems to be confronted. But, to illustrate,
engineers which help a public utility company plan and construct
a power plant traditionally consider their job done if they carry
out the wishes of the client and conform to his specifications.
But is that sufficient today? Does the professional engineer
not also have to take an additional factor into account, namely,
how the power plant influences the living space around it? Does
it contribute unduly to air pollution and health hazards? If so,
is the engineer supposed to warn the client that the type of plant
proposed is not serving social ends but creating hazards? Or
is the engineer to rest content in the thought that it is up to the

legislators and others to pass laws that make the public utility
conform to social needs, which are not an engineering problem
at all? The same questions apply to water pollution, traffic
flow, and a host of other problems accentuated in a highly
urbanized society.

In sum: Does professional practice as professionals view
it today and, even more, tomorrow embrace the client plus
society; or is it to remain faithful to the early tradition, putting
the client first, with social consequences of little concern to
many professional practitioners? Here professionals face a
role redefinition.

THE PROFESSIONAL SCHOOL
IN THE UNIVERSITY COMPLEX

Somewhat removed from the hurly-burly of every-day
professional practice lies the professional school, sometimes
Gothic and ivy-covered and sometimes red-brick and business-
like. As the "central campus" concept is put into force in
university after university, the separated professional schools
scattered in various parts of the city are brought together --
often in high-rise buildings -- to share more fully in the intellectual community of which they have nominally been a part.
This leads to an agonizing reappraisal for all concerned, and
two interesting changes occur.

First, how does a professional school, usually with a strong
administrative leadership of its own, a body of alumni, and
links to extramural professional associations, merge into the
grayness of a central administration? It first asks what benefits it will receive other than those of reduced overhead. If it
still has an undergraduate student body, many of its students
can take courses in other schools or departments and thereby
have a broader exposure than the single professional school
alone could provide. If the student body is primarily graduate,
there are opportunities for cooperative research efforts with
competent faculty members in other colleges, particularly since
so many problems being studied today move one quickly beyond
the confines of a given professional field. There are also
opportunities for joint appointments across colleges, joint programs of study, and a chance for more rational use of what at

best are scarce resources. With such mixing in a university
atmosphere, the stress on practice and techniques lessens and
the emphasis on analysis, understanding, and theory development increases.

The second shift that accompanies reappraisal is a change
in the self-image of the faculty member in a professional school.
In the past, one of the qualifications sought in the faculty member
was successful practice outside the university, on the assumption
that he was being employed to pass the skills of his trade on to a
new generation. If he has never practiced, how can he teach the
neophytes? But as a professional school behaves more and more
like part of its university, faculty members begin to think of
themselves as professors and not practitioners. What is more,
they even go on and get Ph. D. degrees. Still worse in the eyes
of the traditionalist, professors advise their best graduates to
pursue advanced study at the expense of practice, and frequently
bring these bright young men with new-won degrees back to their
faculty or recommend them to some other school's faculty.
These younger men, perpetuating their kind in the academic
hierarchy, do research, develop theory, and try to give their
students an understanding of their profession rather than the
simpler techniques of how to practice it. They do, of course,
develop close working relationships with professional practitioners outside the university, not as fellow practitioners but as
students of practice and professional problems.

This shift in orientation has probably gone much farther
than we professionals think. It can be tested in the case of any
professional school faculty member by asking: What is your
reference group? Where do you seek most prestige and approv-
al--with your university colleagues outside your own school
but on your own campus, with colleagues from the same professional field in other institutions, or with the nonacademic people
prominent in your profession? The answer is never clearly one
or the other, but there is a difference in emphasis which reflects
the extent to which the faculty member has been socialized into
the university, which has very different folkways and pecking
orders from any profession outside the university.

I submit that the professional school and its faculty members are still trying to find their place in the university scheme
of things, while maintaining connections with their profession
outside. The tension in these two requirements will never be
fully resolved and will call for periodic re-examination.

RETHINKING TECHNICAL ASSISTANCE PROGRAMS

The reappraisal of technical assistance programs deeply involves professional people, who are called upon to provide as expatriates much of the expertise in such short supply in a developing country.

Learning About
The Infrastructure

This stock-taking might be faced as a series of questions. First, why does each technical assistance team going abroad tend to repeat the mistakes of its predecessors? The answer lies, I think, in the lack of sensitivity by many professional people to the nature of the infrastructure on which a given profession in the United States or Western Europe depends, and the failure to appreciate the social and cultural context of professional practice at home as well as abroad. The social scientists have been shouting from the housetops of the relevance of such matters to technical assistance for many years, but their voices have not carried to the busy streets below. In 1944, for instance, I was in charge of preparations for a conference in Washington, D.C., entitled "Contribution of Extension Methods and Techniques to the Rehabilitation of War Torn Countries," whose chief theme was the need for American professionals working abroad to recognize the important differences between the U.S. and the host country. In 1945 I edited a book titled Farmers of the World, in which my collaborators and contributors stressed the same theme. In Athens, Greece, in 1953 I spoke to the twenty or twenty-five section chiefs of the United States aid mission on a theme I called "Peasants Are People," a speech in which I described the social characteristics of rural people. I was told that this was the first presentation to be applauded in a year and a half. Afterwards, transportation, health, agricultural and other experts crowded around to say, "If we had only known the truth of what you said before we came to Greece, we would have been so much more effective." They agreed, however, that they would never have appreciated such a talk given in Washington prior to taking their first foreign assignment. Only recently I met with a group of Purdue fellows in agriculture, veterinary science, engineering, and industrial management who had just returned from eighteen-month

internships in Latin America. Their consensus was that the
social and cultural differences they encountered were much
greater than they had assumed. They also agreed that they were
very impatient with any efforts during their pre-departure orientation program to provide the social background of the country
to which they were going.

What is tragic is not that social scientists do not get their
message across to engineers, public administrators, and medical personnel; that is understandable and par for the course.
The tragedy comes when a professional experienced in the com-
plexities of work abroad is unable to communicate what he has
learned to a fellow professional in his own field because neither
he nor his replacement have the concepts they need to talk ana-
lytically about the job to be done. Even more pathetic is the
ease with which the self-confident American professional brushes
off any efforts by others to help him understand what he faces.
This is perhaps one of the major indications of the parochialism
of much professional education today.

Transferring Technology

Another question which illustrates the nature of stock-taking
by thoughtful professionals is, Why is the transfer of technology
so much more complicated than we thought? Professionals are
learning more about the transfer of technology, enough at least
to know how naive they were twenty years ago. The International
Rice Research Institute in Los Baños, the Philippines, is dem-
onstrating that sound research is basic to technological transfer
in agriculture; the research of rural sociologists and others
explains the stages through which acceptance of technology passes
and the factors related to adoption of innovation.

Success

A third question is, Why do some technical assistance
programs become brilliant successes and others fail so miser-
ably? It is clear that many professional people fail to view a
program as a set of social relationships. It is people who are
related to one another in a division of labor and a hierarchical
structure. Knowing much about the technical aspects of a

professional field is no guarantee that one can work effectively with the human factors inherent in a technical assistance
program.

THE PROFESSIONAL SCHOOL IN THE WORLD

What are United States professional schools doing in
response to all the international challenges presented to them?
Perhaps what would help are some of the conclusions and
impressions I gained from a two-year study of how United States
professional schools in eight different fields can more effectively deal with the international challenges which they face.
The reports on the individual professions have been published,
first separately, and now together in a single volume. [1] I
need not go into great detail about matters already treated in
print; rather, I prefer to stress some of the unexpected, even
peripheral results of the study directly relevant to the themes
of this book. The reader should be aware, of course, that I
am reporting on highly personal impressions which do not
reflect the findings of the task forces involved in the study nor
the official position of Education and World Affairs. I do think,
however, that sharing these observations may contribute to a
better understanding of the problems related to increasing the
international perspective of professional schools.

Business Administration

Generalizations on schools of business administration are
complicated by the fact that some are almost entirely undergraduate, others graduate, and some a mixture of the two. The
inquiry dealt mainly with those giving graduate work, though
the undergraduate programs were not completely excluded from
consideration. Business administration faculty members are
well aware of the great plunge by United States businesses into
foreign investment and operations. In their response to this
state of affairs, they are torn between two possible approaches.
One is to infuse international materials into all of the standard
courses, so that for instance, the course in accounting, in
addition to basic principles, would also give some insight into

different accounting systems in other countries. The other
point of view is that a division of international business should
be set up, with the requirement that all students take one or
more courses in this division as part of their regular work.
The second alternative leads into the question of whether there
is a separate theoretical content to international business
which would justify treating it as a separate division. As for
special programs preparing United States students for a career
in international business, the demand is not yet at all clear.
If American businesses think of their companies as multi-
national, then they will move personnel back and forth between
American-based and foreign-based assignments. To be prepared for a foreign assignment and not for a stateside job
would be self-defeating in the opinion of some. The discussion
is still raging, with important figures in the profession coming
out on different sides.

As a sidelight, I must report that the task force trio
representing the business school pulled off a spectacular coup
in delegating the writing of their report. Several task force
meetings had taken place, and discussion was at a high level,
and interest keen. But then came the meeting when I as study
director had to say: "We need the first draft of your report by
the end of this month." This was a dire confrontation on a
Saturday in New York at the Biltmore Hotel. They asked: "Can
you send us some dictating machines?" This I did. But I
heard nothing from them the rest of the day, not even at five
o'clock when people were supposed to report back. But by
nine o'clock the next morning they had produced a most capable
business school faculty member, known to each of the deans on
the task force, who was prepared to write the report under
their close instruction. And this he did, shuttling back and
forth among the task force members. They participated fully
and the report was in every sense their document. Yet it
represents one of the most capable examples of delegation and
supervision that I have witnessed in my career.

Engineering

At first, the agriculturists and the engineers met in the
same task force to talk about common approaches and differences in efforts to internationalize their professional school.

The engineers kept insisting that their profession was non-national; the agriculturists responded, "the hell it is, " or words to that effect. To the engineer, his profession is practiced the same wherever he happens to be. But two modifications later clarified what seems to be a preposterous statement. The first modification was the realization that when the engineer is talking about engineering practice abroad he is talking just about technical engineering and about nothing else. In other words, an engineer may spend five hours each day clearing matters through customs, working out labor arrangements, talking with government officials; he may spend only two to three hours each day on technical engineering matters. However, he does not usually equate the engineer's work role -- what he does from 9 to 5 (or whatever office hours he keeps) -- with his professional role. With this restricted definition of professional role, then, one can claim that it is non-national. But in the engineer's other responsibilities on the job, he uses common sense approaches, or hires some expert to take care of the details for him. He, like the lawyer, claims he can effectively handle any human relations problem he faces because he has been taught to "think. "

A second modification of the non-national theme occurred when the report writing began. The task force realized that engineering was usually performed for a client; a business concern, a municipality, or a national government. And practice did have to be modified to meet the needs of the client. Here national and cultural differences did enter in and, perhaps after all, one could speak of an international dimension to engineering practice.

Law

The task force on law schools recommended the setting up of a new kind of course in law schools wherever a qualified staff member was available to teach it. The recommended course would provide a common basis on which some of the more specialized courses could build. Those working on the law schools report had the advantage of about ten years of a special program in international legal studies funded by the Ford Foundation at ten or twelve of the nation's leading law schools. These programs have done much to develop new

courses, promote international research, and bring about
greater exchange among the legal scholars of different countries. The legal profession, in contrast to engineering, cannot
talk about being non-national, for it is tied in very closely
with the particular legal, governmental, business, family
systems in terms of which it operates. A lawyer is not usually
equipped to practice outside his own country, but as a legal
scholar and adviser he may develop a lucrative and useful
international position.

One sidelight about lawyers that came out in the study was
their interest in and skill in drafting. Their training in this
area is not over-rated in the least. Now and then the Law
Task Force, after what might seem to be an extended harangue,
would adjourn so the task force chairman could proceed with
the drafting of a section to be submitted to the rest for savage
criticism a few hours later. One has to see this to believe it.
Furthermore, in the six regional councils held throughout the
United States to discuss the reports of the study, always the
lawyers had read the report, had marked it up, and had it
physically there ready to discuss. Some other professional
groups never bothered to read the report they were to discuss,
even though heroic efforts were made to get the reports into
their hands well in advance.

A further insight into the legal profession came as the
result of a follow-up effort. Someone suggested that the law
students would take their courses on international topics more
seriously if there were a few questions on the bar examination
touching on these points. An inquiry to this effect was made to
those in charge of the bar examination for a major state. The
bar examiners in their reply rested their case on a 1935 address
by no less a legal dignitary than Roscoe Pound. The reply to
the inquiry stated:

> Our examination does not include questions
> on international law or world affairs. We feel such
> questions would be inappropriate and, in fact, that
> they might violate the Rules of the Court of Appeals
> which require that the examination be held 'on ques-
> tions which a lawyer in general practice may
> reasonably expect to meet.' Our examination does
> contain questions on conflicts between the several
> states as well as foreign nations.

We feel that international law is basically a specialty which can best be pursued in a post-graduate course and as you are aware, there are a number of schools which provide special training in international legal studies.

The reply went on to say that "perhaps the best explanation of the views of our Board is set forth in an address made by Dean Roscoe Pound of Harvard before the National Conference of Bar Examiners in 1935. We feel that the views he expressed in 1935 are as true today as they were when he made his address." Dean Pound's address as excerpted in the letter included the following statements:

Still another difficulty arises from the constant pressure brought to bear upon teachers and examiners alike to make provision for and examine upon special subjects, which it is urged, 'the lawyer ought to know.' It would be well if the lawyer could know everything. But he can't. Stevenson says that the difference between Homer and an ordinary poet is that Homer knew what to leave out. This problem of what to leave out confronts the makers of curricula and the examiners persistently and perennially. If one yields to it, he can seldom make any adequate place for the new subject....

Undoubtedly the lawyer is well advised to study economics and the social sciences. But candidates who come from college, as most are coming to do today, will have done so, and requirements of preliminary training will take care of this matter much better than the bar examiners who can spare so little time for them....There is no more unhappy fallacy current than the idea that no one can be expected to know anything unless he has had a formal course of instruction in it and has been duly examined in it.

And that is where the matter rested.

Medicine

The task force on medical schools had two preoccupations
which it found difficult to shake off, and for very good reasons.
The first was the predisposition to spend their time prescribing
what medical schools in developing countries ought to be doing,
instead of asking themselves what kind of physicians they were
turning out in the United States. The reason was, I am sure,
that some of the task force members were intimately involved
in helping foreign medical schools address themselves to very
critical problems, and these problems remained very vividly
in their minds. The second preoccupation of the task force was
the dependence of United States hospitals, particularly those
not connected with medical centers, upon foreign-trained interns and residents. Since the medical schools did not deal
with these hospitals, what could the schools do to improve the
situation? There was general agreement that the best way to
give the future United States physician an appreciation of world
health problems was to arrange a short foreign tour for the
medical student. One task force member, who is setting up
a new medical school, proposes to require this of every student
where possible. Admittedly, such a foreign assignment, even
for a summer, is hard to work into the crowded medical student's schedule.

In the discussions of the study committee, which discussed
each task force report, the task force on medical schools repeatedly emphasized how similar many of the problems faced
in medicine are to those faced in other professional fields.
The task force urged breaking down some of the isolationism
and parochialism which has existed among professions, even
on the same campus.

Education

The report on education proved the most difficult of all
to prepare. At first I thought this was the result of the vague-
ness of the concepts and purposes often associated with the
field of education, or else the result of the lack of sound
learning and organizational theory, at least as embodied in
the customary practice of the profession. I later decided

that neither was not the real explanation of the difficulty. The
problem lay in the variegated audience to which the report
was supposedly addressed. Teacher training in the United
States is a highly dispersed operation. About half of the
teachers are prepared in liberal arts colleges, many of them
very small and having only one professor of education or perhaps a small department of education. This is one possible
audience which should consider seriously the problem of inter-
nationalizing the teacher's perspective.

Secondly, there is the former teachers college, originally
a normal school but now a state university. It is in the throes
of changing from a pedagogical institute to a well-rounded
academic institution. Its needs and potentialities are different
from other schools', but must be taken into account in any
report.

Finally, there are the well-established colleges of education in major universities. For the most part, these have
relegated international matters to the comparative educationists, to whom they accord low status and little money. The
real power lies in those responsible for educational administration, which is almost entirely American-directed. In these
major colleges of education the problems of internationalization
lie primarily in convincing administration specialists that even
administration can be comparative and that the U.S. educational
system has something to learn from other countries.

Whereas some professional fields are relatively homogeneous, education is decidedly heterogeneous. This may
explain why teachers, through their newly established unions,
are willing to trade their non-existent prestige -- prestige
being the foundation for a professional mystique -- for the
concerted power symbolized by a strike and collective bar-
gaining.

Agriculture

Three things became clear early in the discussions by the
agriculture task force. First, agriculture is not really a
profession in the sense that law is a profession. Agriculture
is rather a collection of separate disciplines, each of which

deals with aspects of the plant and animal world. Professionalization proceeds through the route of the discipline -- agronomy,
dairy science -- rather than through agriculture itself.

Second, the task force concluded that one of the reasons
many agricultural programs sponsored abroad by United States
specialists failed was because we Americans did not understand
the real factors underlying the amazing American performance
in agriculture. In other words, we assumed we knew why we
prospered and tried to apply these assumptions in other countries, where they did not hold up. What is needed, therefore,
is a much sounder analysis of United States domestic experience
if professionals are to try to translate it abroad.

Agriculture, in the third place, differs from other professions in that it takes the client (the farmer) into its confidence
and tries to make him the practicing arm of the profession.
The user then is a part of the profession, a fact which does
not prevail in other professions to the same degree.

Of all the task forces, agriculture and public health each had
collectively the most international experience of a sustained
sort from which to draw in setting forth their findings. More
than any other, the task force on agriculture was able to get
down to cases and infer from them what the colleges of agriculture should be doing. This fact explains why this report
has received such favorable comment -- this fact, plus the
additional fact that the report is so well written.

Public Health

Several of the fifteen or twenty schools of public health in
the United States and Canada are already heavily involved in
international programs. They, like schools in other fields,
face the problem of incorporating what has been learned in
activities abroad to the preparation of regular students expecting to practice in this country. Some schools also have high
proportions of foreign students -- all of course at the graduate
level -- to which they feel a serious responsibility.

The combined task force on Medicine and Public Health
did not attempt to resolve the dilemma of whether to treat

public health matters in a department of preventive or community medicine in a medical school or in a separate school of public health. Suffice it to say that federal legislation which underwrites support for schools of public health is leading to the establishment of such schools in increasing numbers throughout the country, usually with the blessing of the medical school. Public health specialists did seem to be concerned about the problem of the distribution of health services to all sectors of the American population, perhaps because they were more familiar with the many kinds of distribution patterns being experimented with abroad.

Public Administration

Public administration faculty members find that international questions complicate their lives. Here in the United States, one can make a fairly satisfactory distinction between business administration and public administration, but even in this country there are pitfalls. However, when one tries to understand the administrative workings of a socialist country, where the government operates businessess, one cannot divorce the two. A public administrator in many countries abroad is not therefore simply a bureaucrat in a political hierarchy; he may actually be responsible for developing a national economic plan, managing an entire industry, and guiding the entire foreign trade with outside countries. How do American schools of public administration set about training specialists with such confidence?

Of all the task forces, that on public administration did the best job of seeing their profession in terms of future trends, at home as well as abroad. They are not so preoccupied with hardware or material technology as some professions, and are thus more sensitive to the forces affecting social arrangements through which a government tries to get things done. An important leaven in this field has been the Comparative Administration Group, which has had foundation funds to hold summer seminars on comparative administration themes and to disseminate information about international topics. This group holds special meetings at the time of professional conferences and helps its members see administration in a much more international framework.

Most task force members felt that, in most cases, public administration programs under the control of a political science department lacked the strength found where the two were divorced. Certainly, the separate school of public administration has been much more fully involved in international affairs than have the public administration units in political science departments, which for the most part have devoted themselves to detailed aspects of the administration of local government. Is public administration a profession? Many of its practitioners are certainly straining toward recognition as a profession. In the study I am describing we did not try to decide the matter for any field of activity. We simply accepted the current academic usage of the term, call "professional" those schools which were outside the college of liberal arts and its attendant graduate school.

So much then for some of the sidelights emerging from the study on the professional school and world affairs. Perhaps I would have gained different impressions if different people had constituted the task forces; I am obviously generalizing from scanty data, but I have been immersed for some time in discourses by professionals about their international concerns.

THE PROFESSIONAL AS WORLD CITIZEN

National boundaries are becoming increasingly irrelevant to the practice of most professions. In the future -- perhaps twenty-five or thirty years from now -- it will be just as normal for a professional person to take on foreign assignments (which will no longer be called "foreign") and foreign clients as it is today to concentrate on domestic practice.

When this occurs, the professional person will be prepared to recognize and deal with cultural differences in the same way that he now deals with individual differences. If successful in domestic practice, the professional treats no two clients exactly alike. The same holds true in international practice, but success there comes about only if one knows something about the backgrounds from which the clients come.

Furthermore, there will be a heightened sense of supra-
national colleagueship. Already, the professional person in
a developing country is able to maintain a sense of identity
and self-respect in the face of low standards of living and culture by reminding himself that he is not merely a member of
a backward nation but is also a member of a world-wide profession for which he holds the proper credentials. International
exchanges, related to much less expensive air travel, will
bring about on an ever-increasing scale not only the exchange
of published materials but also the opportunity for face-to-face
contact among those interested in similar professional problems
though based at widely different spots on this shrinking planet.

All of this intensified activity, by breaking down much
parochialism, should lead to greatly expanded knowledge of
help in improving practice and developing the underlying theory
on which effective practice must be based. In this, as well as
the situations mentioned above, the professional as a professional will benefit from and feel a sense of responsibility toward
his fellow professionals around the world.

Meanwhile there is the problem of introducing an international dimension into American professional schools, and
clearly this is not simple.

It seems to me that there are four recurrent themes apparent in the experience I have already examined which are
worth attention: increasing administrative commitment, lib-
eralizing the school environment, influencing the professional
system, and developing faculty competence.

Increasing Administrative Commitment

Unless the university administration as well as the administration of the professional school is aware of the international
context in which professionals live, any single unit of the university finds it difficult to make much progress in broadening
its world view. This commitment is shown in the official ad-
dresses which the top administrators give, particularly in
those discourses where they deal with educational priorities;
it is shown in the treatment accorded professors who take
foreign assignments as far as salary raises and promotions

are concerned; it is shown in budget flexibility which provides
funds for comparative research, adding a new professorship
to deal with international aspects of the professional field,
and the kind of structure set up for international programs.
Administrators who have never traveled abroad often return
from their first trip with a much deeper concern than they
have ever evidenced before in making their institution a part
of the modern world.

Liberalizing the Students' Environment

Those most experienced in teaching are the first to recognize the limited role courses can play in changing student
attitudes and even in broadening their horizons. The extra-
curricular milieu at a professional school is just as educational
as the formal curriculum. A friend of mine, at the request of
the student government at the Massachusetts Institute of Technology, made a study of changes in freshmen attitudes toward
a number of matters. She found that when the freshmen first
arrived they were strongly oriented toward the strictly technical engineering pursuits, but by the end of the freshman year
they had learned that the real professional rewards went to
those who were engineering administrators, who in turn bossed
those who stuck to the technical side of the profession. The
freshmen never learned this in the classroom but in the dorm-
itory bull sessions. Similarly, many students report that they
gain much international understanding from foreign students
whom they get to know very well, from a visiting professor
from overseas, and from the comments which professors make
about their trips abroad even though these comments are peripheral to the matters being discussed in class. One can look
at the list of outside speakers scheduled by a professional
school over the course of a year and pretty well gauge the
international interests of that school. A supreme test is in
the accomplishments of those awarded honorary degrees --
that is, the balance between those with domestic or international professional service.

Influencing the Professional System

Educators are quick to point out that preparing new teachers to introduce international materials in their secondary
school subjects is of little effect if their supervisors, school
administrators, and school boards are not interested in such
innovation. In other words, a profession is a total social
system of which the educational and training institutions are
but a part. Unless innovation is diffused as much as possible
into the whole system, it will be much less important in a
single part. It is interesting to note that most professional
associations, especially those including professional schools,
have an international committee of some sort. Most of these
schedule sessions at the annual meetings on some international
theme. So a start is being made. In some cases, the practitioners outside the professional school are further advanced
than the professional school in their understanding of how the
profession is being influenced by forces from abroad.

Developing Faculty Competence

There are two ways for a school to acquire the staff members who can teach courses dealing with the international
aspects of a profession. One is to employ them from outside;
the other is to help professors already on the staff do the study
and gain the experience that will give them the needed competence. In some cases, existing staff members already have
the competence, but have never been provided the outlets for
utilizing it. The competence about which I speak is related to
course offerings: world agriculture, public international law,
international business transactions, tropical medicine, comparative administration, and comparative education. This competence also extends to the ability to advise foreign students
so that they can profit most from their stay in this country and
return to effective practice at home. Those professors who
have some concept of problems in a developing country are
usually most helpful in this respect. Finally, "competence"
includes the supervision of students in comparative research,
which frequently calls for a period of work abroad. The particular mix among these kinds of competence will vary with
each profession.

NOTES

1.   Education and World Affairs, <u>The Professional School and World Affairs</u> (Albuquerque, N. M. : University of New Mexico Press, 1968).

CHAPTER **10** TRAINING ECONOMISTS
FOR SERVICE IN
DEVELOPING COUNTRIES

Gustav F. Papanek

How can the supply of economists trained to work for the
governments of less developed countries be increased?

SEMINARS IN PROBLEM-SOLVING

The first step is to provide some policy-oriented, problem-
solving courses or seminars to graduate students in the field.
A number of professional schools, particularly in medicine,
law, and business, rely very heavily on problem-solving to
teach not only the applied aspects but also the principles and
theories of their field. It is doubtful that economics can usefully imitate them, but it can at least provide some seminars
with this orientation. Even students interested primarily in
theory, history, or methodology could profit from such
seminars; many of the major advances in economic theory and
techniques, from Keynes to input-output and linear programming, have resulted from an attempt to solve problems. For
students planning to deal with the policy problems of less
developed countries, the opportunity to participate in such
seminars is highly important.

The essential characteristic of these seminars would be
their focus on the solution of problems by the application of
economic principles and techniques. Such a seminar can be
a painful but highly educational experience. The student finds

himself suddenly bereft of the assumptions which ease his
intellectual labors in economic principles courses -- adequate
information, ceteris paribus, the absence of transitional,
political and social problems, linear relations and simplifying
assumptions. "Playing" at the solution of real problems obviously does not make a student a competent policy economist,
but it can be a useful first step.

SUPERVISED EXPERIENCE

The second step clearly required is the opportunity to
acquire experience, preferably with guidance from a senior
colleague. In the early 1950's experience in less developed
countries was an asset but not a necessity. Few economists,
nationals or foreigners, had any significant experience with
development problems or with economic policy in less developed
countries. Those who became involved at that time learned
by doing and by their own mistakes, and they learned together.
Economists from the less developed countries had, in most
cases, only begun to return home from training abroad.
Government officials had only begun to shift from concern with
administrative to economic problems. Some foreigners came
from universities, occasionally with little policy experience
even in their own countries. Although many who came from
academia had been concerned with policy at least at some time
in their career, very few had worked in less developed countries.

The situation by the late 1960's had become radically
different in many less developed countries. (A few, more
recently independent or with a poor educational system, are
in the same position as the majority were in the 1950's.) A
good deal of experience has accumulated, much of it not yet
recorded and therefore inaccessible to the outside scholar.
The economist with little or no experience in the less developed
world is seriously handicapped and if he lacks policy experience in addition his usefulness is severely limited. His colleagues, under constant pressure, always desperately over-
worked, usually have little time to transfer their knowledge
and show little patience with the newcomer's discovery of

problems they recognize and relationships they assume almost
automatically.

SOME EXAMPLES

Some examples of these developments may be useful. In
1954, when a Harvard advisory group first began work in
Pakistan, the government had only one or two economists with
advanced modern training. The Pakistani planning commission
was dominated by able civil servants with little formal training
in economics. There was strong sentiment to concentrate on
the preparation of an input-output table, then one of the most
modern techniques, as a basis for a planning model. The few
foreigners who were policy-oriented professional economists
made two major contributions during this early period: First,
they convinced their more academic colleagues -- and especially the inexperienced, recently trained Pakistani ones -- that
the more sophisticated techniques were then inappropriate;
second, they introduced some of the simple techniques useful
in framing government policy and programs -- for example,
cost-benefit calculations, longer-term budgeting, economic
appraisal of tax measures, import-forecasting, foreign exchange gap calculations. Everyone involved learned from experience how techniques, approaches, and policies developed
for the Marshall Plan and for the developed countries needed
to be modified to be useful in Pakistan.

In the late 1960's, by contrast, the Pakistani planning
commission and its counterparts in the provinces have three
or four times as many well-trained economists as they did.
Their work is dominated by professionals. Some of the economists have had ten years or more of experience. Quite
sophisticated techniques are feasible, appropriate, and used.
Economists who join the commission therefore must be well
trained to be accepted. But if experience has not taught them
the limits of their techniques they are quickly ignored as hope-
lessly theoretical by their colleagues. And those among them,
especially foreigners, whose memoranda stress their discovery
of factors long since assimilated into the intellectual baggage
of their experienced colleagues are sometimes regarded as
naive time-wasters. (Foreign advisers, new to the less

developed world, often "discover" the importance of excess
capacity resulting from the import control system or the distorting effects of low tariffs on the import of machinery. They
produce long notes on the advantages of their own complex
scheme for dealing with these problems. Their experienced
colleagues have seen perhaps a dozen such memoranda, are
fully aware of the problems, and have gradually achieved a
substantial modification in the policies by various half-way,
pragmatic steps.)

Even more obvious is the difference between the first
Harvard team and a more recent one, a 1968 team in Indonesia.
Whereas the 1954 group had no one with extensive experience
in less developed countries, in the 1968 team everyone had
such experience, and the average was over five years. This
team is working with Indonesian economists who are first-rate
professionals. Most important, team members can draw on
considerable experience with policy successes and failures in
other countries.

Nowadays, government economists are seriously handicapped by lack of experience. Foreign economists are further
handicapped by lack of experience in a particular country.
The visit by the great economist who comes for a week or a
month to dispense wisdom is becoming less appropriate and
less frequent. It is increasingly obvious that problems are
too complex and that less great men in the country for longer
can do better in dealing with them. (Countries are less eager
now to ask a visiting expert after a month's experience whether
they should devalue the currency.)

EXPERIENCE IN POLICY ADVISING

The obvious reaction of organizations employing economists is to look for those with experience. This principle
limits the number of economists available for work in less
developed countries and makes it increasingly difficult to acquire relevant policy experience. Some economists pursue
the usual academic career and become policy advisers at a
later stage. However, academics who shift to government

after an extensive university career sometimes find an adjustment to policy work difficult and an adjustment to a less developed country even more so. A number of steps can be taken
to enable economists to acquire experience in dealing with
policy problems in less developed countries.

A team approach can provide on-the-job training. In a
team it is possible to combine technical competence with knowledge of how policy is made; the energy and enthusiasm of
younger members with the experience of older ones; and competence in specialized fields with a broad view of the economy.
A team can provide experience to the younger members, without the risk to a country which their lack of experience would
involve. An apprentice relationship is widespread in the professions -- medicine and law provide examples -- and there
are the beginnings of it in economics in large, well-organized
government offices. It is particularly needed in the amorphous,
confused situation which exists in the newly established economic staffs of less developed countries. The quickest, least
costly method for gaining and transmitting experience is in a
team which combines experienced and less experienced members, regardless of whether they are nationals or foreigners.

The second approach to dealing with the need for experience among policy economists in less developed countries is
the development of a career pattern that permits economists
to work for long periods of time in governments of less developed countries without damaging their professional advancement. At the moment most institutions using economists
(that is, institutions in the developed world) do not provide a
well-articulated career pattern that makes experience in less
developed countries, especially in non-research activities, a
major asset, rather than a drawback, to professional advancement. Economists therefore often have to look on a period as
advisers in a less developed country as costly to their career
and are inclined to limit the exposure.

MAINTAINING PROFESSIONALISM

A few economists from developed countries, principally
in the foreign aid programs, often do spend a large part of

their career in less developed countries. Their problems are
somewhat different -- the need to spend a good deal of time
on administrative and diplomatic functions, the difficulty of
remaining in touch with research and with the profession in
general. Their career pattern does include a good deal of experience in less developed countries, but often it involves a
gradual attenuation of their links to their profession.

The problems of economists from the less developed
countries are similar. Some of them, academics concerned
with their professional reputations but with limited access to
research tools, data, and assistance, retreat into the higher
reaches of abstraction. Others, working with governments,
find little opportunity to write, read, reflect, and, above all,
to compare their experience with that of their colleagues in
other countries.

Most economists still come from the developed countries.
Many among them, even those specializing in development,
find it difficult to include in their career extensive work with
governments in less developed countries. Esteem in the profession is, above all, a function of publication, especially the
publication of work which involves theoretical or methodological
advances. Work with governments in less developed countries
has serious drawbacks for publication of this kind. Some of
the work must remain confidential and work pressure leaves
little time for writing. These problems are shared by all
government economists. In addition, in less developed countries data are poor and non-economic factors prominent.
Economists therefore spend much time in data improvement
and in devising solutions that take account of non-economic
factors. This makes generalization and work on the method-
ological/theoretical frontiers of the profession difficult. In
addition auxiliary facilities are scarce -- research assistants,
computers, even desk calculators and reliable assistants who
know arithmetic may be unavailable. Work in less developed
countries also removes an economist from contact with his
colleagues, which is bad both for the interchange of ideas and
for exposure to potential employers. Finally, there is relatively little integration between research on less developed countries and the work of economists advising governments. Even
if he returns to an academic base, the ex-adviser may find
that his research and writing deal with subjects far removed

from his field experience, simply because there is no organized research work at his university dealing with less
developed countries.

Solutions to these career problems can make an important
contribution to increasing the number of experienced economists working with governments of less developed countries.
Such solutions essentially require a recognition that policy
work can be highly rewarding in advancing the discipline.
That is, it is good for economists and for an understanding of
economic casuality, not just for the governments advised.
Given this recognition it is possible to devise institutional
means to provide career rewards for those engaged in advisory or other overseas work. Arrangements under which
economists returning from overseas work are supported and
encouraged while they draw on their experience for further
research and writing would be an important first step. More
difficult, but also more useful, would be widespread arrangements by academic institutions of career possibilities which
clearly envisage alternation between periods in the less developed and the developed countries, the former devoted to
research and advising, the latter to teaching, research,
writing, and catching up. Less developed countries would
be able to obtain advisers who are experienced yet familiar
with recent developments in their profession; the academic institutions would gain faculty members who can bring to teaching and research the extensive field experience now so often
lacking.

SPECIALIZATION AND TEAMWORK

Increased professional competence for government economic advisers involves not only some change in training and
provision for acquiring experience without losing touch with
the profession, it increasingly requires specialization and a
team effort. The group approach has been lauded because it
makes an apprentice program possible. It is needed also because an economic policy staff in a government requires a
critical mass to be professionally effective. One of the staff's
major functions is to consider priorities and interrelationships,
and to do this effectively requires a number of professionals.

Rarely can much be accomplished by fewer than five or six good professionals in a small country. A large economy usually needs a minimum of ten or more competent and experienced economists, nationals and foreigners.

Pakistan: An Example

An example may be useful. In the early 1960's, Pakistan's planning commission was doing much of the staff work on a major increase in the level of the development effort. It was laying the basis for a six per cent rather than a three or four per cent, rate of growth.

This required, first, careful analysis of the policies and programs that could step up the rate of agricultural growth -- what would be the effect of higher and more stable prices; what were the storage requirements to permit price stabilization; what was holding up the fertilizer program and how could the bottlenecks be removed; what would be the effect of price changes on imports, exports and internal consumption; and so on.

Second, someone had to look at industry to forecast the requirements for additional imports and their most likely composition; to devise a sensible strategy for further industrial investment; to consider the role of private enterprise and the government development corporation in carrying it out; and to examine the policy changes required. Some work also had to go on with respect to investment in other sectors -- power and transport principally. Then the government development program had to be put together.

Third, a careful analysis of the foreign sector was required: what increase in exports could be expected and what was the lag with which it might take place; what imports would be required; what private foreign investment might be induced and what foreign public funds would be needed. To calculate foreign aid needs required a large effort, since it called for time phasing of commitments and actual expenditures, a scheduling of different forms of loans and grants, and some consideration of the various sources involved.

Fourth, all of the policies and programs had to be translated into financial terms.   Their effect on budgetary requirements and credit policy had to be examined and the level of
government borrowing considered.   Tax policy alone required
a major effort.

Finally, all the major individual pieces of analysis, plus
innumerable minor ones not mentioned, had to be put together
in a consistent and feasible package.   The amount of foreign
aid expected obviously affected tax, import, and monetary
policy, but the amount of aid in turn was likely to depend to
some extent on the tax, import, and monetary policies the
government was prepared to undertake.   These were related
to likely agricultural output, which in turn depended on price
and subsidy policy.   Priority decisions had to be made and
reasonable consistency assured.   Then the whole package and
individual pieces had to be discussed with the relevant departments, ministries, provinces, foreigners, and international organizations, most of them skeptics.

Compromises were made, requiring adjustments in many
parts of the package; new information required changes in
others.   Mistakes were inevitable.   Some mistakes, weaknesses, and inadequacies could be tolerated, but if they had
been extensive the package would have fallen apart.   For instance -- the U. S. provided $100 million at one time to
underwrite Pakistan's decision to reduce import controls and
free imports.   If the forecast of import requirements had been
too low, the $100 million would have proved inadequate.   Con-
trols might have had to be reimposed, jeopardizing all other
parts of the package.

This example of Pakistani experience emphatically shows
that major economic decisions may involve a complex package
of policies and programs that can be put together only by a
group or team of economists working together and learning
from each other.   The need for a team with a critical mass --
to permit the transfer of experience and specialization and
to cover all important issues -- has implications for the effectiveness of the economist under different circumstances.
The individual can enhance his effectiveness by joining an
economic team.   Foreign institutions supplying economists to
less developed countries are likely to be more effective if
they press for a team approach.   The proportion of the team

supplied by the foreign institution obviously would depend on
the number of nationals available.

THE TECHNOCRATIC INTERNATIONAL

The development of appropriate training remains important, because the number of economists working in less developed countries continues to increase. That many are
foreigners is in substantial part due to the existence of the
Fifth, or Technocratic, International. This is a startling development since the 1950's: the existence in important positions
in the governments of developed and less developed countries
of economists with a similar professional training and outlook.

In the early 1950's, only a few economists played any role
in governments. Among them, and their colleagues on the
fringes of policy, ideological differences were often fiercely
debated. There were strong advocates of widespread government ownership and control, and equally strong advocates of
unbridled private enterprise. Now there are many more
economists with an influence on policy. With greater government experience has come greater flexibility and pragmatism,
more concern with policies that work than with policies that
are ideologically pure. Substantial government intervention,
accompanied by a widespread use of the price system, is increasingly accepted. Other disputes, often all the more
fierce when both sides possessed little evidence, have also become more muted as facts accumulated. For instance, there
is less debate now about models and other mathematical techniques. They are generally accepted as highly useful for
some purposes, but not as the answer to all problems. The
dispute on whether cultivators in less developed countries
respond to economic incentives has died down -- it is pretty
clear that they do, within some definite limits imposed by
risk, ignorance and land tenure problems. One could cite
other examples. As a result of progress towards a professional consensus, foreign economists working in many
less developed countries have immediate and natural allies in
their national colleagues, who share their professional language,
and often their goals.

Increasingly the governments of less developed countries are not monoliths, but a combination of groups with somewhat different approaches and objectives. This greatly eases the moral, as well as the practical, problems of the foreign economist or the foreign economic group. The organizations they are attached to are increasingly pragmatic advocates of economic rationality, professionals acting as "agents of change." The foreign economists then find it easy to be loyal to the organization and to its vision of the country's future, even if the government served includes other tendencies whose objectives and methods are a good deal less congenial. The differences between foreign and national economists are disappearing. The universities' future training, research and institutional involvement in the less developed world needs to take this development into account.

THE CLINICAL YEAR

The number of economists professionally involved in the less developed countries has increased at a phenomenal rate since the 1950's. A majority have probably not performed the traditional academic functions of the profession, but have been working with governments and semi-governmental agencies. A very rough guess would be that at the end of the 1960's some 1,500 economists around the world had a substantial concern with economic policy in and for the less developed countries. Economic performance is of particular importance in poor countries, and it is sometimes crucial to a government's survival; hence these economists often play a major role in government decisions. Both professional training in the broad sense, and the universities as institutions, have only begun to catch up with these developments. A good deal more could be done in both respects.

Training has been almost exclusively focused on theory, principles, and methods and little on practice and application. If economists are going to prescribe on major policy issues under conditions of uncertainty, handicapped by inadequate data and forced to deal with complex, inter-related issues, they will need some training in problem-solving and an opportunity to acquire experience. Analogies are dangerous, but

sometimes useful. Viewed in terms of medical education,
economists now usually graduate after the first two years of
training in anatomy, biology, and so forth. They need the
third, the "clinical" year, which gives them practice in diagnosing economic ills and prescribing for them. Beyond that,
they need a period of internship and residence, when they
apply their training under guidance and supervision, which
minimizes dangers to the "patient. "

To develop training along these lines would involve the
introduction or expansion of policy-oriented, problem-solving
courses and seminars as a regular part of graduate training
in economics. It also requires the use of teams or groups of
economists working together, to provide the required opportunity for apprenticeship or internship training for the younger
members of the team.

The group or team approach is also desirable for other
reasons. It permits the specialization and simultaneous
solution of inter-related issues necessary to deal with the
really crucial problems of an economy which require a policy
and program package, and it can provide a psychological and
professional support to the team members. Universities in
the developed countries who recognize the substantial benefits derived by their economists from participation in government staff work in the less developed countries need to take
account of the advantages of the team approach. Individually,
jointly, or in cooperation with other agencies, they need to
participate in team efforts to increase the effectiveness of
their faculty members overseas.

Some cooperation is also desirable in many cases to deal
with the career problems of development economists. To
acquire the necessary experience in the government of less
developed countries while retaining contact with professional
advances in the developed ones, and to do so without detri-
mental effects on one's professional career, requires a career
pattern which accepts and rewards an alternation between two
worlds -- government in the less developed countries and
academia in the developed ones. Such a career pattern is now
quite rare. Universities may find that it is easier to provide
a flexible career pattern by joint or cooperative effort.

I have discussed adjustments in training patterns and in university practices with reference to development economists with a substantial interest in government policy, but I think these adjustments would apply as well to development economists who contemplate an academic career, though with somewhat less force. Such economists will probably also spend some part of their career in less developed countries and would benefit from training in the applied aspects of their profession, an apprentice system, and a team approach. It even seems likely that these proposals have some applicability to economics as a profession, and not only to the field of development.

CHAPTER **11** GUIDELINES FOR
PROFESSIONAL SCHOOLS

Kenneth R. Hansen

Regrettably, the United States has not credibly led world
efforts to assist the deprived half of the world because of a
strong, enduring, and highly principled national commitment
to their economic, social, and political growth and development
in a climate of self-determination. America's national and
multinational support, involvement, and commitment to the
progress, development, and modernization of the "have not"
countries has dwindled from the high peak of purposefulness
achieved in the late 1950's and early 1960's to the sputtering,
toothless levels of querilous and sanctimonious inaction epito-
mized by the congressional attitudes of the late 1960's --
enhanced and often provoked by a concomitant inability of the
executive branch to crystallize policy, program, and public
support to achieve hopeful progress toward bridging the ever
growing gap between the advanced and underdeveloped halves
of the world.

Indeed, the distressing picture of recent years is one of
(1) relative and absolute reductions year after year in foreign
economic assistance, (2) "Buy American" policies so strict as
to be regressive, (3) a level of debt servicing which eats up
over 50 percent of aggregate new investment, (4) the necessity
of attaching even some 100 percent investment risk guarantees
to the flow of private capital, and (5) a dispirited, apologetic,
and palliative approach to trade, technical assistance, and
educational and cultural exchanges between the "have" and the
"have not" nations.

Surely this is not the best backdrop against which to evaluate the role of the professional, unless one professes that our

national confusion and disinterest are but temporary aberrations
and will go away when the preoccupations of Vietnam, the urban
crisis, inflation, and the balance of payments trauma are erased
from the national scene.

In short, one must realistically perceive the role of the
professional as an agent of change in the less developed areas
within the context of goals and purposes which are set for him
by his society, his government, his institutions of learning and
employment, and in part also his personal interests and private
motivations -- in other words, his perceived purposes. And
where these are not in reasonable harmony, or are lacking in
vital impulse or attractiveness, it is exceedingly difficult to
plot a course for the professional as an agent of change.

I believe that America's actions and sense of purpose and
concepts of vital interests vis a vis the less developed countries
have been in considerable disarray, and that in these circumstances professionals are challenged with the need to evaluate
and indeed change many present public attitudes and national
policies before we as a group can evince a meaningful future
role for the professional as an agent for change in low-income
countries.

THE TRANSFER OF TECHNOLOGY

The more-developed countries have as yet little technology
to transfer when it comes to the problems of the inter-relations
of the peoples of the poor countries with their natural and social
environments -- that is, little to transfer in the area of human
ecology.

When it comes to matters such as those dealt with in the
disciplines of the social sciences -- including politics, public
and private administration, education, communication, urbanization, and some institutions related to agriculture, public
health, and the development or preservation of natural resources
-- there must be a new kind of technical assistance. Broadly
speaking, this type of technical assistance calls for the transfer
to the backward countries of the research and educational
methods of the West, with its genius for problem-solving through

experimentation, analysis, and testing and objectivity and
pragmatism in research method. This assistance consists of
attempting to solve the wide range of problems for which at
present there are no ready or importable answers in the less-
developed countries, but for many of which there are also no
answers in the more-developed countries.

It is truly perplexing and paradoxical that few people view
the problems of low-income and less-developed countries as
modern, that is, as problems arising from modern and current
phenomenon and circumstances as well as from the backwardness of their society. Low-income societies have problems
of urbanization; they have thoroughly modern concerns with
juvenile delinquency, suburban sprawl, air pollution; and
certainly they have their share of concer about fiscal stability,
political apathy and commuter traffic.

They also have unique problems of business organization
and management, mobilization of capital and savings, public
accountability and market research. These problems are not
all susceptible to hand-me-down solutions from the more advanced cultures. And the problems of maximizing the use of
their exceedingly scarce resources in pursuit of objectives of
economic growth, social change, and political stability are
among the more challenging which scholar, action intellectuals,
and modern institutions of learning can tackle.

Clearly there are obvious needs for research and experimentation in all of the activities of the less-developed countries
where development is most dependent on the particularities of
local environment. In agriculture and in many other areas,
different environmental characteristics demand a technology
different from that which exists in the developed countries of
the temperate zones or even in some of the more-developed
countries of the tropical zones. And beyond this, of course,
to make the quantum jump from subsistence to market agriculture requires that many social and cultural as well as technical
problems must be solved.

Irrigation works, fertilizer plants, resources studies of
soil and water can all be accomplished through the simple
transfer of Western scientific and technical knowledge. But
the problems of actually raising the yields of agricultural
products in each locality on a sustained and continuous basis

must be solved through applied local research, and institutions must be created to do this research. Agribusiness, for example, now widely heralded as the means of giving every country its own Imperial Valley, requires an intense application of new research and technology in all aspects of human settlements, investment, and productivity.

Therefore I advance a simplistic proposition: that many of the less-developed countries have unique conditions and special problems which will not yield to the simple transfer of knowledge or transfer of expertise. Technical assistance in these areas must be based upon cooperation between specialists in the developing and developed countries, working and learning together how to solve problems for which at present there are no answers.

And this applies to business and commerce and to education and to public administration and to law just as much as it applies to agriculture. New technologies must be discovered and new insights gained through experiment and applied research and devoted inquiry and cooperation before most of the problems of low-income countries will be adequately identified and solutions sought and, hopefully someday, adequate resources made available from the developed countries to bring about the critical mass of efforts at change which will offer real hope to these areas.

In this endeavor, there are severe limits on the utility of teaching foreign students on a one-by-one basis the clearly irrelevant environmental facts of developed economies and social structures, and the often irrelevant technology addressed to these. There are limits of ecomony and utility in short-term visits by experts in fields of knowledge which must in fact be adapted and made relevant by prolonged study and experimentation in local circumstance.

To make the jump in relevant knowledge -- to apply the framework of theory and understanding achieved in the discipline to the target low-income country and circumstance -- it is clearly necessary that the faculties of professional schools make the necessary commitment to research and study and teaching in the less-developed countries, so they can do the research and study and teaching about these societies in a manner which will develop a body of relevant professional

knowledge and enlist the interest and career commitment of
a corps of knowledgeable professionals.

SOME UNLEARNED LESSONS

Most formal technical assistance and technology transfer
activity is either encapsulated in a particular industrial or
commercial project, or is part of a bilateral or multi-lateral
assistance program, or is contained in a variety of educational
arrangements of a public or private nature.

In some cases, the function is to accomplish a one-time
undertaking, in others to add to the level of effort addressed
to an activity, to make up a deficiency in numbers of trained
people; in some cases the purpose is to develop a new body of
knowledge by study, experimentation, and application of new
technology to new problems.

One might assume that after so many years of advisory
activity, professionals have learned some of the lessons about
organization of advisory, technical assistance and other professional missions and operations in less-developed countries.
That assumption is unwarranted, however, since one can still
see today operations which go sour for the same avoidable
reasons, and one still hears of disappointed and disillusioned
professionals who quit in disgust and despair because of frustration at not being able to play a meaningful role in their overseas assignments.

There is a risk of throwing the baby out with the bath water
if the organizational or institutional activity undertaken in low-
income countries is judged without taking into account the quality
of the professionals engaged.

There is a risk of erring greatly in assessing the worth
and capabilities of a particular advisory effort the environment
for change present in the less developed country is not taken
into account realistically.

And there is a risk of drawing wrong conclusions regarding
the competency and adequacy of professional training if these

are not judged in the correct framework of purpose to which
the professional skills are presumed to have been addressed.

Some examples that I have myself observed:

-      The placement of a foreign economic advisory group
in an organization which has insufficient political mandate and
power to bring about actions consistent with plans or advice.

-      Assignments of technical experts to areas where the
problems were not principally technical, but involved major
issues of administration, management, and policy formulation.

-      Proffering of advice without regard to the instrumen-
talities required to carry them out.

-      Professional advisors who did not evaluate the different
circumstances of the country in which they were operating before judging what was possible.

It would be easy to say that one should avoid these types
of mistakes, that anyone can understand that these things should
not be done. But these things did all happen, and it is in knowing why they happened, of simple common sense, that one can
begin to understand why the institutional and policy framework
behind professional effort in less developed countries is all-
important.

Clearly, when the purposes of an advisory group operating
in a less-developed country are unclear or conflicting or over-
demanding or inflexible, the quality of the professional advisory
effort must suffer some if not all of the same characteristics.
If the organizations through which the professional is to exercise
his leverage on events is wrongly or poorly placed or untimely
or counterbalanced by hostile forces, the professional's effectiveness will be intrinsically limited by these circumstances.

Accordingly, much of what is discussed and determined as
a basis for judging this or that professional effort is a matter
of blind men describing the elephant. I have seen poor results
produced by excellent people and outstanding effectiveness
produced in response to mediocre professional efforts. Much
depends on the purpose sought and on the organizational and
institutional arrangements, just as in the developed societies,

except that in the less-developed countries the responsibility
is infinitely greater, the potential contribution of an individual
awesome, and the opportunities for failure infinite.

Add to this the fact that so many efforts are ill-conceived,
ill-managed, and ineffectual without suffering the penalities of
failure; that there is often a self-perpetuating inevitability to
much of what goes on in the foreign assistance area that many
believe one must look elsewhere to truly make any progress in
the transformation of backward areas through the intervention
of Western technology and developmental efforts.

There are approaches which hint at a viable formula of
this sort, but there is little support for the development of such
institutions in the government, practically none in private industry, and barely enough in private foundations in the United
States; overseas in the low-income countries, there is no clear-
cut demand for any institutional form -- partly because they
have been so continuously exposed over the years to every
marginal type of technical assistance project which could be
invented by ingenious bureaucratic entrepreneurs.

SOME SUGGESTIONS AND
SOME NEW APPROACHES

In search of some way to improve prospects of assisting
in the process of change in low income countries, it becomes
clear that the academic world of the professional schools in
the social sciences has only barely begun to develop the institutional structures and capabilities for a problem-solving
approach of a multidimensional sort -- that is, the creation
of institutions which have the dual function of academic research and problem-solving related to less developed societies.

Every professional can draw from his experience an entire
bibliography of horror stories about maladroit professional
involvements overseas and about the inadequacies of selection,
training, and prior study which may have contributed. I would
guess that it is very difficult to separate cause and consequence
in most cases, however; as I indicated above, it is exceedingly
difficult to distinguish unambiguously between the substantive

professional task and the institutional setting and indigenous circumstances in which the professional finds himself involved in less-developed countries. Accordingly, one often sees very good professional qualification and commitment completely frustrated by unproductive, untimely, or inappropriate administrative and institutional arrangements. Conversely, there are often very successful activities based upon fortuitous circumstance rather than on professional competency.

This leads me to another observation about the professional role in the less-developed societies. The professional is almost inevitably called upon to exercise other administrative or management skills and exceedingly good human judgment if he is to prove effective in such a setting. This is especially true in the framework of public institutions and governmental agencies where the functions often depend on the basic administrative efficiency of the organizations with which the professional works. Inexperienced or narrow professionals are often completely ineffectual in such circumstances, not because of their lack of skill or professional knowledge, but because they were not able to perform in the institutional setting.

A broad general prescription -- consistent with my earlier remarks about the lack of financial resources available to less-developed countries and the bootstrap nature of most development efforts today -- would appear to be a substantial effort by the professional schools to field multi-dimensional institutions of research and problem-solving and teaching, backed by a commitment by faculties to undertake long-term research and teaching efforts in poor countries as a fully recognized and rewarded academic pursuit, that is, that this activity have a fully accepted basis for promotion and status in academia. Such institutional arrangements should involve the on-the-spot research work with graduate students of both areas in real-life problems, and the prospect of interdisciplinary arrangements such as are increasingly being arranged between professional schools in their home environment.

These research problems and teaching activities should encompass all fields relevant to economic, social, and political change, and collaboration could be undertaken with all sectors and sources of sponsorship -- public, private, local, or foreign.

Aside from this core proposition, there are several related suggestions I have to make; some are comments only, but perhaps some colleague will one day incorporate one or another in some grand scheme for professional school reform.

1.   Take the foreign student seriously. Distinguish between viewing him as a possible recruit to the general study and practice of the discipline anywhere, and as someone who will seek or is pursuing a career in his home country. Concern oneself with his future job there with how his knowledge and motivation will permit him to make a specific contribution to problem-solving and intellectual and technological leadership at home. This cannot be done without follow-through by the professional school in both teaching and career counseling and job placement in the low-income country itself.

2.   Accord the professional school faculty member incentives, credit, and honor for devoting his scholarship, his research periods, and his institutions-building contribution to less-developed countries. His is a different operating milieu, he requires departures from the career lines of tenure, promotion, and faculty-related or research-related activity. He should not feel constrained to treat that area of activity as sabbatical-year indulgency rather than as an integral part of his total academic experience and career development.

3.   Have professional schools propose and persuade potential sponsors of projects in low-income countries to undertake complete projects which have continuity, content, and strategic promise. Do not allow the schools to be badgered into incomplete, ill-founded, ill-sponsored partial efforts. Why not take the responsibility to tell the government agency and foundation and host country organizations and leaders what kind of efforts should be undertaken, rather than largely responding to their proposals and doing what they think they would like to have.

4.   Make extensive arrangements for professional school graduates to have a learning and research experience in less-developed countries as part of their educational experience.

Questions of national governmental, private, and institutional policies, approaches, priorities, and sense of human values as related to the less-developed countries remain. These policies and priorities establish a framework of thought and action as a consequence of which the academic professional will be trained and mobilized for tasks in these areas, the business professional will have incentive to pursue opportunities, and the governmental functionary will perform his duties in low-income countries.

THE PROFESSIONAL SCHOOL AS CRITIC

There are questions which reach back into the institutional world of the professional school, the university system, the government agencies, the multilateral organizations, and the heavily-involved parts of the private sector as well as the political leadership of our country. For it is how these institutions perceive their roles and how leaders of national thought perceive the country's world role which will ultimately be the guide to the role and qualifications of the professional.

The truly vital question, therefore, is what the professional's role and contribution should be in this vital area of world affairs.

I believe the professional school should feel uniquely responsible in addressing itself to this question -- indeed, it could make this somewhat a self-fulfilling prophecy -- if it moves into the arena of leadership of domestic thought and policy and into close involvement overseas with vital international issues and overseas programs on a basis coextensive with its responsibilities for scholarship and teaching.

In short, the professional school, if it is to make a relevant contribution, should be in the mainstream of efforts to shape policy, influence values, and encourage or criticize the actions of all those concerned with problems of social, economic, and political change related to the less-developed countries.

To do this adequately calls for deep and continuous involvement in research activities, action programs, and institution-building efforts partially or wholly overseas. It calls for leaders of these schools to perform the function of public and private critic and goad in the domestic scene: contributing to or criticizing the policies and programs of the executive; influencing the legislative actions of the congress; being heavily engaged in the dialogue concerning the principles, practices, and activities of the private sector related to low-income countries; being actively involved in shaping the attitudes and content of informed public opinion which ultimately determine the values of the society.

Lacking this dimension of involvement, the professional school is a vocational training center or a retreat for scholars, functions eminently respectable but not suitable for providing guidance, intellectual leadership, or inspiration as to the social purpose and relevance of efforts of professionals in the low-income countries.

CHAPTER **12** THE INTEGRATED
EDUCATIONAL INSTITUTION:
TEACHING, SERVICE, AND
RESEARCH

Antonio Medina

I started my career in 1948 as an obstetrician and gyne-
cologist with a private practice and devoted part of my time to
the prenatal and family planning services of the Department of
Health of Puerto Rico. I immediately became cognizant of the
vast difference between the two cultural groups, the medically
solvent and the medically indigent.

My first major task was to learn a new language in order
to communicate adequately with the low income clientele; a
great gap existed between the sophisticated terminology I had
acquired and the rather primitive though sufficiently eloquent
ways of expression of the poor. Such terms as "throwing out
an animal" for having a miscarriage, "boiling inside" for heart-
burn, and "to give from one's body" for defecating are only a
few examples of a whole lexicon, very picturesque and very
practical, which I had to learn and which must be learned by
the practitioner before adequate communication, and more
important, rapport, can be established.

Secondly, I realized how important it was for me and my
relationships with this group to comprehend a whole body of
superstitions, beliefs, habits, traditions, practices, and
attitudes if I was to serve them better. To mention a few
examples of beliefs: citrus fruits, especially lime, are believed to cause tuberculosis if taken during the menstrual period;
pineapple and milk taken together, to poison people; a bath during
menstruation or soon after meals is taboo. Among the superstitions that prevail are that some people are capable of causing
harm, especially to infants and young children, through the
"evil eye"; that it is effective to use the "santiguo", the act of

197

rubbing an oil or an ointment on the affected areas of the body while making the sign of the cross and invoking the Holy Spirit; that the bone fixer can handle fractures, dislocations, and sprains (he is often sought). Many a life has been lost, many a fracture rendered incorrigible as a result of these superstitions and practices.

It also took me a while to discover that prescribing has to be based on the reality of a particular situation. What good would it do to prescribe a high protein diet to a pregnant woman or to a child if the family income is such that they can barely afford the minimum basic human needs of food, shelter, and clothing? On the other hand, it was a surprise to find out that even though some high protein foods are provided to pregnant women through public welfare programs, many of the recipients prefer to sell them in order to buy staple foods of low nutritive value. And what about the prescription of salt-free diets in cases of toxemias of pregnancy? In my experience many were the cases of impending eclampsia in which the patient failed to follow medical instructions because she could not afford to prepare both a sodium-free diet for herself and a regular diet for her husband and numerous children and co-residents. Perhaps some readers may fail to see the point: This may not be a problem with most housewives in the continental United States, because meals are seasoned to taste by the individual member of the household, but in Puerto Rico and Latin America in general, the food must be seasoned during the process of cooking. This is well illustrated by the problems of adaptation of Puerto Ricans migrating to the mainland and Puerto Rican troops assigned to American units. Initially, both the patients handled by mainland health agencies and soldiers attached to stateside outfits may suffer unnecessary trauma because this cultural factor is not understood nor taken into consideration.

During the five years of what I call the formative phase of my career -- while I worked as medical officer of the Department of Health in charge of prenatal and family planning clinics, in direct contact with the client -- I went through a series of experiences that created a disquietude within me regarding the significance of my role and function as a physician. These traumatic experiences often led me to question myself as to what I wanted my role to be.

CLINICIAN OR PUBLIC HEALTH DOCTOR?

I was caught in the dilemma between remaining in the clinical field -- a performer of technical acts on a limited number of people seen merely as physical entities who required medical care, or becoming a public health physician truly serving the mothers and children who comprise 74 percent of my people.

In 1953 while still in this dilemma I was appointed consultant in obstetrics in the Bureau of Maternal and Child Health of the Department of Health of Puerto Rico. My new position involved the supervision of programs geared to mothers in the preconception stage of the maternity cycle, that is, potential mothers. Thus, I entered a new phase in my career.

I maintained a limited private practice and devoted more than half of my time and efforts to the duties of my new position, which dealt mostly with the technical supervision of, and consultation services to, the physicians and paramedical personnel detached in the 76 municipalities of Puerto Rico. In this capacity I now had the opportunity to put into practice the knowledge acquired during my formative years in public health. In my periodic personal interviews, discussions, and consultations with the health personnel throughout the entire island, I found myself in the vantage point of discussing and suggesting ways and means of rendering comprehensive rather than isolated health services. All the things I had learned about the values, superstitions, beliefs, habits, and practices of the low-income group were brought into focus during my field visits, for I was by now convinced that we could only bring about change in the health habits and practices of the people by relating our approach to their cultural framework and economic reality.

In 1958, after five years in this position, I was appointed deputy director of the bureau. My primary function was now to assist the director in the planning, implementation, and supervision of the maternal and child health program for the entire Commonwealth. This was the beginning of a new phase in my public health career -- my experience in administration of maternal and child health programs. As my responsibilities required it, I gave up more and more of my private practice. Face to face with the realities of the problems, the needs of the consumers (our mothers and children), and the limitations of

the producers (the health resources), I became greatly alarmed
and preoccupied with the search for solutions. Problems such
as high infant mortality, the alarmingly high incidence of
diarrhea and enteritis, malnutrition among children, widespread
parasitosis, anemia during pregnancy, and the poor and under-
par utilization of maternal and child health services began to
revolve in my mind. In spite of the fact that I served in this
capacity for the brief period of only one year, I again had the
opportunity to participate in the revision of norms and procedures
and in the enactment of certain legislative measures which I
discuss below.

FROM LINE TO STAFF

During this year I also became fully aware of the implications
of the experiment called "Operation Regionalization" which was
sponsored by The Rockefeller Foundation and the Puerto Rico
Department of Health. This experiment aimed at the decentralization of health services and the integration of preventive and curative care in order to cope with the already tremendous expansion
of the health services in the Commonwealth.

Decentralization implied a radical change in the duties of my
position, since the administrative authority of the bureau was to
be delegated to the regional directors; in other words, from a
line officer I was to become a staff officer.

It was both the preoccupation with the search for solutions
to the serious maternal and child health problems and needs, and
the impending reorganization of the Puerto Rico Health Department, which led to my decision of pursuing advanced formal
studies in public health. This also meant the end of my private
practice.

In June of 1960 I obtained the degree of Master in Public
Health with a concentration in Maternal and Child Health from
Harvard University. During my studies I came into close contact with Dr. Martha May Eliot, the internationally known authority, formerly chief of the Children's Bureau of the Department
of Health, Education, and Welfare. Her guidance and wisdom
helped me greatly to develop the insight I had been seeking.

While the curriculum content per se did not have applicability to the reality of Puerto Rico, the conceptualization to which I was exposed proved later to be of transcendent value in my work. I remember thinking at that time what difficulties a mainlander with the same training, but without a deep understanding of our culture, would encounter putting into practice the knowledge acquired. This view is the foundation of the main recommendation I propose below.

My commitment with the Government of Puerto Rico in return for the sabbatical leave that took me to Harvard obligated me to resume my functions as director of the Bureau of Maternal and Child Health, yet deep inside I knew this was to be only a transitory step to the attainment of my now clear goals.

Regionalization in Puerto Rico was made officially effective on July 1, 1960, only a few days after my return. My new duties were primarily those of an adviser and consultant, and little if any administrative authority was given me. Under these circumstances I felt hindered from developing the proper framework for the crystallization of my plans. So I sat tight and waited, trying to derive the greatest possible benefit from my experience on this job. I learned to deal with people at various levels in the government, in voluntary agencies and in private institutions, and much about the intricacies of the systems. I believe that I learned to master my prejudices sufficiently so that they would not interfere with my functioning as what I consider a true public health man. I also learned that compromising is a reality and when wisely utilized achieves real gains.

Thus, while somewhat frustrated, I was aware of my continuous professional growth and I felt stronger than ever about the role I wanted to play in the promotion of the welfare of my people.

SERVICE-ORIENTED TEACHING

Toward the middle of the year I was offered and gladly accepted the position of instructor in maternal and child health (Ad honorem) to be performed concurrently with my other duties. I saw this as an opportunity to see if I had the makings of a teacher, for I believed this a most effective means to serve as

an agent of change -- to impart to the public health worker not
only my real life experiences as a professional and a graduate
student from a Class A school of public health but also my
enthusiasm for, and faith in, the worthwhileness of this work.

CURRICULUM GUIDELINES

A few months later the School of Public Health of the University of Puerto Rico was awarded a grant to establish and develop
a service-oriented teaching program in maternal and child health
and I accepted the position of project director. This fortunate
and unexpected event put me in the position of chairing the newly
formed Maternal and Child Health Unit of the School of Public
Health and therefore of developing a curriculum based on the
following concepts and guidelines which I now had clearly defined
in my mind and shortly thereafter formally stated:

1. Clinical medicine, although representing the core of
the health of individuals, is but a part of the vast concept of
health.

2. The preservation of life and the improvement of health
of individuals is not an isolated enterprise and should be done
within the family setting and the community.

3. The health of an individual is the result of the healthy
biophysiological interaction of tissues and organs within an
integral human system, subject to impacts of mental and
emotional nature, which system interacts gregariously with other
members of a given community.

4. In order to insure the incorporation of these principles
into the student's body of knowledge, the department should continue broadening the opportunities necessary to equip the student
with a deep and thorough understanding of the concept of compre-
hevsive health care, taking into consideration the preventive as
well as the curative aspects in the four components of health;
viz.: physical, mental, emotional, and social.

5. The student should be exposed to, and practice in, real
life situations after he acquires the basic theoretical knowledge.
For this purpose a community should be selected to serve as

laboratory where the faculty and students practice what is
preached in the classroom. Thus, the situation where theory
is taught in a vacuum, is transformed and the university moves
into its continent community.

6. A major purpose of our training program is to provide
each student with a self-participative educational experience
which will help to develop the habits of moral and intellectual
discipline necessary to insure his participation in a process of
continuing learning throughout his professional life. An environment in which the conduct of research is seriously pursued is
viewed as essential in terms of this objective. A student's exposure to a meaningful research environment serves to enhance
his respect for knowledge; it helps him to appreciate more fully
the significance of the historical and evolutionary character of
theory and practice and of their interdependence. Inevitably,
the student in such an atmosphere is enriched by acquiring a
deeper sense of inquiry and a greater appreciation of the chal-
lenge involved in the quest for new knowledge. In the absence
of a research environment, training in public health constitutes
vocational training, the transmission and inculcation of specific
competences and skills. Where relevant research is being
carried on, such training qualifies as graduate study.

7. Our task is to increase our understanding of the unique
and distinctive features regarding the health and illness of our
people and of the significance of this in providing them with care.
The emphasis of our research must accordingly be operational.
As we increase our understanding and our ability to treat community health problems, we must simultaneously develop the
techniques and procedures that are necessary to deal with them.
We must determine the kind, the amount, and the way of deliver-
ing services and of distributing them, consistent with the limitations of our economic situation.

TEACHING-SERVICE-RESEARCH

However, the problem is even more difficult than this. The
research endeavor must be visualized not only in terms of the
practice of community health, recognizing all which this implies
in terms of local coordination, but also against the background
of the relation of health care to national development as a whole.

Community health research should be seen as a means of ensuring that the effort of the health profession is directed to the solution or the control of the actual problems of the people and not merely the rendering of technical acts, however competent.

The product of the research endeavor should be immediately plowed back into the field from which it came as a new or revised service activity. This, it seems to me, is the proper locus for the results of community health research.

The Maternal and Child Health Unit had been in operation for three years when the 1963 mental retardation amendment was passed. This gave me an opportunity to apply for a research grant from the Children's Bureau to study the utilization of prenatal services in Puerto Rico. The grant was awarded on July 1, 1964, a preliminary report of the results of the study has been submitted, and (we are now) in the process of giving the finishing touches to the design of an action program aimed at the improvement of the services.

On July 1, 1966 another grant was awarded by the Children's Bureau through which I, in the capacity of project director, had the opportunity to bring to reality the concept of fusing training and service.

The Cataño community -- a 40,000-inhabitant underprivileged area -- was officially established as the Maternal and Child Health Training Center.

There the students have the opportunity of operating in a setting along the lines described in guideline number 5, that is, a community in which they can serve, learn, and practice in the manner of a public health residency. With my teaching, administrative, and research responsibilities I am in the position to materialize my long-term goals of integrating teaching, service, and research, for all three components of this trilogy interpenetrate and reinforce each other; together they constitute a whole which is greater than the parts and only together can they lead to the formation of a whole public health worker.

CHAPTER **13** A LOOK TO THE FUTURE
AND A BRIEF PLEA FOR
THE COMPARATIVE
APPROACH

Brian Holmes

Present dilemmas regarding the professional training of
educationors for work in low income countries are not likely
to be resolved in the near future. One reason is that the
technical expertise needed is not sufficiently well developed
to meet many problems arising in high income countries.
Educational problems in low income countries are in major
respects different, in some cases less difficult but in others
made more difficult because of the clash of cultural institutions
when new educational ideas and institutions are introduced.

TWO MAJOR PROBLEMS

The absence of any kind of international professional
control of education is serious from several viewpoints. It
makes difficult the professional organization of research on
an international scale. The coordination of the activities of
professional educationists from different high income countries
is virtually impossible. Adoption of policy is outside the control of members of the profession working abroad. The need
for clearly formulated codes of behavior and role specifications
by professional educators is considerable. But each country's
educational aims differ in emphasis, and the United Nation's
commitment in its Declaration of Human Rights to educate as
a consumer good has been questioned and in some cases virtually
abandoned as an educational goal. In short, there is little
professional agreement on aims, little professional expertise
on which effective action can be based, and an inevitable interaction of political and cultural forms on the work of educationists, particularly on those who seek to introduce change.

The other context which creates major problems for
training is the uncertainty prevailing in the world situation.
Indeed its effect is virtually to prohibit effective professional
collaboration among professionals. Perhaps most important
among the factors in this context is the political. What kind
of political world shall we have fifteen years from now? How
politically stable will it be? Will it be a period of revolution,
when rising expectations find expression in violent changes --
military, spiritual, social, and intellectual? And will these
expectations give rise to irrationality; will racism and nationalism dominate political action? What will be the commitment
of high income countries to the low income nations? Will there
be a reaction on the part of taxpayers to aid which seems to
bring in few political returns? Will high income countries be
prepared to commit themselves to a long period of expensive
non-colonial tutelage? Will they wish to provide funds and
personnel through bilateral agreements? Or will multi-lateral
agreements be more usual with the growth and strengthening
of international professional agencies?

What seems certain is that the political strength of the
low income countries in international gatherings will be no
less than it is now. What will the attitude of the governments
of these countries be to the professional activities of personnel
from high income countries? Will they be prepared to use on
a professional basis teachers, administrators, and advisors?
Will it be possible for political considerations to play a smaller
part in professional contracts than at present, either through
international, national, or personal contractual agreements?

The problem of evolutionary non-violent political change
is ever present. If the threat of total annihilation through
atomic warfare has receded somewhat, there seems every
possibility that military force will continue to serve as an
extension of legitimized political action. Education gains
little from conditions of political instability. The contribution
it can make to peaceful political evolution may be slight but
important. The professional training of educators should take
serious account of this possibility.

As for the world economic situation, will Maurice Duverger's
analysis[1] for today still hold? Will there be a few countries,
such as Yemen today, which have scarcely embarked on development? How many will resemble those Latin American countries

which in many respects, and particularly in terms of their
educated elite, are very near the so-called developed or
industrialized countries? Will the majority of low income
countries fall into an intermediate position accepted by many
countries in Africa, the Middle East, and Asia, and by some
in Latin America? Will the economic distances between these
categories of country have widened or been reduced? It seems
that they will have increased, if present trends continue. Under
these conditions, will a Marxian concept for economic growth
-- investment in basic production -- hold sway? Or will the
consumer economy concept of the Western European nations
and North America prevail?

TWO ISSUES

For Western educators two issues will arise. First:
How can they (if they should do so at all) introduce their modern
educational technology into low income countries if the cultural
gap is even greater than today? Should they be prepared to
introduce a much simpler educational technology? And would
such policies be acceptable? The second issue is: should they
be prepared to work under either a Western or a Marxian theoretical framework, or only in a Western framework? In short,
has a choice to be made on moral grounds between education as
a human right and education as investment?

What conditions in low income countries will facilitate or
hinder professional activities in low income countries fifteen
years on? Can a civil service for developing countries capable
of meeting professional needs be invisaged? Can a "primitive"
spoils system based on political choice and the practice of
corruption have given way to a "developed" spoils system based
on political choice and honesty? Or will it be possible to think
in terms of a civil service (of educators) in which choice will
be based on technical efficiency and expertise and honesty?
Because administrators have such a crucial role to play in
developing countries, these questions perhaps bear most directly
on the kind of training administrators should receive. Should
they, in short, be trained as politicians primarily? Or will it
be possible to emphasize increasingly the technical aspects of
their work seen, of course, in the context of a low income

country? Undoubtedly the administrators' role in finding a
working balance between conservative and revolutionary elements will be crucial; this is a political rather than a technical
task.

Finally, will the educational profession in fifteen years
have enough expertise at its disposal to meet the needs both
of high and low income countries? Only if a more conscious
effort is made to make it available. This will involve the
provision of resources for research, inter-professional and
international collaboration, and the growth of international
professional agencies largely independent of international
politics whose continuing task will be to consider the special
skills and knowledge needed if education is to play a role in the
planned development of societies.

To be sure, all the questions I have raised cannot be
answered at once; nor can all uncertainties be reduced. But
effort to reduce ignorance is possible. The last question I
have raised is probably the most pertinent and the one requiring greatest attention. It seems to me that my own profession
still needs to know more about the experiences of other countries
and cultures and should therefore pay special attention to the
comparative approach.

THE PROBLEM APPROACH

Five features of planning are important in the problem
approach to comparative education: (a) the analysis of the
unique national features of commonly experienced problems
bearing on education; (b) the identification and weighting of
contextual factors or conditions which bear on policy outcomes;
(c) the assessment of resources (economic, ideological, administrative, and political) needed if adopted plans are to
succeed, and as assessment of available resources; (d) the
formulation of piecemeal solutions in the form of institutional
innovations designed to meet the stated problem; and (e) the
establishment of processes of decision taking in the light of
predicted outcomes.

The problem approach offers possibilities of strengthening training courses in all five areas. Educational policies have been developed in high income countries which may offer solutions to some problems in low income countries. Policies successful in one low income country might work in another. But the wise acceptance of any policy will depend on ability to predict, however crudely, the consequences of doing so in an alien culture. The major theoretical issue is still whether selective cultural borrowing can be successful. Comparative studies make possible the anticipation of future problems, even though at the moment such studies are not sufficiently well developed to ensure the accurate prediction of a wide range of socio-economic and political consequences.

That I consider massive investment in comparative education worthwhile should be self-evident. But I see such studies as necessarily interdisciplinary and international. I think comparative educators in universities, or in national and international agencies are slowly providing a base on which effective professional training can be based. What is necessary, it seems to me, are comparative centers, international centers where various functions would be served: (a) the centralization of information, (b) establishing consulting services, (c) providing short-term courses for experts going to the field, and (d) undertaking research functions. These centers would take a comparative approach and seek to provide new solutions from the knowledge already distilled in some of the other cultures of the world. I strongly believe that none of education's problems are insoluble. But educators tend to be unaware of the alternatives that have been thought of or have been tried elsewhere. This is, in my mind, what the comparative approach should be about; and this is why I believe the comparative approach can be helpful.

NOTES

1. Martin Kriesberg, ed., <u>Public Administration in Developing Countries</u> (Washington, D.C.: The Brookings Institution, 1963).

PART IV

INTERNATIONAL PROFESSIONAL COOPERATION

14

INSTITUTION BUILDING IN DEVELOPING COUNTRIES

Raúl Devés Jullian

All less developed states generally tend toward a process of anxiety. Universities do not escape this norm, and the winds of desire to change beat on them forcibly and insistently. It is not easy -- even though desirable -- to give quick vent to this anxiety for knowledge. The capacity of a university resides especially in the sum of the individual capacities of a determined number of talents. The formation of these talents is difficult and long, and awareness of their lack is not sufficient to achieve them.

As this road requires solid preparation and maturity and is not always trodden, "change anxiety" can stem from minor solutions, such as a simple change in the administrative, teaching, or economic structure.

In the university "game" there is no room for unperfected natural aptitudes, and neither cleverness, nor the "gift of gab, " nor sagacity, nor leadership in swaying the masses have any real value. Under certain conditions they can produce momentary effects, but they will achieve nothing definitive. Normal ability well directed, patiently educated, and firmly disciplined is much more useful than the most brilliant of brains in a primitive state.

BUILDING A UNIVERSITY

Every university resurgence needs an internal force to bring about its realization.

This internal force must be conscious of the ends to be pursued and of the roads by which they can be achieved. This necessarily leads to the elaboration of a plan, in the sequence of which special consideration should be paid to the following points:

1. Analysis of the existing situation.

2. Analysis of the internal values capable of promoting changes.

3. Final goals desired:

    a. Personnel.

    b. Facilities.

4. Evaluation of the time required to achieve the selection and training of personnel.

5. Completion of facilities as a means of realizing the human change.

6. Maximum and minimum time limit for accomplishing the plan.

7. Analysis of the required economic means.

8. Decision on the time during which the plan will be developed and consideration of the annual and total cost.

9. Search for economic means.

When aid arrives in a university area there should already be a person or persons possessing force to promote change.

These persons or groups of persons will undoubtedly be those who will look out for the success of the plans.

It is not necessarily indispensable, even when it is possible, that this force reside in superior and specialized knowledge. What is most needed is that those who are going to take the responsibility of decision possess the moral quality to act with sagacity and honor, an ample knowledge of the problems to be overcome and the goals to be achieved, as well as a spirit essentially open to the experience and advice of other experts.

The sums invested in education agreements are very important and there are great possibilities of losing force and money if there is not a true sense of asceticism in the use of means, austerity in expenses, and responsibility in the choice of elements.

Experience indicates the absolute necessity of an international association between a master university and the university in the transformation process so that the former can act as counselor in the development of plans, as provider of visiting professors, and as collaborator in the formation of new national talents.

The number of visiting professors in relation to national scholars (abroad) is substantially lower, since it is not always possible to find first-class teachers who can separate themselves from their obligations without causing great upset in their teaching and research staffs.

The difficulties of obtaining visiting professors, especially in such basic sciences as mathematics, physics, and chemistry, are very difficult to overcome. If the developed countries really want to influence universities, some system must be found whereby there could be maintained an appreciable stock of excellent professors destined to be sent abroad for reasonable periods.

One of the most important points in achieving positive work in a university through contact with a more highly developed university consists of the concentration of action on areas sufficiently small as to produce real impact. In other words, one must attempt to change the criterion of one section of the university in depth before exercising a weak and unproductive action upon the university as a whole.

The best formula consists of choosing the area size when the economic and human means have been determined, or establishing the economic and human needs once the areas have been chosen. By way of example, I can say that if one relies on a small sum of money it would be preferable to expend the effort on a professorship for a man involved in determinate research, aiding him fully, rather than distribute the sum among various petitioners or sections within which it would operate weakly and produce nothing satisfactory.

Another of the reasons a concentration of action is convenient is that it should succeed in creating a climate of
effervescence at the point where it is applied. When various
persons have been subject to influence in depth on a small area,
the contact between them succeeds in setting the atmosphere
in motion, changing habits and raising the level of those around
them. If, on the contrary, the areas are very large, the means
will absorb the renovators and these, not having contact with
persons of a proper level, will feel frustrated or they will remain influenced by the inadequate atmosphere. As a consequence,
the intellectual investment made will be lost or the participants
will go elsewhere for means more challenging to their capacities.

In the process of renovation it is necessary to work with
the most absolute coldness in separating elements troublesome
to development, either because of their inadaptability to changes
or because of their inability to follow them. No consideration,
sentimental or otherwise, must prevent the elimination of such
an obstacle.

The master university must have a clear awareness that
the primary need in the training of professionals in the developing
countries is not for quantity but for quality. This consideration
conditions the capacity of the visiting professors. They must
have the best training for the mission which they will exercise
at the highest and most modern level, so that the renovating influence in the visited country places its followers in the van-
guard of knowledge.

On the other hand, the prestige of the master university,
which is fundamental in promoting the confidence of the university student, depends exclusively on the intellectual and
moral behavior, as well as the scientific and technological
knowledge, of the visiting professors.

Education is a social responsibility and, as a consequence,
its importance is much superior to the interests of individuals.

Age is an important factor in development plans. In a university which is stagnant or of slow development, there is not frequently found a team of persons of mature age susceptible to
advancing or absorbing the effects and mentality of change. Even
persons well trained and personally capable will have a certain
grain of resistance sufficiently important to retard the process.

Not touching only on the achievement of a scientific or technological advance, even when it is indispensable, the disposition
and philosophy favorable to change must produce a common
vocational attitude. Young teams are more susceptible and
definitely more capable of building a new university. They also
have the advantage of a longer-term profit on the investment,
as well as better penetration in the confidence of the students.
Economic problems do not encircle them as insistently as in
mature age and vocation can delineate their lives in a clearly
collegiate process.

Any university development plan which only promotes education and is not capable of producing research as a logical
consequence will fail.

No program between universities can be permanent. It
must necessarily have limitations in time and economy. The
process of intense change will cover a determined period and
will succeed in realizing a series of pre-established objectives.

The local university, after this initial impulse, will have
to continue progressing through its own intellectual forces, its
own economic resources and its facilities. But it is necessary
to consider that neither its intellectual force nor its physical
means will allow it to maintain the level achieved if a certain
type of connection is not adopted with the associate university.

This connection must be sufficiently strong to produce
vitality and sufficiently economical to achieve its permanence.
In general, it should be made with the private resources to each
university and through normal local organizations, aided by certain very agile and economical administrative organization.

The nerve-center of this union must be common research in
matters of mutual interest.

The interchange of professors and scholars during the plan
promotes intellectual and human contacts useful toward the
stipulated end. Common ambitions are awakened and the same
horizons in science and technology interest men of different
latitudes.

Communication systems today are simple, rapid, efficient
and economical and distance is not a factor which can seriously
hinder joint research.

The materials with which the more developed universities are supplied and will be supplied in the future are and will be difficult for the universities in developing countries to obtain. If live contact is maintained in the way expressed, laboratories, computers or other instruments of greater economic value will be able to be used following the road of joint research, and the academic life of the expanding universities will not be retarded by lack of physical facilities.

One must also remember that advances are produced in some isolated points within the university and as a result contact among the most excellent men will never be massive nor will it cause any disturbance in the academic and economic life of the universities. On the contrary, the inter-communication of talents of both institutions will be highly favorable to all since it will permit counting on a complementary intellectual force of great value and efficacy at insignificant cost.

Good relations among people are produced when equal treatment allows identical advances. To the extent that scientists and technicians of the new nations place their knowledge on the same level with the developed countries, so will under-development come quickly to its end.

The mission of the wealthy countries is, above all, to furnish their intellectual force generously and efficiently to the poorer ones. No one can economically, socially, or politically save a man, country, or continent if that man, country, or continent does not have the intellectual and moral capacity adequate to make correct use of the resources at its disposal.

Thus, my conclusion is very clear: more knowledge; more professors; fewer business promoters; understanding rather than money.

It is my opinion that the greatest efforts should be made to import "seed" talent for the educational field, and not executives who come to do things that can be done by professionals.

It is neither good sense nor very conducive to good relations with the developing countries sending foreign technicians, professionals, or scientists who arrive en masse in the country to perform mercantile operations which eventually can be developed by nationals. On the other hand, the visit of professors, coming to prepare new directive frameworks for the country and instilling in them all their modern knowledge and research procedures, shows a real feeling of friendship, the transmission of science and culture a feeling of generosity.

I believe that underdevelopment exists in the mind of man, and while this mind is not changed, educated, and transformed, other efforts would be in vain.   There are parallel economic, political, and social actions which must take place to make possible the change, but it is the individual, conscious, and responsible human being that makes a people great, promotes the welfare of his fellow men, makes justice possible, and contributes to the internal and external peace of human societies.

CHAPTER **15** THE INTERNATIONAL
INSTITUTE APPROACH

Vernon W. Ruttan

The research institute and the university represent alternative methods of organizing professional resources to produce
technical, social, and cultural change. I argue that in societies
characterized by a highly developed infrastructure linking the
university to the other public and private institutions involved
in technical, social, and economic change, education and research within the framework of the traditional academic disciplines and professions represents an effective link in the total
system devoted to the production, application, and dissemination
of new knowledge. I further argue that the same academic disciplines and professions, when transplanted into societies where
such an infrastructure does not exist, rarely become forceful
agents of technical, social, or cultural change. If developing
countries are to overcome the technical and institutional barriers to economic growth they must adopt a pragmatic search
for patterns of institutional organization of professional resources rather than adopt either a "classical" or a "land grant"
university ideology as a model.

U. S. technical assistance programs in agriculture have
been organized around three patterns or models. Perhaps the
most familiar is the "counterpart model." This is the situation
where individual U. S. scientists employed by U. S. technical
assistance agencies work in close cooperation with individual
scientists in national research, educational, or operating program agencies. A second pattern might be characterized as
the "university contract model." The university contract model
has typically been employed where institution building has represented a major objective of the technical assistance activity. Frequently, the institution building objective has involved, either
explicitly or implicitly, positive assumptions with respect to the

relevance of the land-grant philosophy or the land-grant experience to the solution of technical and social problems of the
host country. A third research and/or training "institute model"
has also been widely employed. The institute model has typically been employed when it was felt that working within the framework of existing institutions would be subject to such severe
limitations as to hamper the achievement of the technical assistance program objectives.

THE INSTITUTE MODEL

I trace the emergence of the international research and
training institute model within the context of the agricultural
program of the Rockefeller Foundation. Both the technical
accomplishments and the production impact of the Rockefeller
Foundation program in agricultural sciences in Latin America
and Asia have been adequately reported in both the professional
and the popular literature. [1] I therefore focus my primary attention on the manner in which the organization of professional
resources has evolved in order to meet the program objectives.
The program objectives themselves have been stated primarily
in terms of the invention, introduction, and diffusion of a new
biological and chemical technology. The measure of the success
of these efforts that has been adopted by Foundation scientists
and administrators has been primarily in terms of increases in
the national average yield and of national output of key agricultural commodities, particularly wheat, corn, and rice.

MEXICO: AGRICULTURAL SCIENCES

The Rockefeller Foundation agricultural sciences program
was initiated in 1943 with the establishment of the Office of
Special Studies (Oficina de Estudios Especiales) in the Mexican
Ministry of Agriculture. Field research programs were first
initiated with wheat and corn. The program later expanded to
include field beans, potatoes, sorghum, vegetable crops, and
animal sciences. A common pattern of staffing was followed
for each commodity program. [2] A U. S. specialist was brought
in as each commodity program was initiated. Each specialist

assembled a staff of young Mexican college graduates who were
trained in research methods and practices as part of the research program rather than through a formal program of graduate studies.

In retrospect the staffing program adapted by the Foundation,
centered around a project leader for each commodity, did have
one major limitation. This can be illustrated by comparing the
relative progress of the wheat and corn programs. The wheat
program achieved technical success earlier and its impact on
yield per hectare and on total wheat production has been greater
than for the other commodity programs. New wheat varieties
were being distributed to farmers by the fall of 1948. By 1956
the production impact was sufficient to make Mexico independent
of imported wheat. The rapid progress of the wheat program was
clearly related to the special competence of the early leaders of
the wheat program in the field of plant pathology and genetics and
the fact that stem rust was a dominant factor limiting wheat
yields. Improvement of corn yields was much more complex.
In addition to a more complex set of biological factors, the institutional considerations involved in seed multiplication, distribution, and diffusion were more difficult.

Multidisciplinary Teams

In situations where the technical, production, and organizational problems were relatively complex, requiring contributions from a broad spectrum of biological and social scientists,
the staffing pattern worked out during the early years of the
Mexican program was not entirely consistent with rapid progress
in the solution of research and production problems. In these
more complex situations a multi-disciplinary team approach
emerged as a more appropriate strategy than the simple commodity program approach of the early years. The problem of
successful integration of social scientists into the project teams
was, however, never successfully solved in the Mexican program.

Internship

A major source of strength in the success of the Rockefeller Foundation program in Mexico was its economical use
of the scarce professional manpower available in Mexico both
at the beginning and throughout the program. The shortage of
professional manpower and of indigenous educational resources
was conducive to the development of an internship system which
intimately linked professional education with investigation. In
1943 there was not a single Mexican in the field of agricultural
sciences with a doctoral degree and only a few with a masters
degree. By the end of 1945 the Office of Special Studies employed 7 Rockefeller Foundation scientists and 25 Mexican
"interns." Even at its peak in the late 1950's the Rockefeller
Foundation staff in Mexico consisted of less than twenty scientists. By 1963 over 700 young Mexicans had served for one or
more years as interns in the Oficina de Estudios Especiales.
About 250 of the best interns had received fellowships for study
in universities in the United States or elsewhere. There were
156 Mexicans with M.S. degrees and 85 with Ph.D. degrees in
the agricultural sciences. Of the twenty-seven interns who
entered the program in the first two years, all but 4 were still
engaged professionally in the field of agriculture in Mexico in
1963.

Disengagement

By 1963 agricultural science had been successfully institu-
tionalized in Mexico. [3] On December 30, 1960 the Office of
Special Studies was dissolved and merged into a new National
Institute of Agricultural Research under Mexican direction.
After an emotionally painful two years' disengagement, the
Rockefeller Foundation program and staff in Mexico was re-
organized into a new International Center for Corn and Wheat
Improvement.

The significance of the disengagement is that it is symbolic
of the fact that Mexico has succeeded in building into the fabric
of professional life the acceptance of agricultural science as a
career service in which men could enter with confidence that
their contributions would be rewarded both in money and in
professional recognition.

It is also significant that on May 14, 1963 advanced degrees in the agricultural sciences were conferred for the first time in Mexico. Mexico's new capacity to produce trained manpower in the agricultural sciences is developing in response to the demand for scientific manpower generated by the success of the initial thrust of the technical revolution in Mexican agriculture. The dramatic technical revolution of the past two decades did not, however, depend on the existence of graduate training in the agricultural sciences in Mexico nor did it draw significantly on the skills of large numbers of Mexican scientists trained in the United States and elsewhere.

THE PHILIPPINES: IRRI

The establishment of the International Rice Research Institute (IRRI) in the Philippines in 1962 represents a second major landmark in the evolution of the agricultural science program of the Rockefeller Foundation. The IRRI was jointly financed by the Ford and Rockefeller Foundations. It was established as an international research and training institute rather than as a component of a national ministry of agriculture. It was staffed by an international team of scientists representing eight different nationalities. Recognition of the complexity of the problem of achieving higher yield potentials and the multi-disciplinary competence that would be required to solve the biological problems of higher yield potential and to achieve rapid increases in total national and regional output were recognized and carefully structured into the staffing plan. Specialties on the staff were agronomy, plant breeding and genetics, soils, plant physiology, plant pathology, entomology, chemistry and biochemistry, microbiology, statistics, agricultural economics, agricultural engineering, and communications and sociology. [4] An intensive program of seminars and research program reviews was initiated to focus the efforts of the diverse multi-national and multi-disciplinary team on a common set of objectives and to achieve the complementarity among the several disciplines necessary to invent, introduce, and diffuse a new high productivity rice technology.

The location of the IRRI in Los Baños, adjacent to the University of the Philippines College of Agriculture (UPCA), made professional resources available to the IRRI that had not

been available in Mexico.   The UPCA had already developed
relatively strong departments in several fields of agricultural
science.   Joint appointments of IRRI staff to the UP graduate
school strengthened this capacity.   This arrangement permitted many of the IRRI trainees to work toward M. S. degrees
under the direction of an IRRI member while simultaneously
engaged in a highly complementary research "internship" at
the Institute.

In my judgment the typical research scholar or intern at the
IRRI has emerged from this training with greater personal research capacity and a higher level of sophistication with respect
to research strategy and relevance than most graduate students
from the less developed countries who complete either M. S. or
Ph. D. degrees in U. S. graduate schools.

Within six years after the initiation of the research program
at the IRRI a series of new rice varieties with yield potentials
roughly double that of the varieties that were previously available to farmers in most areas of Southeast Asia had been developed and are now being disseminated to substantial numbers
of farmers.   In some areas this process has proceeded far
enough to have a measurable impact on aggregate production. [5]

THE ORGANIZATION OF RESOURCES

The significance of the Rockefeller Foundation experience,
both in Latin America and in Asia, goes well beyond the impact
of the new wheat, corn, and rice technology which has been invented.   The significance of the experience is the evolution of
an institutional pattern for the organization of scientific resources which can be replicated for a wide variety of crop and
localities with a reasonable probability of success.   It is now
possible to organize a multi-disciplinary team of biological,
physical, and social scientists capable of inventing a new high
productivity biological and chemical technology for crop production and to make this technology available to farmers in a
form that they are capable of accepting within the relatively
short period of five to ten years.

What are the implications of the two cases for the organization of professional resources to induce change in underdeveloped countries?

The United States is characterized by a highly developed
institutional infrastructure linking the university to other private
and public institutions involved in technical, social, and economic change. In societies where such an infrastructure has
developed, research and education within the framework of the
traditional academic disciplines and professions have represented an effective link in a larger system devoted to the production, application, and dissemination of new knowledge.

Nevertheless, even in advanced countries one is aware of
problems. For example, in spite of its initial problem-solving
orientation, agricultural economics in the United States has acquired most of the organizational and cultural characteristics
which are typical of other fields of science or academic disciplines. Problems that are defined within the discipline or the
field of science carry an increasingly heavy weight relative to
problems that are defined outside of the discipline in the choice
of research strategy, objectives, and methods. This trend is
reinforced by a rise in private sector research in agricultural
economics relative to public sector research. This is particularly true of applied problem solving research. Appropriate objectives of public sector research have become less
obvious.

One result of these developments is that academic public
sector research is increasingly directed to problems that are
of interest to other economists. Both of these developments
are functional in a society characterized by a highly developed
institutional infrastructure linking the university to other private
and public institutions which are directly involved in the conduct
and management of economic affairs. They would be highly dis-
functional in a society which has not yet developed such an infrastructure.

The American pattern of academic and professional organization, when transplanted into societies where the presumed institutional infrastructure does not exist, rarely performs as an
effective instrument of technical, social, or cultural change.
In my judgment this is one of the major factors responsible for
the substantial frustration involved in attempting to utilize the
"university contract model" as an instrument to induce technical,
social, or cultural change in developing economies. The institution building approach to the replication of either the "land
grant" or the "classical" university in developing countries has
rarely been productive in terms of either technical or cultural

impact. The more typical result is to burden the developing
country with an over-extended academic bureaucracy which is
unable to make effective use of the limited professional capacity available to it.

If developing countries are to overcome the technical and
institutional limitations that separate the performance of the
world's low and high income economies, they must make efficient use of the professional competence which represents
their single most limiting resource. This implies a pragmatic
search for patterns of institutional organization which permits
a nation to have access to the professional competence available to it and to focus this competence directly on the critical
barriers to technical, social, and cultural change. [6]

The research institute pattern which has evolved in the
Rockefeller Foundation programs in Latin America and Asia
is an example of one such pattern that has been exceptionally
effective in situations where the institutional infrastructure
linking science to the rest of the economy is lacking. I would
not hold up this model as a solution in other situations. Rather
it is illustrative of the desirability of a pragmatic rather than
an ideological approach to the organization of professional manpower for the solution of development problems.

NOTES

1.   See, for example, A. T. Mosher, Technical Coopera-
tion in Latin America (Chicago: University of Chicago Press,
1957) pp. 100-126; L. M. Roberts, "The Rockefeller Foundation
Program on the Agricultural Sciences, " Economic Botany, XV
(1961), 296-301; Ralph W. Richardson, Jr. , "A Pattern of
Practical Technical Assistance: The Rockefeller Foundation's
Mexican Agricultural Program, " Agricultural Science Review
(Winter, 1964). E. C. Stakeman, Richard Bradfield, Paul C.
Mangelsdorf, Campaigns Against Hunger (New York: Cambridge
University Press, 1967); Delbert T. Myren, "The Rockefeller
Foundation Program in Corn and Wheat in Mexico, " in Clifton
R. Wharton, Jr. , ed. , Subsistence Agriculture and Economic
Development (Chicago: Aldine).

2.   Sterling Wortman, "Approaches to the World Food Problem" (unpublished paper presented at Southwest Agricultural Forum, Tulsa, Okla., January 19, 1967).

3.   Charles M. Hardin, "The Responsibility of American Colleges and Universities: Definition and Implementation" (unpublished paper read in Section O of the American Association for the Advancement of Science, New York, December 28, 1967).

4.   Stakeman, Bradfield, and Mangelsdorf, op. cit., p. 298.

5.   These developments have been widely reported in the popular press, typically in a highly exaggerated form, for a more careful assessment see International Rice Research Institute, Annual Report: 1967 (Los Baños, Philippines, 1968); E. A. Jackson, "Tropical Rice: The Quest for High Yield," Agricultural Science Review (USDA-ESRS), (Fourth Quarter, 1966); S. C. Hsieh and V. W. Ruttan, "Environmental, Technological, and Institutional Factors in the Growth of Rice Production: Philippines, Thailand, and Taiwan," Food Research Institute Studies, VII (1967), pp. 307-347.

6.   T. W. Schultz, "Efficient Allocation of Brains in Modernizing World Agriculture," Journal of Farm Economics, IL (1967), pp. 1071-1081.

CHAPTER **16** THE INTERNATIONAL
CONSORTIUM

P. K. Kelkar

In the development of the Indian Institute of Technology
(IIT) Kanpur, we who were involved kept before us international
standards right from the beginning. It is necessary to consider
the manner and the nature of growth of IIT Kanpur against this
background. One of the characteristics of modern times is that
one has to accomplish in a given interval of time a lot more in
breadth as well as in depth than what was considered possible
in the past. Further, whatever the project, quick results are
expected. This exposes all those involved to certain dangers
which are inherent in such an undertaking. There is a tendency
to compromise on various issues in the interest of speed and
also to minimize the efforts needed to keep good human relations.
Then again, if one wishes to bring about changes for which there
is no traditional support or parallel, one has to pay special attention to the reactions of one's colleagues who have to bear the
main brunt of innovation. In making a choice, there is always
a tussle in one's mind between what appears to be ideal and what
is actually possible. One has to be prepared for continuous
efforts to reduce this gap at every opportunity.

The three most important elements which constitute an
educational institution are the students, the faculty, and the
physical facilities. These have to be interwoven in a manner
by which academic activity at a high level becomes possible.
What distinguishes a first-rate institution from an indifferent
one is the kind of climate that exists there. The climate cannot
be imported as a part of foreign aid but has to be locally generated. The ingredients of the aid therefore have to be so assembled that together they will assist in the creation of the right
climate and the right attitudes of mind in the institution which
is being assisted. The pattern of the American aid to the Indian
Institute of Technology Kanpur has to be viewed against this

background. It is not commodities only that are of significance
but also men.

Beginning in 1960, negotiations went on between the United
States Agency for International Development (AID) and the
Government of India (GOI) about the best way of assisting IIT
Kanpur in its development. It was thought at first that a sister-
hood relationship between an American institution or university
and IIT Kanpur would be the best way of channeling the assistance.
Several institutions were sounded out and at one stage it appeared
that the Massachusetts Institute of Technology (MIT) might agree
to have such a relationship. But ultimately MIT indicated its inability to do so unless an MIT team had an opportunity to study at
first hand and assess the situation in India. It was thought this
would involve too much time, and negotiations were opened with
Ohio State University. In the meantime, the Ford Foundation
sponsored a study team of three persons from MIT to visit India
specifically to assess whether it was possible to assist IIT Kanpur
in a positive way. The team was in India in January-February
1961. Before coming to Kanpur the team paid a visit to the other
IIT's and several of the engineering and technological institutions
in the country. It was in Kanpur on February 6, 1961 and spent
the whole day in Kanpur. It became obvious during the course
of discussions that the main advantage which Kanpur had was that
the institution was quite new and started from a scratch. It,
therefore, offered full scope for new ideas and experimentation.
Further, it became apparent that the task of assisting in the establishment of this institute was too big for any one institution
to handle singly. This was the beginning of the idea of a consortium which was ultimately formed. It was the formation of
the consortium which made possible the viable and potent collaboration necessary in the setting up of a substantial technological
institution aiming at international standards. The team returned
to MIT and reported favorably. At this stage it was finally decided to pursue this further instead of formalizing the relationship with Ohio State University. This decision was crucial and
was jointly taken by AID and GOI.

The leader of the three-man MIT team took the initiative to
explore the possibility of forming a consortium of institutions
and universities to assist IIT Kanpur in its development. He was
successful in his efforts and a consortium of nine institutions
and universities was formed. These were (1) The California
Institute of Technology, (2) The Carnegie Institute of Technology
(now the Carnegie-Mellon University), (3) The Case Institute

of Technology (now the Case Western Reserve University), (4)
Ohio State University, (5) The Massachusetts Institute of Technology, (6) Princeton University, (7) Purdue University, (8)
The University of California, and (9) The University of Michigan.
ESI, the Educational Services Incorporated (now Education Development Center), was associated with this group as the con-
tracting and administrative agency. A steering committee
came into being consisting of representatives of the nine institutions and the ESI; the leader of the MIT team which visited
Kanpur became its first chairman.

RECIPROCAL VISITS

At this stage it was felt that a team representing IIT Kanpur
and GOI should visit the United States to have discussions with
the steering committee and visit each one of the institutions forming the consortium. This proved to be a very useful exercise.
For those who have not been previously exposed to the American
educational scene it is difficult to visualize the striking difference
that exists between the largely classical Indian approach to education and the current American approach. It is not only a difference in degree but in kind. Although each one of the nine institutions had a character of its own and distinguishing features, all
of them seemed to have the same basic philosophy of education,
similar motivation, and an unmistakable drive toward the pursuit of academic excellence. The relationship between education and society and industry seemed to be far closer than what
was thought possible consistent with high academic standards.
Above all, the most outstanding characteristic seemed to be
willingness and ability to grow continuously, modify, change,
and try out new ideas not only in response to the needs of con-
temporary life but of the future that is yet to be.

The visit of the Indian team to the States was followed by a
visit to India of the members of the steering committee. They
had an opportunity of acquainting themselves with the working
of many of the existing engineering and technological institutions in the country, including the other IIT's which had been
established earlier. They were not only able to appreciate the
difference between the traditional and modern but also saw how
difficult it was going to be to establish a viable relationship between the modern and sophisticated on the one hand and the

classical and unsophisticated on the other.   Finally the team
came to Kanpur and spent nearly three days.   The members
paid a visit to local industrial establishments and met some
of the prominent industrialists in Kanpur.   Then there were
discussions about the future planning of IIT Kanpur.   Many
organizational matters were discussed in detail, and the
visiting American faculty were to play vis-a-vis to the Indian
faculty and the director.   It was felt that the most fruitful mode
of operation would be a parallel approach, with integration only
in the advisory capacity along with freedom for a visiting faculty
member to participate in the actual implementation of the academic program according to his desire and the needs of the
situation.   This meant that all visiting personnel was directly
responsible to the program leader, and any step to be taken on
the Indian side in relation to them was in consultation with the
program leader.   Experience has shown that this was a very
effective basis for mutual cooperation.

The next stage was to finalize the arrangements by which
the American aid would be chaneled through the steering committee to IIT Kanpur.   A contract was signed by the U. S. Government with Educational Services Incorporated which brought into
being the Kanpur Indo-American Program (KIAP).   The Government of India and AID entered into an agreement to assist the
Indian Institute of Technology Kanpur in its development.   The
aid to the institute was to be routed through the Kanpur Indo-
American Program set up by ESI on the advice of the steering
committee.   The role of the steering committee was to negotiate
the contract with AID, to recruit American visiting staff, and
to review from time to time the progress of IIT Kanpur and the
operation of the whole program.   The role of ESI on the other
hand, was to give administrative support to the steering committee through KIAP, implement the policies laid down by the
steering committee, and act as a purchasing agent in America
for IIT Kanpur.

SEPARATE ADMINISTRATIVE OFFICE

The first program leader, who was also the leader of the
MIT team which visited IIT Kanpur in 1961, arrived in March
1962; he was soon followed by an administrative assistant.   A
separate administrative office was set up for the program leader

on behalf of KIAP, and he had another office in IIT Kanpur from
which he would carry out most of his work. This separate administrative office was a very important step. It took on the
entire responsibility of settling in Kanpur every member of the
American visiting staff and looking after his personal needs
during his stay in Kanpur. Within eight days of his arrival in
India, a visiting expert was ready for work in the institute because of this facility. The standard of living and the personal
needs of the American visitors were substantially different
from those of the corresponding Indian staff. Further, closer
links with ESI could be established through the local KIAP office.
The expense involved in this operation, therefore, was quite
justified.

RECRUITMENT

The recruitment of all academic visiting personnel was
restricted to the consortium institutions. This meant that there
was some common academic background irrespective of the institution from which a particular person came. The response
of the academic community of each institution to the appeal to
take up an assignment at Kanpur has been different. Although
all age groups and all the disciplines in IIT Kanpur were involved, the choice generally speaking was limited. The important point in the selection process was the adequacy and the
quality of the academic background of the individual concerned.
The next important consideration was personality and adeptness
at human relationship. In general every person going to IIT
Kanpur was expected to take his family along with him. The
steering committee took extreme pains and care in selecting
the right type of person. The final acceptance rested with IIT
Kanpur, subject to the formal approval of GOI. For maximum
effectiveness of the program the visiting academic personnel
had to be maintained above a certain minimum level. Generally
speaking, no person on regular assignment stayed for less than
a year or more than two years. There were a few short-term
appointments. To support the academic program, a few technicians were also recruited; they spent not less than one year
or more than two years in Kanpur. In addition, some administrative staff also was recruited. Further, an architectural consultant, a medical consultant, and a school consultant were also
a part of the program of assistance. Thus every facet of the

activity of IIT Kanpur was in collaboration with visiting personnel associated with it.

IMPORTANCE OF PERSONAL QUALITIES

        Looking back, it seems on balance that the entire process
of collaboration has proved to be fruitful not only from the point
of view of IIT Kanpur but also in terms of the valuable experience which the visiting professors and others have carried
back with them.   There are many intangible components of the
gains involved.   At no time has the visiting faculty acted as a
substitute for the Indian faculty.   The academic standing of the
visiting professor was important initially for gaining quick respect from the students and the faculty.   But what counted most
in the long run was the personality characteristics of the visiting professor.   To get on as quickly as possible, he had to
establish good human relationship with his colleagues.   In the
long run, however, it is the total behavior that counts.   He not
only comes in contact with the academic community and students
but also with the other staff.   Besides, he has the opportunity
of mixing with the local community.   Then there is travel within the country.   All these are experiences for which he has to
be appropriately prepared to derive the maximum benefit from
such contacts.   Every visiting individual has at the back of his
mind the thought that his country is giving aid to this institute,
and this fact forms a parameter in the pattern of his behavior.
Then again, his standard of living and his ability to spend is far
more than most of the people with whom he has to work.   This
by itself, however, is not enough reason for acquiring respect
from others.   There must be some inherent qualities in the individual which are a product of personal efforts and culture.
It is these which will carry him through his stay successfully.
What one has to appreciate is that things done differently are
not necessarily wrong or immoral.   One has to be careful in
passing any judgment, as this is likely to have far-reaching
consequences.   A superior or condescending attitude will rarely
result in establishing genuine friendship.   It must be realized
that the stay in Kanpur is a mutual experience and not one-sided.

        Every visiting individual passes through four phases, gen-
erally speaking.   The first phase is of excitement and elation.
The second phase is of involvement and frustration.   The third

phase is of adjustment and appreciation. The fourth phase is of departure and wistfulness. It seems India gets into the blood of most people which makes them forget most of the bad experiences and have instead a feeling of nostalgia for their stay and a hope of some day paying a return visit. There are, of course, exceptions -- individuals who never want to return. The younger people who come like to take advantage of this experience for their professional advancement; the older people wish to give an edge to the experience they already have. There is a certain amount of maturity and detachment associated with older people. From the inception of the program to 1968, the total number of visiting academic staff was 68; of non-academic staff, 24. The lowest number visiting at one time was 10 (October-November 1962); the highest, 31 (November-December 1964 and August 1965). Of the 68 academic staff, 15 came from the University of California. The minimum number of staff sent by any institution was 5.

It would not be right to say that every one who came here was equally successful. By and large failures were very few and even these had some positive aspects. As a result of the experience so far, it may be possible to arrive at some conclusions regarding the background which the visiting academic staff should have. To begin with, it must be realized that the whole family becomes a part of the system and not just the individual professor. Academic training tends toward narrow specialization. This is necessary to acquire the requisite degree of competence and depth in one's area of interest. This by itself is not adequate preparation for taking up an assignment in a low-income country like India. A person must acquire breadth of interests and must be capable of carrying on conversation and argument when confronted with situations and opinions with which he is not familiar. He must learn to check the tendency to pass moral judgments and he should try to bring about changes in behavior patterns through consent and not through coercion. One's high standard of living is not necessarily an advantage in dealing with people with a low standard of living. In addition to the current information about the country, the person must become reasonably well acquainted with its historical background, particularly from the social point of view. It would be valuable if the person before taking up a foreign assignment is exposed to social work in his own country and has an appreciation of the need for it. If the person has cultural interests and also a hobby it will go a long way in increasing his area of experience and in making his stay more meaningful,

not only for himself but to all those who come in contact with
him. He must learn to apply standards with discrimination.
He cannot always apply international standards or standards
with which he is accustomed to in his own country. He must
not approach his job with ready-made solutions but evolve these
locally through a process of mutual participation. In this context it is useful to remember that just as anger begets anger,
so does originality beget originality and idealism beget idealism.
It would be particularly useful if a person before he leaves his
country goes through an appropriate short course in the psychology of behavior. Above all, one must learn to have patience.
It will thus be seen that a person wishing to take a visiting appointment should have precisely those qualities which would make
him a good citizen in his own country.

The most important aspect of the whole process of collaboration is the mental attitude of the key people involved. If there
is no basic understanding of the priorities then many things can
go wrong. Particularly in the early stages the dialogue between
the program leader and the director should be meaningful and
continuous. Appreciation of each other's point of view with out
too much argument goes a long way in arriving at quick decisions.
Both of them should have sufficient understanding of the psychological background of people in the two countries. For the successful implementation of a program of this type merely conscious efforts are not enough; the inner energies of all the key
persons associated with the program have to be released. Cultural and traditional differences play a significant role. It is
useful to remember that it is not only some individuals from
both the countries that are involved, but also the two governments. This brings constraints which are likely to lead to frustration unless they are dealt with skillfully and with a great deal
of patience. The old adage that it is not enough to be right, one
must also appear to be right, is particularly relevant in dealing
with governments and public bodies. In all that is attempted, it
must always be kept in mind that this is the host country's institution, and the joint efforts are to be directed toward that end.

The basic purpose of an educational institution will not be
served if it grows in isolation. It must always strive to be a
part of the environment in spite of its inner drive towards the
achievement of academic excellence. There should always be
a viable relationship established between what is, what can be,
and what ought to be. Care should be taken that the institute
succeeds in all three of its missions: the creation of knowledge,

the transmission of knowledge, and the utilization of knowledge. Although the scientific attitude of mind will provide the integrating principle for all the fields of study, the environment should give support to that branch of knowledge and experience which is not amenable exclusively to unaided scientific and rational approach. In addition to narrow specialization, there should be scope for breadth as well, and the possibility of being able to modify one's personality through one's own efforts.

Given the right attitude of mind and adequate motivation, it is always possible for a visiting individual to be productive and at the same time enrich his experience in terms of human relations. In order that he performs his duties satisfactorily, adequate administrative support has to be given to him in terms of his personal needs. The administrative setup in which each visiting individual becomes directly responsible to the program leader and through him to the institute has proved to be very satisfactory in its operation. Certain qualities and appropriate training are necessary for a national of an advanced country to be able effectively to participate in a project in a low-income country. This is equally true of participating individuals from the low-income country. There is something intangible associated with countries having a long history and traditions which often unknowingly affects the visiting individuals at the subconscious level. Thus they carry back with them memories and feelings which have no rational explanation. It is the whole family of the visiting individual that is involved in this process. The giving of aid and the receiving of aid is a two-way transaction. Nothing can be given without taking something and nothing can be taken without giving something in return.

The setting up of IIT Kanpur has been a major undertaking where a unique opportunity was provided for the American nationals to come together voluntarily with the Indian nationals and work together in the pursuit of a common ideal. Looking back, I have no doubt at all that it has been a worthwhile undertaking.

CHAPTER **17** EPILOGUE:
PROFESSIONALS AND
DEVELOPMENT

Jack C. Westoby

One of the dangers of a book of this kind is that it may
serve unwittingly to strengthen the professional's sense of his
own importance. If this were to be so, this book would have
done more harm than good. Generally speaking, we professionals already have a somewhat exaggerated idea of their
power to influence social and economic change. It is as well
to remind ourselves from time to time that, in the last analysis,
it is not the engineers who build bridges; it is not the agronomists who grow food; it is not the public health officers who
build hospitals; nor is it the foresters who create and indus-
trialize forests.

Yet all these have a role to play, and a not unimportant
role, in bringing about economic and social change. How effective they are in that role depends in part on their formation,
and on the attitude with which they approach their tasks. They
can only be fully effective in the long run if they are working
with individuals and groups who share the aspirations of the
common people, and with institutions that are designed to give
expression to those aspirations and to harness the common
people to the development tasks.

SCOPE OF TASKS

The tasks which face the forester today and tomorrow
in the developed countries are much more complex, and much

238

more responsible, than those which faced him yesterday. He
will be much more concerned with what I loosely term "social
forestry", the management of the forests to provide an expanding flow of those physical benefits and social values which the
forests are capable of generating for the community, and he
must seek to do this at minimum cost for the community. At
the same time he must grow a timber crop, as economically
as possible, for a wide range of forest industries which because of technological progress and changing pattern, are
bringing about radically different calls on the forest.

All this is equally true of the professional forester in a
developing country. But there are two important differences.
The first is that the professional forester in most developing
countries has, practically from the outset of his career, to
resolve issues of such complexity, and to take decisions of
such moment, as his colleague in the developed country will
probably not be called upon to take in the first ten years of
his professional service, if, indeed, he is ever called upon to
take them. The second is that the professional forester in the
developing country is obliged to be development-oriented.

Most foresters entering their professional career in the
developed countries take service with a public forestry authority, with private forestry estates, or in the forests of industrial companies. Their first years are still years of apprenticeship. This is when they learn to become "dirt" foresters.
They carry out a variety of technical, and often menial, assignments. They absorb the wisdom of their elders and betters
in the profession. For many young foresters these are the
years of disillusion, of complaints that their technical knowledge and mental capacities are under-utilized. These are the
years of maximum drop-out from the profession. The plain
fact is that in most developed countries professionals are
under-utilized and uneconomically deployed. Many of the tasks
on which they are engaged could equally be carried out by
competent technicians. Those professionals who survive this
period of their service (and a surprisingly high proportion do)
are given new assignments of progressively increasing responsibility, and eventually get the opportunity of applying the
problem-solving and decision-making capacities they carried
out of school, if in the meantime these capacities have not
atrophied.

But in many developing countries, so acute is the shortage
of professional foresters that the young forester starting his
career is likely to find himself plunged immediately into tasks
involving heavy functional or area responsibilities. The problems that come across his desk, or that confront him in the
field, are frequently of a complexity that his training and
limited experience have ill-equipped him to resolve. Moreover, many of the problems are different in kind from those
which faced his expatriate predecessors in pre-independence
days. He is now compelled to approach all his tasks with a
development orientation. This is because governments in the
developing countries are coming to understand that the forestry
sector is capable of making a special contribution to the process
of overall economic growth. The reasons for this derive from
improved understanding of the relationship between the forestry
sector and other sectors of the economy. The forester in a
developing country can no longer content himself with being a
tree-tender. He has to become a forest-mobilizer, and set
about managing, developing, and industrializing his forests in
the interests of the total development effort.

Hence, a senior forester in a developing country is called
upon daily to explain to, argue with, and negotiate with planning
officers, development institutions, finance and trade ministers,
potential investors, industrial consultants, equipment suppliers,
bankers, and so forth; and he must strive to do this in language
which all these can understand. And the pity of it is that the
forestry school from which he graduated probably had no concept of how important it would be to him to get acquainted with
this language. Not surprisingly, his judgment is often in error.
But the miracle is that so many of this new generation of
forestors in the developing countries learn to swim so quickly
and so well in seas that would daunt their contemporaries in
the developed countries. The miracle is all the more astound-
ing in that the senior forestor in the developing country does
not have at his beck and call the massive institutional support,
research services, specialized staff, and documentation facilities that his fellows in the developed countries enjoy. And
never forget that he normally has to operate with forces that
are under-trained and inadequate in numbers, and on a shoe-
string budget.

In short, the job of a professional forester in a developing
country is not only different; it is a good deal tougher. Once
we Westerners appreciate this, we can begin to get some understanding of what is wrong with the education the forester gets
in our North American and European institutions. We can also
get a glimmering of the kind of people we need to send from
our own ranks to help him in his tasks.

AVOIDING ILLUSIONS

Before discussing what steps can be taken to remedy present deficiencies in the formation of professional foresters
for service in the developing countries, it will perhaps be useful to turn for a moment to some of the disappointments that
have been experienced in technical assistance programs, disappointments that have led to disillusion. Disillusionment is,
of course, a necessary precondition for effective action. Most
of us concerned with the development business started out with
a number of illusions. The important thing is to shed these
illusions, to shed them as quickly as possible, and to do so
without losing one's faith and purpose. But much disappoint-
ment would be avoided, and a great deal of time saved, if we
could reduce the number of illusions we start out with.

Institutional vs. Technical Problems

One widespread illusion is the notion that the expatriate
professional in the developing country is, or can be, a princi-
pal agent of economic and social change.

How did this illusion arise? It arose, I think, because
we professionals assumed that, of the various shortages holding back development, capital and know-how were the most
important. This has proved to be an erroneous assumption.
But from this assumption we mistakenly deduced that injections
of walking know-how would somehow transform the situation.
The early days of technical assistance (and perhaps I should
interject at this point that I am speaking mainly of multilateral

aid programs in forestry and forest industries, the only area
in which I can claim detailed, first-hand knowledge) were the
days of the expert adviser. These were the days when the
shelves of ministers, senior administrators, and senior professionals in the developing countries began to fill up with impressive technical reports, containing masses of noble advice.
A large number of these reports have been collecting dust ever
since, largely because the means necessary to implement the
advice have not been available.

Not all advisory missions of this kind were failures, of
course. There were many successes to report. But the degree of success was more closely related to the objective
capacity to implement advice than it was to the quality of the
expert. Though we speak glibly of developing countries, there
is a world of difference between Mexico and Paraguay, between
the United Arab Republic and Rwanda, between India and Laos.

In those countries which have already advanced some way
on the development path, and have already acquired some institutional strength, it is relatively easy to identify and define
problems, and most of the problems have a higher technical
content. In these circumstances, it is not too difficult to
tender suitable advice, and there is some assurance that the
advice, once tendered, can be implemented. In such cases,
technical assistance advisory missions did succeed in removing
many significant impediments to development. But the more
general case was that it was not easy to identify the problem,
or, if the problem were identified, it was seen to be intimately
related with a host of associated problems, the solution of
which was a prerequisite for the solution of the original problem. Moreover, most of the associated problems were institutional rather than technical in character.

In short, the fruitfulness of a professional forester's
contribution to economic and social progress is at least as
much dependent upon the institutional context, the outlook of
the individuals and groups with which he is working, as it is
upon his own intrinsic and acquired qualities. In circumstances
where investment regularly succeeds advice, where the people
as a whole are involved in building for their own benefit, where
a determined assault on nature is being made in the interest
of man, the professional appears not as a forlorn proselytizer

of development, but as an invaluable accelerator and lubricant of the development process. He is there to ensure that the effort of the people is used as economically and productively as possible.

It would be naive to suppose that these hopeful conditions exist in most low-income countries. From this it does not follow, however, that our professional is a creature born before his time. To understand why, we must turn our attention for a few moments to some features of the present conditions of low-income nations. Many of them have large populations; most of them have extensive and under-utilized natural resources; all of them have, in all senses except that of realized demand, huge and pressing needs. As against this, they still produce and consume relatively little. They share a world with nations which have achieved, over two centuries of turbulent and aggressive social history, a stage which has been dubbed that of high mass consumption.

These nations have not become noticeably less turbulent or aggressive, and they show at the moment few signs of extending their mass consumption to the low-income countries. It would be both simplistic and pessimistic to expect the process of development in low-income countries to be broadly a repetition of the recent history of the metropolitan nations. Nor is it possible to predict what course the development path will take. It has been truly said that men make their own history, but in conditions that they do not choose. But we do know something about these conditions today.

One of Latin America's outstanding economists, Celsio Furtado, has pointed out that "the speed with which modern technology must penetrate the underdeveloped world in order to overcome initial resistance and ensure continuity of development inevitably provokes a series of social reactions incompatible with the preservation of most of the pre-existing structures."[1] One of the permanent headaches of all those who are seriously engaged in development assistance is that their efforts are intended to help peoples, whereas their dealings are for the most part with governments. At the end of the day, the professional has to decide whether he is for stability or for development, whether he is for order or for justice. Having reached his decision, he has by no means

acquired a license to intervene directly in the political life of
the country to which he is assigned. But he will have acquired
a depth of view which will enable him to see where his efforts
can best be applied, and what emphasis he should give to his
work, to ensure that they have a lasting impact. He will
achieve this depth of view only if he has taken pains to acquaint
himself with the true nature of the economic, social, and
political tensions that rend the country in which he is to serve,
has rid himself of preconceived notions, and has won through
to a sympathetic understanding of the problems which are going
to frame his own particular mission.

The touchstone for judging the success or failure of technical assistance is how much it contributes to improving the
capacity of the social and institutional order for utilizing as
fully as possible the creative and productive capacities of the
population. Technical assistance is only really successful if
it is geared to promoting development from within. It is not
simply a question of transferring skills; these skills have to
become firmly rooted, capable of growth, and attack a wide
front.

If I may use a bellic image, usurping the privilege of ivy-
covered professors in ivy-covered walls, the development
battle is not won by an invasion in which "progress" establishes
its bridge-heads in a backward land; it is rather won by helping
the local liberation army to remove stagnation, to destroy the
structures that perpetuate underdevelopment, and to keep
growing and building up its own command.

This tells us much about the qualities needed in the professional who is to join the development battle. Obviously he
must be honest and competent; but he must also be free from
preconceived ideas, he must be adaptable to unfamiliar circumstances, he must be sympathetic to strange ideas, and he
must be tolerant of the shortcomings of others. In short, he
must have the curious, open, and fresh mind of the truly in-
telligent, and this means that he must be young, if not in years
at least in heart.

NOTES

1.   Celsio Furtado, "U. S. Hegemony and the Future
of Latin America," The World Today, 1966.

ABOUT THE CONTRIBUTORS

GUY BENVENISTE
   is Associate Professor of Education, University of
   California at Berkeley. A graduate of Harvard University, he holds a Ph. D. in Sociology from Stanford
   University. Before starting his academic career, Dr.
   Benveniste worked as a development economist for fifteen
   years, first with the Stanford Research Institute, then
   successively with the United States Department of State,
   the International Bank for Reconstruction and Development,
   and the International Institute for Educational Planning of
   UNESCO. He also served as consultant to the U. S. AID
   Agency, the Pan American Union UNESCO, the President's
   Scientific Adviser, and to the Mexican Government. In
   1965 he returned for his Ph. D. at Stanford, and now teaches
   in the field of educational planning and development at
   Berkeley. He is co-author of Handbook of African Economic
   Development, also published by Praeger, and of many
   articles and papers in professional journals dealing with
   science, education, and development.

WARREN F. ILCHMAN
   is Associate Professor of Political Science at University
   of California, Berkeley. A graduate of Brown University,
   he holds his Ph. D. in political science from the University
   of Cambridge in England. He started teaching in the
   Department of Political Science at Berkeley in 1965. Dr.
   Ilchman is the author of Professional Diplomacy in the
   United States, published by the University of Chicago Press
   in 1961, The Time-Dimension in Institution-Building (with
   Norman T. Uphoff), published in 1968 by the University
   Consortium on Institution-Building, and is joint author of
   two forthcoming volumes, The Political Economy of Change
   (with Norman T. Uphoff) and Comparative Administration:
   Synthesis and Analysis (with Todd R. LaPorte). He has
   also written articles and reviews on the same subjects in
   the professional literature. Professor Ilchman was a
   recipient of the Harbison prize in 1968 offered by the
   Danforth Foundation for outstanding teaching. In 1969 he
   headed a major research project in India dealing with the
   political, economic, and social aspects of unemployed
   school leavers.

NILS CHRISTIE

is Professor at the Faculty of Law at the University of
Oslo, Norway where he has been associated as a Criminologist since 1959. For six years he was a Research
Fellow with the Norwegian Research Council. He received
his M. A. in sociology from the University of Oslo in 1953
and his Ph. D. from the same university in 1960. He is a
member of the Institute of Criminology at the University
of Oslo, of the Scandinavian Research Council for Criminology and is editor of the Studies in Criminology.
In 1966 he received honorary mention for his book Umge
Norske Lovovertredere from the Sociéte Internationale de
Criminologie in Montreal. He is the author of three other
books on criminology published in Norway and the author
of some 40 articles which have been published in scientific
journals.

ADAM CURLE

is Professor of Education and Psychology at Harvard
University and Director of the Center for Studies in Education and Development at Harvard. He is a graduate of
Oxford University in England where he received his Ph. D.
in Philosophy in 1950. He has been Professor of Education
and Psychology in England and in Ghana and from 1956 to
1959 he was advisor to the government of Pakistan, working
with Harvard University. He has written numerous books
and articles on educational planning and problems in developing countries including Educational Problems of
Developing Societies, also published by Praeger.

RAÚL DEVÉS JULLIAN

is a member of the engineering and construction firm of
Deves, Del Rio y Cia, Ltda. in Santiago, Chile and has
been active in Chile as a civil engineer, an industrialist,
a financier and government official at different times.
Until the spring of 1968 he was Dean of the Faculty of
Physical Sciences and Mathematics at the Catholic University of Chile. He received his Bachelor's degree in mathematics in 1933 from Sagrados Corazones, Valparaiso,
and a degree in engineering in 1939 from the School of
Engineering, Catholic University, Santiago.

JOHN FRIEDMANN

is Director for the Ford Foundation of the Program of
Urban and Regional Development in Chile and Visiting
Professor at the Catholic University of Chile on the

248

Committee for Urban Development. From 1961 to 1965
he was Associate Professor in the Department of City and
Regional Planning at MIT prior to which he had been head,
of the Economic Development Section, United States Operations Mission in Korea with AID, and Regional Planning
Advisor and Visiting Professor at the University of Bahia,
Brasil, also with AID. Between 1952 and 1955 he was an
industrial economist with the Department of Regional Studies
Tennessee Valley Authority. He received his Master's
degree in Planning and Ph.D. in 1955 in Planning both from
the University of Chicago. He is a member of the American
Economic Society and the Regional Science Association and
in 1967-1968 was vice-president of the Regional Science
Association. He is the author of numerous publications and
articles on development and planning.

KENNETH R. HANSEN

is a consulting economist in Palo Alto, California. From
1964 to 1967 he had been Vice-President of Corporate
Planning for the Syntex Corporation in Palo Alto. During
the previous ten years he had been Assistant Director of
the Bureau of the Budget, Field Director of the Harvard
Economic Advisory Group to Iran, Assistant to the Vice-
President of Marketing and Supervisor of Foreign Market-
ing.Research for the Atlantic Refining Company, as well
as Assistant Administrator and Deputy Director of Foreign
Operations Administration Mutual Security Agency and
Mutual Defense Assistance Control. He is the author of
a number of articles on economic planning.

BRIAN HOLMES

is a professor in the Department of Comparative Education,
Institute of Education at the University of London. He
graduated from the University College of London in 1941
majoring in Physics. In 1946 he received a diploma in
Education from the University of London and his Ph.D. in
Comparative Education from the same university in 1962.
He is an Associate of the Institute of Physics and a Fellow
of the Royal Society of Arts. In 1956 he received the Boyd
H. Bode Memorial Lecture award from the Ohio State
University and in 1965 was honored with the New York
University, Department of Education Centennial Lecture
Award. He has published a number of books dealing with
comparative education, as well as articles in leading
journals in the field.

P. K. KELKAR
is Director of the Indian Institute of Technology at Kanpur,
India, and prior to 1959 had been for three years deputy
director and planning officer with the IIT at Bombay. For
thirteen years he had been (professor and) head of the
Department of Electrical Engineering and Vice-Principal
of the Victoria Jubilee Technical Institute at Bombay. He
graduated from the Indian Institute of Science in Electrical
Engineering in 1933 and received his Ph. D. in Electrical
Engineering in 1936 from the University of Liverpool,
England. He is a member of the Institution of Electrical
Engineers, London, a member of the Board of Governors
of four colleges and institutes in India in addition to mem-
bership in several engineering and technical societies in
India. He is the author of a number of technical papers
and reports.

ANTONIO MEDINA
is Associate Professor and Chairman of the Department of
Maternal and Child Health at the University of Puerto Rico.
From 1948 to 1961 he had been with the Puerto Rico Department of Health, for the final three years as chief of the
Bureau of Maternal and Child Health. He received his degree of Doctor of Medicine in 1943 from The George Washington University, Washington, D. C. , and M. P. H. in 1960
from Harvard University. He is a member of the American
Public Health Association, the Puerto Rico Medical and
Public Health Associations and the Association of Teachers
of Maternal and Child Health. Among his many published
writings are books on maternal and child health problems
and programs with particular reference to Puerto Rico.

GUSTAV F. PAPANEK
is Director of the Development Advisory Service and
Lecturer in the Department of Economics at Harvard
University. From 1958 to 1966 he had been Deputy Direc-
tor and then Acting Director with the same departments.
For a year he was Project Field Supervisor of the Harvard
Advisory Group to the Planning Commission of Pakistan
and has served in the past as Consultant to the Taxation and
Development Harvard University Law School and Deputy
Chief of the Program Planning for South and Southeast
Asia, Technical Cooperation Administration for the U.S
Department of State. He graduated from Cornell Univer-
sity in 1947 in Agricultural Economics and received his
Ph. D. in Economics in 1951 from Harvard University.
He is a member of the American Economic Association,

American Farm Economic Association, Society for Asian
Studies, and Society for International Development. He is
the author of Pakistan's Development - Social Goals and
Private Incentives published in 1967, as well as several
articles on planning and development.

EUGEN PUSIĆ
is Professor of Public Administration at the University
of Zagreb, Yugoslavia. For ten years he was Head of
Division and Bureau Chief of the Ministry of Social Welfare
of the State of Croatia and from 1953 to 1955 was Assistant
Secretary. He received a Doctorate of Law from the University of Zagreb in 1939 and in 1955 a Diploma of Public
Administration from the Institute of Social Studies, The
Hague. He is President of the International Council on
Social Welfare as well as a Fellow of the Institute of Social
Studies at The Hague, and has received the Božidar Adžija
Prize for best book of the year in the social sciences in
1965. He is the author of six books and over 300 articles in
political science, public administration, and social welfare
and development, including Urban Government for Zagreb,
Yugoslavia, also published by Praeger.

VERNON W. RUTTAN
is Professor and Head of the Department of Agricultural
Economics at the University of Minnesota, St. Paul,
Minnesota. For two years he was Agricultural Economist
with The Rockefeller Foundation, supervising agricultural
economics research and training at International Rice Research Institute, Los Baños, Philippines. From 1954 to
1963 he was Professor at Purdue University, West Lafay-
ette, Indiana. Concurrently he served as a member of
President Johnson's Task Force Committee on Farm Bar-
gaining Power, Washington, D. C., and has been consultant
to the Agency for International Development, to the RAND
Corporation, the Rockefeller Foundation, and Stanford Research Institute. He graduated from Yale University in 1948
in Economics and received his Ph. D. in 1952 from the University of Chicago. He is a member of Economic Associations in the United States and the Philippines and has three
times received the American Farm Economic Association
Publication Award. He is the author of numerous articles ar
monographs in the field of agricultural economics.

IRWIN T. SANDERS
is Vice-President of Education and World Affairs in New
York. Prior to 1967 he was Associate Director of The

Ford Foundation in New York for four years. He has been
Department Chairman at Boston University and the University of Kentucky, and Lecturer at Harvard University. He
graduated from Washington & Lee University, Lexington,
Virginia in 1929 and received his Ph. D. in Rural Sociology
from Cornell University in Ithaca, New York in 1938.
Prior to receiving his Ph. D. he spent eight years with the
American College at Sofia, Bulgaria, first as tutor and
later as Dean of the College. He is a member of the American Sociological and the American Anthropological Associations, as well as the Rural Sociological Society, and has
received the Royal Order of the Phoenix from the Greek
Government, the Distinguished Professorship from the
University of Kentucky, and awards from the Social Science
Research Council and the American Philosophical Society.
His list of publications includes over 70 articles and books
covering a thirty-year period on world-wide sociological
problems.

C. DWIGHT WALDO

is Professor at the Maxwell School of Citizenship, Syracuse, New York. He spent twenty years with the Department of Political Science at the University of California,
Berkeley, part of the time as Director of the Institute of
Governmental Studies at Berkeley. During World War II
he had been Associate Business Economist with the Office
of Price Administration, and Administrative Analyst with
the U.S. Bureau of the Budget. He graduated from Nebraska State Teachers College, Peru, in 1935 and received
his Ph. D. in 1942 at Yale University. He is the well-
known author of numerous books and articles on public
administration and political science.

JACK C. WESTOBY

is Deputy Director of the Forestry and Forest Industries
Division of the Food and Agriculture Organization of the
United Nations in Rome, Italy. He has been with that
organization since 1952, formerly in the capacity of
Economist-Statistician and later as Chief of the Forestry
Economics Division. He graduated in 1935 from University College, Hull, England, in Economics. He is a member of the Royal Statistical Society, the Commonwealth
Forestry Society and in 1965 was awarded the MacMillan
Lectureship by the University of British Columbia. He
has been author or joint author of all major forestry re-
source statistics published by FAO in the last fifteen years.

252

HAROLD L. WILENSKY

is Professor of Sociology at the University of California,
Berkeley. Prior to 1961 he was with the University of
Michigan and for four years was with the Center for Advanced Study of Behavioral Sciences. He graduated from
Antioch College, received his M.A. in 1949 and his Ph.D.
in Sociology in 1955 from the University of Chicago. While
in Berkeley he has served on various advisory committees
and councils and has been on the editorial board of journals
devoted to sociological problems. He received the McKinse
Foundation Book Award for Organizational Intelligence as
one of four outstanding management research books of 1967
He was also co-author with Paul Lazarsfeld and William
Sewell of The Uses of Sociology, published in 1967 by Basic
Books, as well as the author of innumerable articles published in journals relating to industrial relations and social
welfare.